BOSTON'S MASSACRE

Boston's Massacre

ERIC HINDERAKER

The Belknap Press of Harvard University Press

CAMBRIDGE, MASSACHUSETTS · LONDON, ENGLAND

2017

Library of Congress Cataloging-in-Publication Data

Names: Hinderaker, Eric, author.
Title: Boston's massacre / Eric Hinderaker.
Description: Cambridge, Massachusetts : The Belknap Press of Harvard
University Press, 2017. | Includes bibliographical references and index.
Identifiers: LCCN 2016038804 | ISBN 9780674048331 (alk. paper)
Subjects: LCSH: Boston Massacre, 1770. | United States—History—Revolution,
1775–1783—Causes. | Boston (Mass.)—History—Revolution, 1775–1783.
Classification: LCC E215.4 .H66 2017 | DDC 973.3/113—dc23
LC record available at https://lccn.loc.gov/2016038804

For my parents

Contents

Maps and Illustrations

MAPS AND ILLUSTRATIONS

MAPS

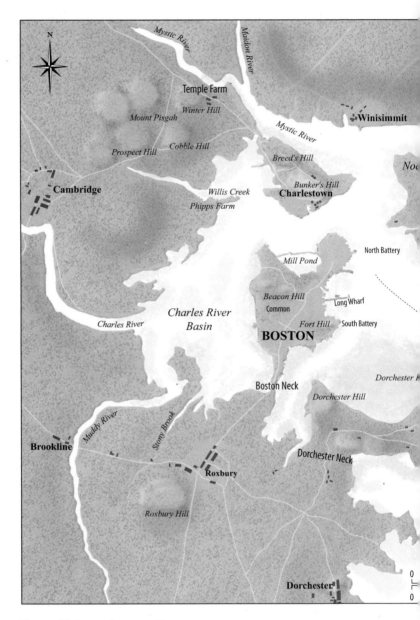

Boston Harbor and surroundings, 1770

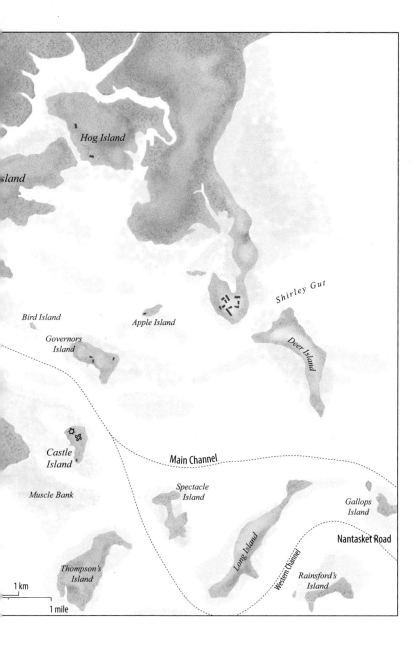

Hog Island

...land

Shirley Gut

Bird Island

Apple Island

Deer Island

Governors
Island

Castle
Island

Main Channel

Muscle Bank

Spectacle
Island

Gallops
Island

Nantasket Road

Long Island

Western Channel

Thompson's
Island

Rainsford's
Island

1 km

1 mile

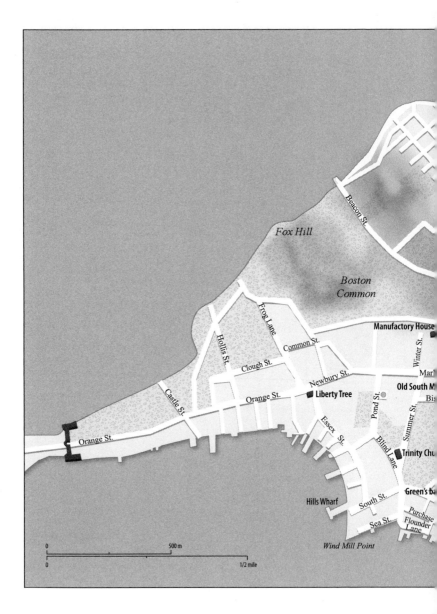

Town of Boston, 1770

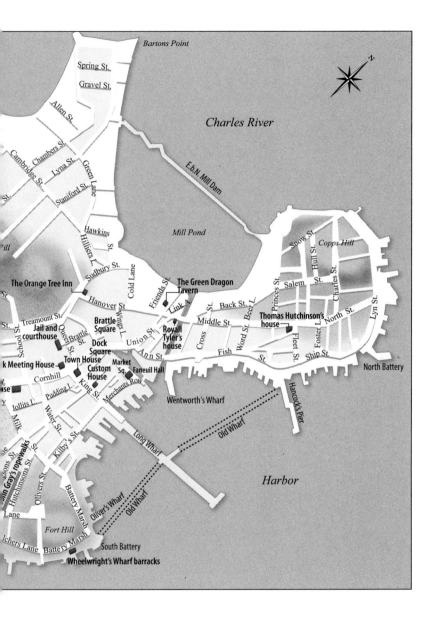

Bartons Point

Spring St.
Gravel St.
Allen St.

Charles River

Cambridge St.
Chambers St.
Lyna St.
Green Lane
Staniford St.

E.b.N. Mill Dam

Hawkins
Hilliers L.
Sudbury St.
Cold Lane

Mill Pond

Snow St.
Copps Hill
Hull St.
Salem St.
Charles St.

The Orange Tree Inn

Friends St.
Link A.
The Green Dragon Tavern

Hanover St.
Wings L.

Back St.
Beer L.
Princes St.

Salem St.

Lyn St.
North St.

Treamount St.
Jail and courthouse
Queen St.
Brattle
Brattle Square
Dock Square
Union St.
Royall Tyler's house
Middle St.
Word St.

Thomas Hutchinson's house

Foster L.
Fleet St.
Ship St.

Cross

Fish St.

North Battery

School St.
k Meeting House
Town House
Custom House
Market Sq.
Faneuil Hall
Ann St.

Merchants Row

Cornhill
Jollits L.
Pudding L.
King St.

Wentworth's Wharf

Hancock's Pier

Milk
Water St.
Kilby's St.
n Gray's ropewalks

Long Wharf
Old Wharf

Harbor

Hutchinsons St.
Olivers St.
Battery Marsh

Oliver's Wharf
Old Wharf

Lane
Fort Hill
chers Lane
Battery Marsh
South Battery
Wheelwright's Wharf barracks

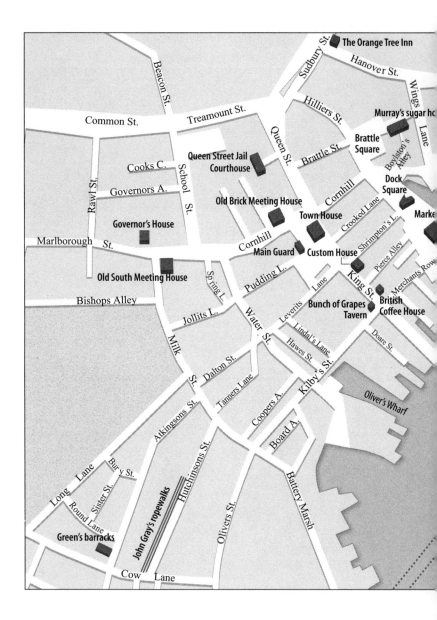

King Street and central Boston, 1770

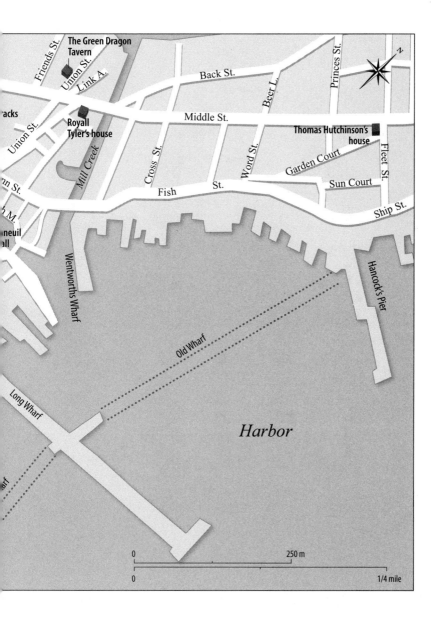

BOSTON'S MASSACRE

Introduction

A LITTLE AFTER 9:00 P.M. on March 5, 1770, a detachment of British soldiers fired into a crowd of townspeople on King Street in Boston, in the Massachusetts Bay Colony. The result—the "Boston Massacre"—has echoed through the pages of newspapers, pamphlets, and history books ever since. It is perhaps the most densely described incident in early American history (with more than two hundred eyewitness accounts), yet the descriptions are sufficiently contradictory to make the unfolding sequence of events surprisingly hard to pin down. To say what happened would seem to be a straightforward task, but in many ways the Boston Massacre remains an irreducible mystery.

This book is about three things: an event and the contexts that shaped it; the competing narratives that developed to shape contemporary understandings of the event; and the evolving memories of the event as it was invoked in later years as a symbol of American identity. The human mind does not simply recall everything it sees, recording an objective and unerring account of events as they happen. Instead, in moments of stress, it picks up patches of highly subjective impressions. Only through narrative—only by subsequently devising a story that threads those patches together into a meaningful pattern—do the instantaneous effects of a dramatic episode like the shootings in King Street acquire a form that can be recalled, interpreted, and argued for. The Boston Massacre offers an unusual opportunity to observe impressionistic flashes gradually take on the shape of competing narratives, and then to trace the evolution of those narratives across a long span of time.[1]

In the abundant literature on historical memory, most of the attention has been given to momentous events. One large body of work in memory studies relates to the place of catastrophe — especially the Nazi Holocaust — in the historical experience of Jews. In U.S. history, memory studies have paid close attention to the ways in which the Civil War is remembered, especially among southerners.[2] The Boston Massacre is very different from the Holocaust and the Civil War. In a critical way, it is precisely their opposite: while those later occurrences were so monumental in scale and implication that it was difficult to assimilate their meanings, the Boston Massacre was, by comparison, an inconsequential skirmish. Similar scrapes occur often, and are just as quickly forgotten. But the shootings in King Street were not forgotten. They were amplified and politicized in ways that made the Boston Massacre seem to be an event of transcendent importance. This use of historical memory differs dramatically from the cases that dominate the literature on the subject, and it deserves careful and extended consideration.[3]

Simply to call the Boston shootings a "massacre" was to make a claim for the event's significance. Townspeople immediately referred to the shootings as the "bloody massacre" in King Street; within weeks, that phrase had repeatedly cropped up in print. Though it is inflammatory, the term "massacre" is also vague. According to the *Oxford English Dictionary,* its primary definition in the eighteenth century was "the indiscriminate and brutal slaughter of people or (less commonly) animals; carnage, butchery, slaughter in numbers; an instance of this." In modern usage, a massacre seems to require a high body count. But in the early modern sense of the word, the "cruel and atrocious murder of a single individual" could constitute a massacre. It was identifiable by the spirit in which it was undertaken, its wantonness and brutality. To invoke the term was to make a rhetorical claim with political significance: this shooting was no "unhappy disturbance," as the soldiers' apologists wanted to argue. It was intentional and cold-blooded, and the soldiers could not be excused for their actions. The Boston Massacre is a phrase that contains within itself a judgment, an indictment, a conviction.[4]

Boston was the crucible of the American Revolution. It was not the only place that mattered in the era of independence, but it was the place where all the elements of the familiar story came together. Thirteen (or perhaps more) of Britain's North American colonies would surely have attained their independence without the crises in Boston; in all likelihood, they would have had to fight a war to win it; and it is possible that they would have called that war a revolution. But even if all these things came to be, without Boston every aspect of the American Revolution — the time line, the events, the unfolding narrative of conflict and war — would be so different as to be unrecognizable to us. Without Boston, there would have been no destruction of the East India Company tea; no Coercive Acts; no Lexington and Concord; no Continental Army forming on the Cambridge Common. There would have been no First Continental Congress, no John or Abigail or Samuel Adams, no Paul Revere, Joseph Warren, or Mercy Otis Warren.

If Boston was the crucible of the Revolution, its military occupation beginning in the fall of 1768 was the catalyst with the power to transform all the other elements taking shape there into something uniquely volatile and malleable. And the events of March 5, 1770 — the Boston Massacre — applied the heat necessary to energize that catalyst and transform local conditions into something new: mutable, protean, unpredictable. If it were not for the shootings in Boston, 1770 might have been a year of reconciliation between Britain's Parliament and its North American colonies. The signs were favorable. But events

{ 3 }

in Boston ensured that 1770 would not be remembered that way. The Boston Massacre decisively shifted the direction of relations between Britain and its North American colonies. It was the sine qua non of the American Revolution as we know it.

A PORT TOWN sited on a peninsula that was almost an island, Boston had connections to the British Atlantic that were indispensable. But both the community of Boston and the British Empire evolved dramatically during the first three-quarters of the eighteenth century, in ways that endangered their relationship. Boston's population ceased to grow after 1740 (a unique circumstance among the port towns of British North America), a fact that profoundly colored its community dynamics and political culture. It developed a complex, prickly relationship with Great Britain, which was itself undergoing dramatic change in the eighteenth century. A relatively weak and isolated island kingdom wracked by civil war and revolution through much of the seventeenth century, Britain emerged in the eighteenth century as a rising European power. Characterized by an increasingly efficient fiscal-military state, with a powerful navy, a growing army, and a political culture that galvanized the nation around a muscular defense of imperial interests, Great Britain entered into a series of European wars that spilled more and more into the Atlantic and onto American shores as the eighteenth century progressed.

In this process of militarization, the town of Boston and the colony of Massachusetts Bay had been enthusiastic partners. With deeply rooted militia traditions and a strong, assertive sense of Protestant English identity, New Englanders were especially well prepared to join in the task of fighting Catholic New France. Massachusetts Bay soldiers participated in the military campaigns of the eighteenth century in large numbers, while its merchants supplied the provisions and ships that carried the effort forward. Britain's victory in the Seven Years'

War validated New Englanders' confidence in the righteousness of their cause and the efficacy of their institutions. The superiority of their locally controlled militias and their representative assemblies had been proven against the centralized, authoritarian practices of the Catholic French.[5]

But as Great Britain evolved into a more efficient war-making state, it had become a more centralized and authoritarian power as well. In the seventeenth century, it was an article of faith in England that a standing army in peacetime was a dire threat to freedom, and this presumption remained strongly in force in British North America — and especially in New England, where the republican ideals of the seventeenth century underlay every aspect of law and government. In Great Britain, the Glorious Revolution of 1688 marked the beginning of a long era of sustained European warfare and growing imperial commitments. Those wars overturned earlier assumptions about the place of armed force in public life. A peacetime standing army became indispensable to the crown and Parliament. But many fundamental questions about the army's relationship to both civilian populations and subordinate institutions of government remained unanswered.[6]

When Parliament decided to station a large body of troops in North America following the Seven Years' War, and political and military leaders subsequently chose to dispatch four regiments to Boston as a peacekeeping force, they were marching onto an unmapped landscape. The shootings in King Street that came to be called a massacre were one result. But they occurred only after seventeen long months of military occupation: a period marked by confusion, outrage, and endemic conflict. The clash between local and imperial authorities derived from Bostonians' deep attachment to older republican principles, which were incompatible with the eighteenth-century rules under which British officials sought to manage imperial relations.[7]

If Boston was especially sensitive to these changes, it was also especially well equipped to resist them. Its town meeting form of government gave local politics a distinctly popular cast, while several decades of economic stagnation helped to shape a local political apparatus that was adept in expressing supplication, grievance, and resistance. During the 1760s a network of local associations developed to mobilize public opinion and, on occasion, orchestrate crowd actions. British authorities came to see Boston as their most intransigent North American community, while Bostonians, more than the residents of any other colonial settlement, resisted compromise and interpreted their conflict with Great Britain as a matter of fundamental principle.

Three themes drive the narrative that follows. First, how did military and civilian officials of the British Empire negotiate their authority with leaders of Boston — that unusually independent and uniquely unified colonial town? Though the power of British officials was theoretically expansive, in practice it was limited by custom, legal precedent, and practical considerations; as a result, it was exercised in convoluted and ambivalent ways that did more to confuse than to clarify the relationship between crown and town. Second, how did Boston's leaders achieve their unusual level of independence from crown authority and forge the unified front that the town presented to British officials? And third, how is a chaotic event like the Boston Massacre assimilated into historical memory? What were its legacies, and how have its meanings been politicized in the months, years, decades, and centuries since it occurred?[8]

After Chapter 1 explores the competing accounts of the shootings that appeared immediately afterward, Chapters 2 through 4 set the context for Boston's occupation. Chapters 5 and 6 describe the seventeen-month period when British troops took up residence in the town, while Chapters 7 and 8 examine the long and uncertain period from the shootings through the trials of the accused. Finally, Chapters 9 and 10 consider the legacies of the Boston Massacre, first in the era of the American Revolution and then in the centuries that followed. Tracing a long chronological arc from the mid-eighteenth century to the present, the book asks its reader to consider the relationships among events as they unfold, full of uncertainties, ambiguities, and controversies; the narratives they can inspire, which often take the form of heated arguments; and the lingering, one-dimensional memories that eventually take their place.

EVENT, NARRATIVE, MEMORY: it is a sequence that can be generalized into a three-stage interpretation of the way historical consciousness evolves. It begins in confusion, when the basic facts of an occurrence are unclear and participants are trying to make sense of what has happened. It proceeds to a period of contestation, when competing interests construct alternate narratives, each highlighting some aspects of the event while suppressing others. In this period, the narratives evolve as observers try out various formulations of their views, but they gradually develop into coherent and self-sufficient explanations and interpretations.

The contest between competing accounts of an event can have a long life, but it cannot last forever. Eventually, the particular issues that energized competing interpretations fade, the contest's heat diminishes, and the inheritors of an occurrence like the Boston Massacre lose a fine-grained sense of what was at stake in the original controversy. They are left with a dim, residual memory that can lie fallow for decades, serving as a vaguely recalled icon of American experience but divorced from its original contexts and uncontroversial in its meanings.

But new contexts can bring new meanings to the fore. Initially, memories of the Boston Massacre provided a vital spark of outrage in the growing conflict with Great Britain. But at the end of the American Revolution, the usefulness of that function faded. Recollections grew more ambivalent, and the event fell into disfavor in public memory. When memories of the Boston Massacre were revived in the nineteenth century, they came with a surprising new twist: Crispus

Attucks, one of the men killed in King Street, was recast as the most important figure in the shootings. A sailor of mixed African American and Wampanoag ancestry, Attucks was taken up by Boston's African American community in the decades before the Civil War as the first martyr in the struggle for American liberty. This rhetorical move triggered a decades-long dispute in Boston about whether Attucks and the other victims were lawless rioters or a patriot vanguard. Eventually that conflict was settled and the Boston Massacre resolved, once again, into a vague and uncontroversial memory.

In more recent times, the Boston Massacre has been invoked for political purposes when the firepower of the U.S. government has been directed against its citizens. It happened during the Vietnam War; more recently, it has framed discussions of the militarization of policing in the twenty-first century. And as race has become increasingly salient to those discussions, Crispus Attucks has again been invoked, this time as a new kind of symbol of African American citizenship. Identified in the nineteenth century as the first martyr of American independence, in the twenty-first century he has become the first African American victim of unrestrained police brutality.

With the passage of 250 years, the Boston Massacre occupies a timeworn niche in the American memory palace. It is a half-forgotten event in a shared patriotic past. But competing interpretations can still be reenergized. Controversies long laid to rest, smoothed under a blanket of warm reminiscence, can suddenly rise from their slumber with surprising force. It is worth recalling the contexts that made the Boston Massacre a unique and powerful occurrence. In a shocking, dramatic episode that unfolded in less than an hour, the shootings in King Street shone a bright light on the landscape of late eighteenth-century British North America like few occasions before or after.

CHAPTER 1

A War of Words

O N THE NIGHT of March 5, 1770, in the uncertain light of a quarter moon reflecting on snow-covered streets, a detachment of British troops fired into a crowd of civilians in front of Boston's Custom House. Three were killed on the spot; two others died of their wounds a short time later. The story of the Boston Massacre has often been told: several newspapers gave detailed accounts a week after the fact; two pamphlets followed shortly thereafter, with strikingly divergent descriptions of the events leading up to the shootings; the soldiers' trials eight months later generated more eyewitness accounts and produced another narrative. More than two hundred eyewitnesses offered testimony related to the shootings. All these accounts are mind-numbingly repetitious—yet they also differ dramatically, in both their details and their narrative strategies. Boston's newspapers and the account published by the town highlight the aggression of the soldiers, while the version of events sympathetic to the soldiers stresses premeditation and violence on the part of the townspeople. The testimony given at the trials, and the narrative it supported, differed from all the preceding accounts. If one considers the Boston Massacre story as a series of narratives that unfolded in real time rather than as a disconnected body of individual recollections, its malleability is its most striking feature.

This account of the Boston Massacre begins with words, not actions, because the truth of what happened on the night of March 5, 1770, was disputed from the beginning. Both the facts of the case and their meaning were examined repeatedly in the months and years following the massacre. Local officials deliberated immediately after the event to determine a sensible course of action. Then, in subsequent months, the court of popular opinion chewed over the details as narratives and images circulated in Boston and throughout the British Atlantic. Late in the year the court of law had its say, as the soldiers were brought before the bar on charges of murder. Finally, with the case decided, the Boston Massacre took its place in the political culture of Boston and Massachusetts Bay, where it continued to serve a useful rhetorical function for many years. None of these processes, however, got to the bottom of the matter. Competing accounts were fundamentally incompatible, and even now key elements of the story are matters of conjecture, not fact. The shootings triggered a war of words in which truth was the first casualty.

On March 12 three Boston newspapers offered accounts of the shootings. Two—those in the *Boston Evening-Post* and the *Boston-Gazette, and Country Journal*—were especially detailed. They shared key features in common: they portrayed the soldiers as ferociously aggressive; they contended that the conflict began in scuffles between soldiers and "youths" or "lads"; and they highlighted the self-control of townspeople, who avoided further violence and instead proceeded to a peaceful resolution of the conflict.[1] In the *Gazette*'s account, several soldiers of the 29th Regiment set the tone for the evening with their unprovoked belligerence. For no clear reason, they were "parading the Streets with their drawn Cutlasses and Bayonets, abusing and wounding Numbers of the Inhabitants."

The action began to unfold, not in King Street where the shootings would happen, but a block north, in a narrow alleyway off Cornhill leading to a sugar warehouse owned by James Murray, where two companies of the 29th had their barracks. Just after 9:00 P.M., two Boston "youths"—Edward Archbald and William Merchant—passed by the alley. A soldier stood there "brandishing a broad sword of an uncommon size against the walls, out of which he struck fire plentifully." A "person of a mean countenance armed with a large cudgel" kept him company. Archbald warned Merchant to be careful of the sword; in response, "the soldier turned around and struck Archbald on the arm, then pushed at Merchant and pierced thro' his cloaths inside the arm close to the arm-pit and grazed the skin." Merchant retaliated by hitting the soldier with a stick. This encounter prompted the man with the cudgel to run into the barracks; he returned momentarily with two more soldiers, "one armed with a pair of tongs the other with a shovel." The soldier with the tongs "pursued Archbald back thro' the alley, collar'd and hit him over the head with the tongs."

The commotion, according to the *Gazette,* brought people out into the street. John Hicks—a "young lad"—responded to the attack on Archbald by knocking down the soldier with the tongs. Then, "more lads gathering," they drove the soldiers back to their barracks. "In less than a minute 10 or 12 of them came out with drawn cutlasses, clubs and bayonets, and set upon the unarmed boys and young folks, who stood them a little while, but finding the inequality of their equipment dispersed."

Samuel Atwood next approached the alley from Dock Square. After the boys departed, he observed the ten or twelve soldiers as they proceeded to run down the alley toward the square. He asked "if they intended to murder people? They answered Yes, by G—d, root and branch! With that one of them struck Mr. Atwood with a club, which was repeated by another." Atwood, unarmed, turned away to protect himself. He "received a wound on the left shoulder which reached the bone and gave him much pain. Retreating a few steps, Mr. Atwood met two officers and said, Gentlemen, what is the matter? They answered, you'll see by and by."

To this point in the *Gazette* account, it is difficult to understand why bloody-minded soldiers suddenly began striking townspeople and threatening worse. The chaos and unprovoked violence of the scene is shocking — and also a little implausible. After wreaking their havoc near the barracks and vowing to murder townspeople "root and branch," the soldiers next set off on a rampage. They made their way first to Dock Square, then into King Street, and finally up Cornhill, threatening violence and "insulting all they met in like manner, and pursuing some to their very doors." Curious townspeople filtered into the street to see what the commotion was about. The dozen rampaging soldiers (along with the two officers who issued an oblique threat to Atwood) now fall out of the *Gazette* narrative.

Soon, thirty or forty people — "mostly lads" — had gathered in King Street. Suddenly, Captain Thomas Preston and a party of soldiers "with charged bayonets" marched east two blocks from the Main Guard. The soldiers were "pushing their bayonets, crying, Make way!" Forming up in front of the Custom House, they continued "to push to drive people off, [and] pricked some in several places." In response, the townspeople grew "clamorous, and, it is said, threw snow-balls."

In response to the clamor and snowballs, "the Captain commanded them to fire." With "more snow-balls coming, he again said, Damn you, Fire, be the consequence what it will!" One of his men then discharged his musket. In response, "a townsman with a cudgel struck him over the hands with such force that he dropt his firelock; and rushing forward aimed a blow at the Captain's head, which graz'd his hat and fell pretty heavy upon his arm." The other soldiers "continued the fire, successively, till 7 or 8, or as some say 11 guns were discharged." The account concludes with one final, shocking indignity. As townspeople rushed to the aid of the victims, the soldiers who had just fired into the crowd now tried "to fire upon or push with their bayonets the persons who undertook to remove the slain and wounded!"

In the *Gazette*'s account, all the aggression is on the side of the soldiers, and the townspeople are mostly boys. Thomas Preston, the officer of the day, leads a detachment of soldiers to the Custom House in response to the gathering crowd — small and unthreatening, merely curious about the soldiers' noisy havoc — and then orders his men to fire upon the provocation of a few snowballs. The shooting is over in an instant.

After the shooting, as the *Gazette* would have it, "the Bells were set a Ringing" to alert townspeople to the crisis. "Great Numbers soon assembled at the Place where this tragical Scene had been acted." Three men were killed on the spot; two were "struggling for life." (By the time the *Gazette* went to press, a fourth had died.) Six more were less grievously wounded. But the townspeople remained calm. Though angry, spirited, and unafraid, they allowed cooler heads to prevail and justice to pursue its quiet course to a fair resolution of the night's dolorous events.

"Tuesday morning presented a most shocking Scene," the *Gazette* narrative concluded, "the Blood of our Fellow Citizens running like Water thro' King-Street, and the Merchants Exchange the principal spot of the Military Parade for about 18 Months past. Our Blood might also be track'd up to the Head of Long-Lane, and through divers other Streets and Passages." The *Boston Evening-Post* ended its account with a direct indictment of the troops' intentions. "An apprehension of a settled plan for a general if not universal massacre, from such barbarous outrages, in conjunction with their former attacks and continued menaces," it contended, "justly alarmed the people."[2]

One-sided as they are, the *Gazette* and *Evening-Post* accounts offered the most detailed explanation available to townspeople who had not been on the scene themselves. A sense of outrage already ran high; this version of events only fanned the flames. It was elaborated in a pamphlet quickly assembled by the town and published for circulation in Britain. *A Short Narrative of the Horrid Massacre in*

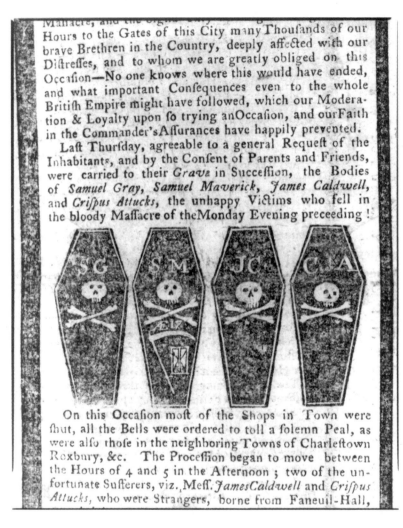

Hours to the Gates of this City many Thousands of our brave Brethren in the Country, deeply affected with our Diftreffes, and to whom we are greatly obliged on this Occafion—No one knows where this would have ended, and what important Confequences even to the whole British Empire might have followed, which our Moderation & Loyalty upon fo trying anOccafion, and ourFaith in the Commander'sAffurances have happily prevented.

Laft Thurfday, agreeable to a general Requeft of the Inhabitants, and by the Confent of Parents and Friends, were carried to their *Grave* in Succeffion, the Bodies of *Samuel Gray, Samuel Maverick, James Caldwell,* and *Crifpus Attucks,* the unhappy Victims who fell in the bloody Maffacre of theMonday Evening preceeding !

On this Occafion moft of the Shops in Town were fhut, all the Bells were ordered to toll a folemn Peal, as were alfo thofe in the neighboring Towns of Charleftown Roxbury, &c. The Proceffion began to move between the Hours of 4 and 5 in the Afternoon ; two of the unfortunate Sufferers, viz.,Meff. *JamesCaldwell* and *Crifpus Attucks,* who were Strangers, borne from Faneuil-Hall,

The Boston-Gazette, and Daily Journal for March 12, 1770, included a detailed account of the shootings. Paul Revere engraved four coffins to represent the four victims who had died at the time the paper went to press: Samuel Gray, Samuel Maverick, James Caldwell, and Crispus Attucks. A fifth victim, Patrick Carr, died soon after, and the *Gazette* printed another coffin to mark his passing.

Boston, written by a committee appointed to the task, was approved by the town meeting on March 19, two weeks after the event and only a week after the *Gazette*'s first report. It was printed by month's end by Benjamin Edes and John Gill — the publishers of the *Gazette* — and shipped off to London on a chartered vessel. Though it was intended for a British audience and did not circulate widely in Boston until the summer, it captured the sentiments and prejudices of the town precisely. According to the *Horrid Massacre,* the soldiers were hostile to Bostonians from the moment they arrived, seventeen months prior to the shootings. They joined forces with the customs commissioners, a group of tax collectors who had resided in Boston since 1767, much to the unhappiness of many townspeople. The pamphlet's narrative, and the eyewitness accounts that follow, indict soldiers and commissioners alike.[3]

The *Horrid Massacre* contended that the soldiers in Boston plotted the events of March 5 for several days beforehand. William Newhall, for example, testified that on Thursday, March 1, he overheard a soldier of the 29th Regiment say, "*There were a great many [Bostonians] that would eat their dinners on Monday next, that should not eat any on Tuesday.*" This remark implied not only that the soldiers generally seemed to be spoiling for a fight, but also that they had a specific plan in mind for Monday evening. The depositions of half a dozen other witnesses pointed toward the conclusion that "there was a general combination among the soldiers of the 29th regiment at least, to commit some extraordinary act of violence upon the town." Various soldiers initiated the action in the hours prior to the massacre, when "many persons, without the least provocation, were in various parts of the town insulted and abused by parties of armed soldiers patroling the streets." More than half a dozen depositions described a mob of soldiers leaving Murray's barracks and charging through the streets with "naked cutlasses" and bayonets, shouting threats and wreaking havoc as they went.[4]

The *Horrid Massacre* claimed that "very few persons" had gathered in King Street in the vicinity of the Custom House until the rampaging soldiers made their way there. The "outrageous behavior and the threats" of these soldiers caused someone to ring the bell of the Old Brick Meeting House (New Englanders called their churches meeting-houses), "which bell ringing quick, as for fire, it presently brought out a number of the inhabitants, who being soon sensible of the occasion of it, were naturally led to King-street." As townspeople rushed into the vicinity of the Custom House, they found that "a number of boys" had gathered around the sentry there. It was unclear whether the boys mistook the sentry for one of the rampaging soldiers, or whether the sentry "first affronted them"; in any case, they were exchanging "much foul language." Then, in response to the sentry "pushing at them with his bayonet," the boys started to throw snowballs. The sentry called for help from the Main Guard, and Captain Thomas Preston, the officer of the day, marched to his aid with seven or eight soldiers carrying "fire arms and charged bayonets." To take up their position, they pushed "through the people in so rough a manner that it appeared they intended to create a disturbance." Without any provocation except a few more snowballs, Preston—"in great haste and much agitated"—ordered his men to fire, and repeated the order. One gun fired, "then others in succession, and with deliberation, till ten or a dozen guns were fired." About seventy or eighty people had gathered in King Street by the time the shooting commenced.[5]

Not all the shots were fired from the soldiers standing in front of the Custom House. The *Horrid Massacre* places particular emphasis on the testimony of seven witnesses who claimed that unidentified individuals were also stationed at second-floor windows inside the Custom House and firing guns at the crowd. Samuel Drowne even reported that he saw a figure at one of the windows: stooping (and therefore tall), holding a handkerchief to his face (presumably a hastily improvised disguise), and firing a gun (*"which he* [Drowne] *clearly discerned"*). The implication of this testimony was unmistakable. Conspiring with the soldiers who had turned on an innocent citizenry were the customs commissioners themselves, in what could only have been a premeditated attack on the townspeople.[6]

In sum, the *Horrid Massacre* describes an event that was planned and orchestrated by a cabal of soldiers and customs commissioners, in which locals were unwitting and innocent bystanders. The streets of Boston were crowded with townspeople only after the ringing of the bells, which came in two stages: first at the Old Brick Meeting House, in response to the rampaging soldiers; then at meetinghouses throughout the town after the shootings. The townspeople were incensed but orderly. As in the *Gazette* version of events, they resisted the urge to vigilantism and instead sought a more measured and official form of justice. Buttressed by ninety-six depositions whose text ran to more than sixty pages, the *Horrid Massacre* constituted a prima facie indictment of the soldiers' conduct and a powerful argument for freeing the town of Boston from their oversight. Though the depositions conflicted in many details, their general drift was clear, and the pamphlet's central message was one of unambiguous aggression against a peaceable citizenry.

At the same time that local justices of the peace were hearing depositions on behalf of the town, British officers began to collect testimony of their own on the order of Lieutenant Colonel William White. John Robinson, one of the customs commissioners stationed in Boston, left town on March 16 with a packet of twenty-eight depositions; eventually, they were printed as the appendix to a pamphlet entitled *A Fair Account of the Late Unhappy Disturbance at Boston in New England,* which laid out its own version of the story. It differed dramatically from the versions printed in the *Gazette,* the *Evening-Post,* and the *Horrid Massacre.* Like the *Horrid Massacre,* the *Unhappy Disturbance* highlighted the long-running tensions between soldiers and townspeople in Boston. It stressed that the "ill disposition of the inhabitants" was so strong that it had become "unsafe for an officer or soldier to walk the streets." One inhabitant warned that townspeople intended to "kill all the officers in town." The pamphlet attributes the massacre to the soldiers' "natural desire of defending themselves" in the face of an attack "by at least an hundred people, armed with bludgeons, sticks, and cutlasses."[7]

According to John Gillespie, one of the deponents in the *Unhappy Disturbance,* townspeople had begun to mass in the streets during the afternoon of March 5. A group of about three hundred people had assembled near the Liberty Tree in the South End around 3:00 P.M. By early evening, Gillespie reported that townspeople were out in force, walking the streets in groups of three to six and armed with clubs. He encountered a total of forty or fifty people walking in these armed groups when he was making his way through the South End around 7:00 P.M. In front of the Custom House, at about the same time — in early March, dusk would already have been fading into night — a group had gathered around the sentry, "standing almost close" to him. They began to throw ice and snowballs. When he warned the group to leave him alone, a "gentleman dressed in a red cloak" approached and spoke to the locals, whereupon they crossed the street and remained at a distance. An hour later most of them were still there, some armed with "large clubs and sticks."

By about 8:00 P.M., according to Sergeant Major William Davies, "a large body of inhabitants" was out in the streets near the North End (several blocks from the Custom House), "some with firearms, others with cutlasses and bludgeons." Then around 9:00 P.M., a bell began to ring. "We thought it for a fire," Gillespie noted, "but the landlord said it was to collect the mob." At about that time, Davies reported that a crowd of several hundred people was gathered near the marketplace, a short distance from King Street, "tearing up the butchers stalls for clubs." He reported that this group, shouting threats against the soldiers, "divided into three divisions, of some hundreds in each," and set off for different parts of the town. A soldier with a severe head wound "and one of his fingers almost cut off" reported that "the towns-people were murdering some soldiers in the street." All this activity, according to the *Unhappy Disturbance,* "shews that the inhabitants had formed, and were preparing to execute, a design of attacking the soldiers on that evening."[8]

The Custom House and the sentry posted in front of it "seem to have been a principal object of the people's fury." After the bell began to ring, the crowd in King Street stepped up their harassment. They "surrounded the centry, and began to attack him by striking at him with clubs, swearing they would be revenged on the soldiers." When he was pelted with ice and sticks, he retreated up the steps of the Custom House to its front door, where he loaded his musket, hoping to deter the crowd. "But it had not this effect; for the people assembled in greater numbers, and set him at defiance, crying, *"Fire, fire, and be damned."* The sentry, "being thus hard pressed," requested assistance from the Main Guard. Captain Preston led a detachment toward the Custom House "with their arms in a horizontal posture, and their bayonets fixed." When a bystander asked Preston whether he intended to have his men fire on the crowd, he replied, *"By no means."* Preston "spoke often to the mob, desiring them to be quiet and disperse. . . . But his humane endeavours were to no purpose." The crowd continued to pelt the soldiers with sticks and ice.[9]

When one of Preston's grenadiers was struck by a large stick or a piece of ice so forcefully that it "made him stagger," he and the soldier next to him "fired their pieces without any order from Captain Preston for that purpose." More shots followed; three townspeople were killed immediately, and eight wounded. After the last shot was fired, Preston "sprung before the soldiers, and waving his sword or stick, said, 'Damn ye, rascals, what did ye fire for?' and struck up the gun of one of the soldiers who was loading again; whereupon they seemed confounded, and fired no more."[10]

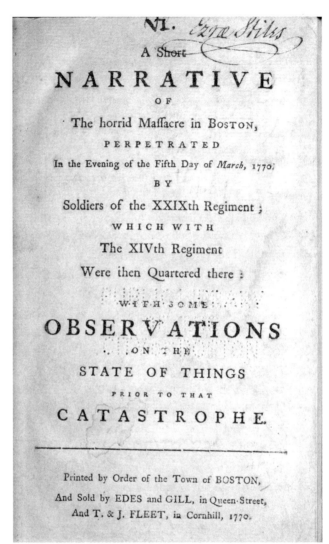

A Short

NARRATIVE

OF

· The horrid Maſſacre in BOSTON,

PERPETRATED

In the Evening of the Fifth Day of *March*, 1770,

BY

Soldiers of the XXIXth Regiment ;

WHICH WITH

The XIVth Regiment

Were then Quartered there :

WITH SOME

OBSERVATIONS

ON THE

STATE OF THINGS

PRIOR TO THAT

CATASTROPHE.

Printed by Order of the Town of BOSTON,

And Sold by EDES and GILL, in Queen-Street,

And T. & J. FLEET, in Cornhill, 1770.

The *Horrid Massacre (above)* and *Unhappy Disturbance (opposite)* offered sharply contrasting descriptions of the shootings on March 5, 1770, and the events leading up to them. Both included numerous eyewitness depositions. Both were originally intended to circulate in Great Britain, though the *Horrid Massacre* was available in Boston by midsummer.

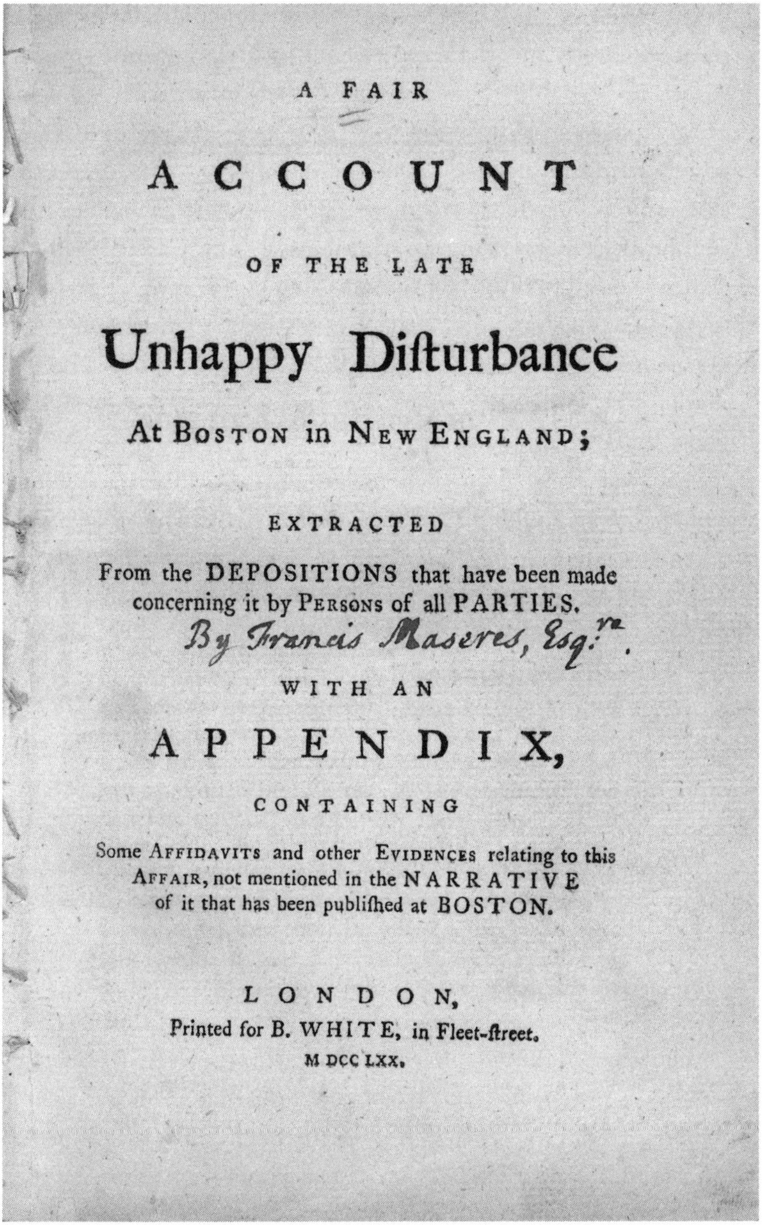

A FAIR

ACCOUNT

OF THE LATE

Unhappy Difturbance

At Boston in New England;

EXTRACTED

From the DEPOSITIONS that have been made
concerning it by Persons of all PARTIES.

By Francis Maseres, Esqre.

WITH AN

APPENDIX,

CONTAINING

Some Affidavits and other Evidences relating to this
Affair, not mentioned in the NARRATIVE
of it that has been publifhed at BOSTON.

LONDON,
Printed for B. WHITE, in Fleet-ftreet.
M DCC LXX.

In truth, both pamphlets impose considerably more order on the narrative of events than an honest accounting of the appended eyewitness testimony would allow. Estimates of the crowd in front of the Custom House varied from thirty or forty to seventy or eighty. One deponent said that the crowd numbered some two hundred until Preston and his men took up their positions, at which point "so great a part of the people were dispersed at the sight of the armed soldiers, as that not more than twenty or thirty remained in King Street."[11] Descriptions of the crowd's behavior vary widely. One deponent says the people in the street were some twenty yards off from the soldiers, "standing still," while other accounts describe a "mob," "many of them armed with large clubs and sticks," that "began to abuse the soldiers in the grossest terms."[12] Two deponents describe themselves standing among the soldiers, taking Preston by the sleeve, striking at the grenadiers' muskets as they began to fire, and being knocked down by the guns or poked at with bayonets. One of them claimed that, after the first shot was fired, he knocked the gun out of the offending soldier's hands.[13] One witness reported that a soldier's gun was knocked to the ground by a piece of snow or ice before the firing commenced, while another claimed that, before any shots were fired, a grenadier was knocked off balance by a stick thrown at him from the crowd.[14] According to one witness, Preston gave the order to fire; when his men failed to act, he shouted, "Damn your bloods, fire, be the consequence what it will." Then, after a series of shots, this same deponent described Preston jumping in front of his grenadiers and demanding, "Damn ye, rascals, what did ye fire for?"[15]

Preston's own version of events is, if anything, even more harrowing than that of the *Unhappy Disturbance*. He reported that Boston's townspeople were in "great commotions," and that a hundred people had surrounded the sentinel in front of the Custom House and begun to threaten him with "Clubs & other weapons." As Preston debated what to do, a townsman told him that the crowd intended to carry off the sentinel and murder him. When Preston marched a detachment of soldiers to the Custom House, he wrote, the crowd grew even "more outragious." Preston said that he took up a position between the soldiers and the crowd and pleaded with the people to "retire peaceably." Instead, "they advanced to the point of the Bayonets, struck some of them, and even the Muzzels of the pieces, and seemed to be endeavouring to close with the soldiers."

As Preston continued to exchange words with a few bystanders, one of his men "received a severe blow with a stick, step'd a little on one side and instantly fired." As Preston tried to intervene, he wrote, "I was struck with a Club on my Arm which for some time deprived me of the use of it." Meanwhile, the first shot prompted a "general attack . . . on the men by a great number of heavy Clubs, & snow Balls." In response, "three or four of the Soldiers fired, one after another, and directly after three more, in the same confusion and hurry."[16]

Preston, of course, had good reason to blame the assembled crowd. His account was written from jail, and he feared for his life. Though no one else had quite so much at stake, every deponent had his own reasons to shade his testimony to favor either the townspeople or the soldiers, which goes a long way toward explaining why their versions of events vary so dramatically.

Two and a half centuries after the events of March 5, 1770, occurred, many of the factual disputes about them cannot be resolved: we cannot arrive at a definitive account of *the* "Boston Massacre." Yet we can do a great deal to explain how it came about and to explore its consequences. When we examine the larger contexts of the massacre, we cannot fail to recognize that essential changes in British governance pushed Boston toward a crisis. More important, the character of Boston itself comes into focus. Events of the 1770s would show that this small port community, perched on a tiny North Atlantic peninsula, had the power to shape the fortune of the Western world's greatest empire. Even as *the* Boston Massacre remains an enigma, Boston's massacre — a global event shaped by local sensibilities — rises in sharp relief.

FEAR, UNCERTAINTY, DETERMINATION, RAGE: in the wake of the shootings, every shading of powerful emotion must have run through the agitated crowd. While townspeople began to attend to the dead and wounded, Preston hastily formed up his party. Warned that an angry mob several thousand strong was gathering a block away "and had sworn to take my Life with every man[']s with me," Preston marched his men back to the Main Guard.[17]

Bells were ringing in every steeple. The town drums were beating to arms, many inhabitants were crying, "Turn out with your guns," and some considered breaking out the town's muskets, which were stored in Faneuil Hall. Preston, too, ordered his drummer to beat to arms. The soldiers in the Main Guard hastily assembled outdoors, where the rest of the 29th Regiment soon joined them. Preston ordered them to take up the position known as "street firings." This formation, in which the soldiers were arrayed in files, with the foremost man kneeling in a firing position — originally conceived to help Europe's early modern soldiery cope with urban rioters — was intended to give the soldiers control of the upper end of King Street. After his small squadron was nearly overwhelmed by the crowd in front of the Custom House, Preston was determined to assert control. Under his direction, the men were "divided and planted . . . at each end of the street to secure their rear, momently expecting an attack." Numbering in the hundreds, the soldiers must have constituted a formidable presence. As James Bowdoin pointedly noted, this was a formation that "plainly manifested a disposition to commit a further massacre."

Having sent urgent word to Lieutenant Colonel William Dalrymple, the commanding officer, Preston prepared for the worst.[18]

As the surging crowd pressed in on the soldiers, Thomas Hutchinson, the acting governor of Massachusetts Bay, was rushing to the scene. Despite the chaos in Boston's streets, he had managed to spend the evening quietly at his home in the North End. When he heard bells ringing, he assumed they were signaling a fire and did not stir himself. But then, as he wrote, just a bit defensively, to Thomas Gage, the British commander in chief for North America, "I soon found there was another cause and one upon another came running to my house to inform me that unless I went out immediately the whole town would be in arms and the most bloody scene would follow that had ever been known in America." Hutchinson hurried out into the night. As he made his way toward the center of town, he met Joseph Belknap, Jonathan Mason, and Samuel Whitwell, who were on their way to get him. The three turned around and accompanied Hutchinson. As they tried to pass through Dock Square, a crowd of angry townspeople threatened Hutchinson. The four men were forced to retrace their steps, pass through the house and backyard of Royall Tyler — a member of the Governor's Council who had been out in the streets a few minutes earlier, only to retire inside when he saw the temper of the crowd — and then find a safer route.[19]

In King Street, Joseph Belknap pointed out to Hutchinson the blood in the snow. Then they pushed their way toward the soldiers through the crowd. Belknap later recalled that he thought the soldiers, arrayed in their files with "Guns all leveled down [the] Street," appeared to be "just ready to fire."[20]

As Hutchinson approached the troops, Isaac Pierce spotted him and called out to Preston, "There is His Honor, the Commander in Chief."

"Where?" asked Preston.

"*There,* and you are presenting your firelocks at him."[21]

Hutchinson was "push'd by a vast throng of people" toward the troops, "almost upon the Bayonets," until he found himself standing next to Preston. "How came you to fire without Orders from a Civil Magistrate?" demanded Hutchinson, with "some emotion" in his voice. Both men knew—as did most of the townspeople in the streets that night—that, by the law of both England and Massachusetts Bay, troops could be used in a domestic police action only by order of local authorities. In this case, it was Hutchinson himself who should have given such a command.[22]

"I was obliged to, to save my sentry," answered Preston. Hutchinson thought that Preston seemed offended by the question.

"Then you have murdered three or four men to save your sentry," snapped Pierce angrily.

"These soldiers ought not to be here," Hutchinson told Preston.

Preston replied, "It is not in my power to order them away."[23] This was a little disingenuous. He could not abandon the Main Guard, but he certainly could have ordered his men into a less threatening position. While he waited for his superiors to decide what to do, Preston was taking no chances with the crowd.

Next, Preston asked Hutchinson to go into the guardhouse with him so he could explain his position more fully. Hutchinson was tempted—he later wrote that he thought Preston was holding back in their conversation in the street—but he also realized that it would look to the assembled crowd like he was colluding with Preston if he did. He refused Preston's request. Instead he conferred with Lieutenant Colonel Maurice Carr, commander of the 29th Regiment, and persuaded him that "the regiment should retire to their barracks and the people to their houses." But neither was prepared to give way first.[24]

The crowd, meanwhile, was pushing forward. Belknap suggested that Hutchinson should enter the council chamber, on the upper floor of the Town House. Standing at the head of King Street, alongside the files of soldiers to the south and the surging townspeople to the east, the Town House was the seat of Massachusetts government. It had a balcony looking out onto King Street from which Hutchinson could address the crowd. The crowd began to chant, "The Town House, The Town House," urging Hutchinson to go inside.[25]

CHAPTER 2

Town and Crown

THE TOWN HOUSE was one of Boston's two principal nodes of political activity. The Governor's Council met upstairs at the east end of the building, while the House of Representatives convened at the west end. (Together, these two bodies composed the Massachusetts General Court.) It was familiar ground to Thomas Hutchinson. Born and raised in Boston, Hutchinson entered politics early. He was elected to the Massachusetts House of Representatives for the first time at the age of twenty-five and served there for more than a decade, with three years in the Speaker's chair, before rising to other offices. He was appointed to the Governor's Council in 1749 and as chief justice of the Massachusetts Superior Court in 1760. He had also served as the colony's lieutenant governor since 1758; upon the resignation of Francis Bernard, he became the acting governor in August 1769. Now fifty-eight, Hutchinson was the most experienced political leader the colony had ever known, but also, because of his accumulated offices, one of the most controversial.[1]

The second focus of political action in Boston was Faneuil Hall, where the town meeting assembled. The proceedings of the town meeting were open to anyone who chose to attend, and a large proportion of the town's adult male inhabitants could cast a vote. Since the passage of the Stamp Act in 1765, the town meeting had been

Boston's principal forum for expressing public discontent over crown policy. Since Hutchinson had become acting governor, leading voices in the town meeting, including James Otis Jr. and Samuel Adams Jr., had been sharply critical of him.[2]

Now Hutchinson was in the middle of a chaotic scene. "With irresistible violence," he later recalled, "I was carried by the crowd into the Council Chamber." One of the people waiting for him there was William Molineux, a Boston merchant and radical Whig who had long helped to orchestrate local crowd actions. "Many Things are attributed to him," wrote fellow merchant John Rowe, "& tis believed he was first Leader of Dirty Matters." Hutchinson and Molineux despised each other. Hutchinson was cautious and moderate to a fault; Molineux was fiery and impetuous. Both considered themselves men of principle, but the principles they followed could not have been more different. Like-minded townsmen admired Molineux's zeal, but to Hutchinson's close associate Peter Oliver he was a "most infamous Disturber of the Peace." Now he approached Hutchinson to warn him that the crowd would not disperse unless the soldiers gave ground first.[3] The governor knew that he had to act decisively or the shootings that had already occurred would be remembered only as a prelude to the catastrophe that was about to unfold.

Hutchinson stepped onto the balcony and addressed both the soldiers and the crowd. He looked out on a boisterous group of enraged townspeople — contemporary accounts estimated four or five thousand — many armed with clubs or cutlasses, while the soldiers remained in firing position below him to his right. He urged the crowd to disperse and assured them that justice would be done. They refused to leave until the soldiers had given way, so Lieutenant Colonel Carr formed up his regiment, and the men of the 29th "marched off down Pudding Lane," leaving the acting governor of the Massachusetts Bay Colony to deal with the crowd. Around 1:00 A.M., once the soldiers were gone, most of the townspeople retired to their beds, leaving a smaller crowd of perhaps a hundred who remained in King Street, waiting to witness the progress of events.[4]

Hutchinson's night was far from over. Some members of his council were already present in the chamber; he sent for Lieutenant Colonel William Dalrymple, the ranking officer in town, to join them. Two justices of the peace, Richard Dana and John Tudor, issued a warrant for the arrest of Captain Preston and the eight soldiers who had been under his command at the time of the shootings. The sheriff brought Preston to the council chamber, where several eyewitnesses testified that they heard him order his men to fire into the crowd. The justices' inquiry concluded shortly after 3:00 A.M., and Preston was immediately committed to the Boston jail. By 4:00 A.M. the streets were quiet. Later in the morning, eight more soldiers—William Wemms, James Hartegan, William McCauley, Hugh White, Matthew Kilroy, William Warren, John Carrol, and Hugh Montgomery—joined Preston in jail; together they awaited the outcome of events.[5]

On Tuesday morning, the Town House and Faneuil Hall were both alive with activity. At around 11:00 A.M., after a short and presumably disturbed night's sleep, Hutchinson arrived at the Town House, where the Governor's Council was already assembled. "I found all the selectmen of the town and a great part of the Justices of the county waiting for me," he wrote, ". . . to represent to me their opinion of the absolute necessity, in order to prevent a further effusion of blood, that the troops should be at such a distance as that there might be no intercourse between the inhabitants and them." Hutchinson summoned Dalrymple and Carr to confer with the council.[6]

Meanwhile, an enormous crowd was gathering at Faneuil Hall—not just the town's voting population of perhaps fifteen hundred, but some three to four thousand people, too many for the hall to hold (in the afternoon the crowd moved to the more spacious Old South Meeting House). Beginning its own deliberations at 11:00 A.M., the town meeting recalled Boston's selectmen from the State House council chamber and sent in their place a committee specially designated to present its demands to the governor. In the long day that followed, they repeatedly petitioned Hutchinson to remove the troops from town; he repeatedly answered that he did not have the authority to do so. He did, however, have Dalrymple's ear. By early afternoon Dalrymple had agreed to remove the 29th to Castle William, the fort that stood on an island in the harbor. After considering this proposal, the townspeople replied "that nothing less will satisfy them, than a total and immediate removal of the Troops." Dalrymple told Hutchinson that he would also order the 14th Regiment to withdraw if the governor requested it. Hours later, exhausted and alarmed by the town's persistence, Hutchinson asked Dalrymple to withdraw the 14th as well.[7]

THE WRANGLING between town and crown captured in miniature the increasingly polarized character of politics in Massachusetts Bay. The colony charter prescribed a mixed form of government in which the crown was represented by a royally appointed governor, while assembly members were elected annually in town meetings. In an especially unusual provision, a new council was chosen each year as well. The assembly and the previous year's council together nominated twenty-eight prospective councilors; the governor could not alter their selections, but he did have the power to disallow any nominees he chose. The assembly's role in selecting council members made the Massachusetts charter more democratic than that of any other royal colony, while the involvement of prior council members and the governor's veto power imparted a measure of stability to the advisory body the governor relied upon for guidance, and leverage, in his dealings with the assembly and its constituent towns.[8]

Historically, Boston's representatives often found themselves at odds with a majority in the assembly, who styled themselves a country interest and sought to limit the influence of the colony's leading port town and commercial center. As Hutchinson later recalled, "There was a jealousy lest the town should obtain too great influence." But as resistance to the imperial reforms and tax measures of the 1760s gained momentum, Bostonians "became the leaders," and the assembly lined up behind its members. Hutchinson believed that the two James Otises, father and son, led the shift in sympathies on the part of the "country towns." James Otis Sr. represented Barnstable for many years in the assembly, where he had consistently supported Governor William Shirley in opposition to Boston's members. (Shirley, governor of Massachusetts Bay from 1741 to 1749 and again from 1753 to 1756, was the most successful crown representative in the province's history.) But in 1760 the new governor, Francis Bernard, chose to appoint Thomas Hutchinson — a man with many connections but no legal training — as chief justice of the Superior Court rather than the elder Otis. From that time forward, the father became Hutchinson's inveterate enemy. He also became, according to Hutchinson, a "strong advocate" for Boston "and drew much of the country interest after him." His son, James Otis Jr. — now a Boston lawyer — was elected to the assembly for the first time in 1761 and thereafter helped to cement the connection.[9]

At the same time that the assembly drew together behind Boston's leaders, the council grew more sympathetic to the assembly's concerns. For most of the colony's history, the Massachusetts council had functioned much like councils in other colonies, the process of election notwithstanding. Its members tended to be well-to-do gentlemen; generally, they advised the governor in a spirit of cooperative goodwill that often made them the governor's natural allies when he clashed with the assembly. But by the late 1760s, as the imperial crisis deepened, the governor often found the council to be unreliable in its support, and he began to exercise his veto power over its members more vigorously. After the Stamp Act crisis, Otis and the country party began putting up slates of candidates for the assembly; in the process, they gained leverage over the composition of the council and absorbed it into partisan politics as never before. The year 1768 — when Governor Bernard and General Gage decided to station troops in Boston to suppress radical activity — was an especially fractious one. (It was also the year in which Bernard described the election of councilors as "the Cankerworm of the Constitution of this Government.") In 1769 the assembly refused to reelect four members of the previous year's council — "nearly the whole that had not joined in opposition to the governor." In their place was a cadre of new faces, many from Boston and all supporting the radical cause; they included James Bowdoin, John Hancock, James Otis Jr., and Artemas Ward. Governor Bernard responded by vetoing an astonishing eleven candidates, leaving him with a council of only seventeen. Yet even those seventeen were unreliable allies for the colony's beleaguered governor.[10]

If the governor, council, and assembly together made up the superstructure of colony government, the town meetings — and especially the Boston town meeting — often supplied its ballast and heft. Town meetings had a dual character. Much of the time their business was routine and crushingly dull, but in moments of crisis they could become a ready-made force, quick to organize and irrepressible in their actions. The town meeting is an often invoked but little understood institution. It made municipal government in New England far different from that of any other region in British North America. Elsewhere, towns were generally constituted under corporate or municipal charters and managed accordingly, with municipal officers operating largely independently of their constituents. In New England, by contrast, town meetings served as the foundation for all local political activity. The franchise was broad enough to allow a large proportion of adult males to vote, and all men — "whether Inhabitant or Foreigner, free or not free" — could attend and deliberate.[11]

The functions of the town meeting were diverse and often mundane. It annually elected the town's selectmen and its representatives in the assembly, as well as a panoply of local officials, from tax collectors, constables, and overseers of the poor to viewers of shingles and fences, market clerks, surveyors of hemp and flax, cullers of staves, sealers of leather, hogreeves, and scavengers. Local residents dictated much of its business as they petitioned the meeting for relief or compensation for their services, sought permission to undertake a new development, or proposed a solution to some problem. In response to petitions and matters that came from the floor, the town meeting acted as both a petty legislature and an all-purpose management board. It arranged for public funerals upon the death of noteworthy citizens; it crafted rules designed to restrain local hog populations when they disturbed the peace; it arranged to cut or pave new streets; it approved the construction of public markets and established regulations for them; it set salaries for schoolmasters; it protected public property and granted permission for private building projects that impinged on the public interest. It also voiced the concerns of the community by crafting letters and petitions aimed at the colony's governor, council, or assembly.[12]

Involvement in the town meeting was time-consuming, and participation was by no means universal. Its annual cycle of meetings began in March, when it convened daily for three or four days running to elect a slate of local officials and begin to attend to the year's business. It met again in May and September. In between these regularly scheduled sessions, the meeting convened irregularly as needs dictated; it might reconvene, for example, to hear the report of a committee and consider some recommended course of action. During the mid-1740s, the meeting gathered about a dozen times a year; in 1770, when the shootings in King Street caused its activity to balloon, it met on nineteen days, including eight days in March. Double sessions would sometimes consume the entire day. Moments of high drama aside, regular attendance at the town meeting demanded more patience than many residents could muster. Boston had a voting population of around fifteen hundred in the third quarter of the eighteenth century, and just over a third of eligible voters typically participated. On average, between 1763 and 1774, 555 votes were cast in Boston's town elections. (In May 1770 turnout was a below-average 513.) This represented a typical turnout of perhaps 37 percent.[13]

Thus, while it was an unusually open institution, the town meeting was also susceptible to being led by a coterie of interested individuals who could anticipate and orchestrate local issues. The first man to capitalize upon this possibility was Elisha Cooke Jr. Early in the century, Cooke opposed an effort to incorporate Boston as a municipal borough whose charter would have replaced the town meeting with a mayor and aldermen. Then he claimed his place at the center of a group of local leaders who emerged after 1719 to dominate local affairs for nearly two decades. Cooke died in 1737, and his circle died with him. But the group that came to be known as the Boston Caucus, led by James Allen, Nathaniel Cunningham, and Samuel Adams Sr., revived its activities and methods in the 1740s. They soon gained enough influence to be regarded as leaders of the town's "popular" party, with the ability to influence the attitudes and direct the actions of a large proportion of Boston's residents.[14]

Though Hutchinson was a native Bostonian, by 1770 he had been at odds with local leadership for many years. The divergence was partly philosophical, partly temperamental, and — in the end — deeply personal. Hutchinson's forebears were among the earliest migrants to Massachusetts Bay, and from the beginning they occupied themselves in trade. Merchant activity in Boston was a precarious undertaking; it required constant adjustments and innovations and repaid only the most painstaking attention to detail. The Hutchinsons persevered through steady, unspectacular effort. Thomas's father, a colonel in the Massachusetts militia who served, like his son, on the provincial council, capitalized on the opportunities available in Boston as effectively as almost anyone of his generation.

Thomas, a serious and precocious boy, was twelve years old when he enrolled in Harvard College in 1723. At the same time, his father gave him "two or three quintals of fish"—that is, two or three hundred pounds of dried, salted cod, the lifeblood of the New England merchant. Like the good servant in the parable of the talents related in the New Testament gospels, Hutchinson parlayed this small stake into the beginnings of a great fortune. By the end of his college years, Hutchinson later recalled, he had already amassed some £400–500: a respectable annual income for a London gentleman of the time, and an extraordinary stake for a Boston teenager just embarking on his career.[15]

When Hutchinson entered public life a decade or so later, Massachusetts Bay was wrestling with one of the most persistent problems facing the residents of an isolated Atlantic outpost: an anemic money supply. The General Court agreed to print 7,000 pounds in paper currency in 1690 as England entered an era of imperial warfare and the colony struggled to meet its expenses. The earliest issues of paper currency were essentially loans taken out against future tax revenues. At around the same time, Britain adopted a new paper currency of its own: pounds sterling. Backed by the silver supply controlled by the Bank of England, pounds sterling became the most reliable currency available in the British world. By comparison, the colonies' paper issues tended to be unstable and inflationary. While they could facilitate economic transactions within the colony, they had no value in the transatlantic market. They could bear hard on merchants like Hutchinson, who had to mediate between the local exchange economy and the British Atlantic, and who were therefore especially vulnerable to the inflationary tendencies of colonial currencies.[16]

Hutchinson and other economic conservatives came to see paper currencies as a profound threat to the colony's economic well-being. William Douglass, a like-minded physician and historian who was a contemporary of Hutchinson's, complained:

> I have observed, that all our *Paper Money* making Assemblies have been Legislatures of *Debtors,* the Representatives of the People who from Incogitancy, *Idleness,* and *Profuseness,* have been under a Necessity of mortgaging their Lands; Lands are a real permanent Estate, but the Debt in *Paper Currency* by its Multiplication *depreciates* more and more; thus their Land Estate in nominal Value *increases,* and their Debt in nominal Value *decreases;* and the large Quantities of *Paper Credit* is proportionably in Favour of the Debtors, and to the Disadvantage of the Creditors or industrious frugal Part of the Colony: this is the *wicked Mystery* of this *iniquitous Paper Currency.*[17]

Douglass captured Hutchinson's sentiments precisely. As an industrious, frugal creditor with transatlantic obligations, Hutchinson worried that paper money would bleed away his wealth, while the colony's feckless debtors would benefit by his loss.

In opposing paper money, Hutchinson ran up against strong popular sentiment. Most residents of Massachusetts Bay were hardworking, cash-poor farmers. Their wealth, as Douglass suggested, was in land. But they often lacked the currency they needed even to pay their taxes, and they could trade only in face-to-face settings where cash wasn't required. Instead they recorded their exchanges with neighbors and relatives in crabbed notations inked into the personal account books that nearly every adult carried. Paper currency enhanced their liquidity and expanded their options. John Colman was, like Hutchinson, a Boston merchant, but one who favored a more abundant supply of local cash to lubricate the economy. In

1739 Colman led a group that petitioned the General Court for the right to create a land bank. Residents of the colony would be able to borrow money from the bank against the value of their land or personal property. Though the land bank was a private company rather than a public enterprise, its backers hoped to generate a new form of money for the colony, one that held its value and circulated in the countryside as well as in Boston. The General Court granted the land bank its charter. In September 1740 it already had more than twelve hundred subscribers; by 1741 it had issued £49,000 in loans.[18]

But for all its initial success, the land bank also had powerful enemies, including Hutchinson and then-governor Jonathan Belcher. At their urging, in 1741 Parliament disallowed the charter that had created the land bank, leaving its largest investors holding the bag. Deprived of this money supply, and needing to raise funds for military expenditures during the War of the Austrian Succession, the General Court issued paper money throughout the 1740s. The colony's most expensive venture in that war—the campaign to capture the French fortress at Louisbourg on Cape Breton Island—was also its most astonishing success. Word soon reached Boston that Parliament was considering a payment of £180,000 to compensate the colony for the cost of the Louisbourg expedition. While the payment was still only a rumor, Hutchinson persuaded the General Court to accept a plan to retire the colony's old notes and use the silver as the basis for a new currency. A majority of the General Court—perhaps believing that the payment was a remote possibility at best—was rather easily persuaded to support the idea, while the colony's advocates for a more generous monetary policy were taken by surprise. James Allen, Boston's other representative in the assembly and one of the backers of the old land bank scheme, could only fume in response. Like his supporters in the Boston town meeting, Allen opposed the hard money plan, and after it was passed he rose to condemn the General Court for its action. The legislature responded by ejecting him from his seat and ordering a new election.[19]

CURRENCY REFORM, a triumph for Hutchinson, brought misfortune to others — among them, some members of that circle of men known as the Boston Caucus who emerged to dominate the town meeting during the 1740s. Its most prominent victim was Samuel Adams Sr., father of the more famous Revolutionary-era leader of the same name. Adams was one of the principal shareholders of the land bank, and with the other partners he became legally liable for its debts. Adams was hounded until his death in 1748 for the recovery of his share. (A decade later, Boston's sheriff threatened to sell the father's estate out from under the son, Samuel Adams Jr., but the younger Adams managed to fend off the proceedings and finally, it seems, escape the burden of the land bank debts.) James Allen — who would so vehemently oppose Hutchinson's hard money scheme — was another partner in the land bank; he was also the elder Adams's son-in-law, having married his daughter Mary.[20]

The rise of the Boston Caucus coincided with the economic distress and dislocations of the 1740s, which were linked in turn to the decade of warfare that ran from 1739 to 1748. Much of the town was in trouble as a result of the war, and its leaders labored to broadcast Boston's difficulties. In March 1743 the town meeting petitioned the General Court for tax relief. According to its plea, Boston had been "almost entirely Stript" of its direct trade in fish to Europe, while its West Indies trade was "almost reduced to Nothing." As a result, commerce in Boston had declined by 50 percent since 1735. In that year, Boston shipyards had received orders for forty new vessels; in 1742 they received only two. This sudden contraction in the local economy caused a sharp increase in poverty; charges for poor relief had more than doubled since 1735. At the same time, the downturn drove productive laborers — skilled craftsmen, fishermen, small traders and shopkeepers — out of town in large numbers. Boston's economic woes, the town's petition lamented, "must Necessarily Oblige a great many of Our Useful Tradesmen to leave the Town as many have already done." The number of taxables had fallen more than 12 percent, from 3,395 to 2,972, while the local tax rate had increased by nearly 28 percent.[21]

In fact, while the distress of the 1740s had immediate causes, it was part of a longer-term pattern of decline. In 1700 Boston had the most robust maritime economy in British North America. Only London and Bristol ranked ahead of Boston in the number of vessels registered in the port. Townspeople participated in the growth of maritime enterprise not only as laborers, but also as investors, to a surprising degree: in the early eighteenth century, 544 of Boston's adult males, who numbered perhaps 1,800 overall, owned a share of at least one vessel. The town's population grew by 30 percent during the 1720s and the 1730s, despite devastating waves of smallpox in 1721 and 1730. By 1740 Boston had some seventeen thousand residents and appeared to be entering an era of sustained prosperity and growth.[22]

But it didn't come. Instead, against all expectations, Boston fell into the shadow of other ports, large and small, while its economy suffered waves of contraction. In contrast to every other port town in British North America, the city's population ceased to grow: in 1770 Boston was smaller than it was in 1740. Its merchants faced stiff new competition from Philadelphia, which tapped a richer agricultural hinterland than Boston; from New York, which challenged Boston's dominance in trade with the British Isles; and from smaller New England ports like Salem, Marblehead, Newbury, Portsmouth, and Newport, which began shipping dried fish directly to the West Indies and the Mediterranean and captured a growing share of the shipbuilding industry that had become so important to the region's economy.[23]

The midcentury wars—the War of Jenkins' Ear (1739–1748), the War of the Austrian Succession (1744–1748), and the Seven Years' War (1754–1763)—created opportunities for wartime contracting that partially offset the effects of this stagnation, but they did so selectively. The biggest winners were a relatively small number of merchants whose connections won them large contracts. The greatest beneficiary was Thomas Hancock, uncle to John; Andrew Oliver (brother-in-law to Thomas Hutchinson), John Erving, and Charles Apthorp also did well. Beyond the obvious success of these few individuals, however, the wartime legacy was mixed. It brought a much greater demand for maritime labor, and with it a rise in wages, but also dramatic price inflation and ruinously high taxes. On balance, the effects of these wars were complex enough that they offered a kind of camouflage to the longer-term pattern of stagnation that Boston was experiencing by comparison with its neighbors and rivals.[24]

This was the context in which the Boston Caucus came to the fore in local politics. It was James Allen who revived the methods of Elisha Cooke Jr.; along with the elder Adams, Nathaniel Cunningham, and a larger cohort of around twenty men, the Caucus sought to orchestrate the affairs of the town. The town meeting pursued tax relief from the province in the 1740s; then, when that was not forthcoming, it apparently facilitated a widespread pattern of tax evasion. The town elected its own tax assessors, tax collectors, and auditors, and during the turbulent years of the 1740s and 1750s it returned the same men to office in these positions over and over—including Allen, who served repeatedly as an auditor—despite the fact that tax receipts fell hopelessly into arrears. As local officials granted de facto tax relief to Boston's citizens, the town's selectmen were forced to borrow money from local merchants to fill the gap and meet immediate needs.[25]

The Caucus envisioned itself as the vessel for local interests, and its natural enemies were the colony's crown appointees: the royal

Thomas Hutchinson, by Edward Truman (1741). Hutchinson's portrait was painted only once, on his visit to England in 1741, when he was still a young man but already accomplished and well-to-do. This image captures Hutchinson's sense of supreme self-confidence.

governor and the circle of officials to whom he granted offices. Although they were appointed by the crown, many of Massachusetts Bay's governors were prominent locals with overseas connections; this was true of Joseph Dudley, William Tailer, William Dummer, Jonathan Belcher, Spencer Phips, and, eventually, Hutchinson himself. These men especially galled the Caucus, and the feeling was mutual. In 1741, when Thomas Hutchinson was in England acting as an agent for the Massachusetts Bay Colony, Governor Jonathan Belcher wrote to him, "I dont wonder, you find such Prejudices among the King's Ministers, against this Province when I consider what pains have been taken here, for 25 years past, to treat the Crown, with all possible rudeness, and ill manners, and altho' the first beginner and Principal Agitator [Elisha Cooke Jr.] is dead, yet you know, he dropt his Mantle (forgive the Prophanation of the words) on a Creature [James Allen], who still carryes it, to higher Lengths."[26]

THE IMPERIAL CRISIS of the 1760s and 1770s brought another generational transition in Caucus leadership. Samuel Adams Jr. stepped forward to follow in his father's footsteps; along with prominent locals like James Otis Jr., William Molineux, Joseph Warren, and William Phillips, he played a key role in shaping the town meeting to the needs of another era of crisis. The new Caucus used the town meeting as a mouthpiece for expressing collective grievances. It had a distinctive voice — sometimes plaintive, often outraged, always standing on principle — that gave shape and focus to the town's collective rhetorical identity. Over time, the Caucus became a crucial bridge between the local institutions of government and the extra-institutional, out-of-doors activity for which Boston became famous.[27]

Adams and Otis emerged by the mid-1760s as the town's preeminent radical leaders. It may have been only a matter of coincidence that each had deep personal reasons to despise Thomas Hutchinson, a key figure in provincial politics throughout the crises of the post–Seven Years' War era and, beginning in August 1769, the acting governor of Massachusetts Bay. For both men, the animosity was grounded in their fathers' experiences with Hutchinson.

Samuel Adams Sr., who would later lose so much in Hutchinson's attack on the land bank scheme, was a maltster who enjoyed enough success to build a substantial home on Purchase Street overlooking the harbor. The younger Samuel attended Boston Latin and, like Hutchinson, Harvard College. His father then apprenticed him to the merchant Thomas Cushing, but Cushing quickly concluded that Adams was ill suited to trade and persuaded his father to end their arrangement. Next, his father gave Samuel a cash stake of £1,000 — a much larger sum than the two or three quintals of dried cod that had laid the foundation of Hutchinson's fortune. In a foreshadowing of Adams's lifelong impecuniousness, it evaporated without a trace. As a final resort, Adams became a partner in his father's malt house, which, after his father's death, he soon ran into bankruptcy. While he served as a tax collector for the town, his accounts ran hopelessly into arrears. "He affects to despize Riches, and not to dread Poverty," wrote his cousin John. "But no Man is more ambitious of entertaining his Friends handsomely, or of making a decent, an elegant Appearance than he."[28]

After his father was passed over for the position of chief justice of the Superior Court, James Otis Jr. had his own reasons to despise Hutchinson. Otis and Adams inherited the mantle of the Boston Caucus and, beginning with the imperial crises of the mid-1760s, came to the fore in local affairs. Both men were active in the Boston town meeting; Otis also served in the assembly. They also made regular contributions to the local newspapers. Their pieces were signed with pseudonyms, but usually there was little doubt in Boston about their authorship. Together they crafted the voice of Boston's

Samuel Adams, by John Singleton Copley (ca. 1772). Copley's portrait shows Adams in a moment of high drama, standing before Hutchinson, his council, and Lieutenant Colonel William Dalrymple on March 6, 1770, and demanding that they withdraw the troops. Adams points to the colony's charter with his left hand while his right clutches a copy of the town's instructions to its representatives in the General Court following the Stamp Act, a document Adams helped to draft. Adams cuts an imposing figure in the dress of a respectable tradesman.

republican conscience, expressing outrage at Parliament's constitutional innovations and directing their hectoring fury at the crown officers in their midst. No one received more of their withering criticism than Thomas Hutchinson.[29]

While the Caucus emerged to manage the affairs of the town meeting, its efforts were paralleled by other organizations that were created to shape opinions and, when necessary, mobilize action. In 1751 a group calling itself the Merchants' Club began to meet regularly at the British Coffee House and the Bunch of Grapes tavern to discuss issues affecting the town's commercial life. Boston's merchant community was fractured and diffuse, but the Merchant's Club was composed of men who were closely affiliated with the Caucus and sought to synchronize the views and actions of the local merchant community and the town meeting. Sometime around 1760, this loosely organized club gave way to the Boston Society for Encouraging Trade and Commerce, which further unified the town's commercial interest.[30]

Clubs and associations with explicitly political aims multiplied in the 1760s, spurred by the post–Seven Years' War crackdown on smuggling and the Stamp Act crisis. Boston was not unusual in this: these parliamentary efforts to impose new forms of control on the colonies were interpreted throughout British North America as an unconstitutional intrusion upon provincial prerogatives. What is striking about Boston is the characteristic way in which it mobilized its resources to protest the acts. Beginning in the 1760s, a rapidly expanding web of clubs and private associations organized a complex pattern of responses. The Caucus remained a vibrant force; by 1770 it had divided into three distinct but overlapping groups: a North End Caucus, a South End Caucus, and a third caucus that met in between. The Loyal Nine, ostensibly a social club, was formed in the summer of 1765 and, alongside the Caucus, helped to organize resistance to the Stamp Act. It served as the core of a much larger group called the Sons of Liberty, which was active by 1768. The Caucus and the

James Otis Jr., by Joseph Blackburn (1755). Painted when Otis was thirty—in the same year he married Ruth Cunningham, daughter of a wealthy Boston merchant—Blackburn's portrait depicts him as a man of comfort and refinement. Otis was one of Boston's most articulate and capable lawyers. He argued the writs of assistance case of 1761 so effectively that John Adams described him as a "flame of fire." By the late 1760s, mental illness made him increasingly erratic. Struck ferociously on the head by customs commissioner John Robinson during the occupation of Boston in the fall of 1769, Otis was thereafter almost wholly absent from public life.

Sons of Liberty were aided by the so-called Union Club, whose members were drawn from gangs of North End and South End youth. These gangs had staged massive brawls on Pope's Day every year since the late seventeenth century. During the protests against the Stamp Act, the Union Club—under the leadership of a charismatic shoe-maker, Ebenezer McIntosh—put its energy at the disposal of the Loyal Nine. In this same period, town leaders who were not them-selves merchants began to attend meetings of the Merchants' Club and, as the imperial crisis developed, ensured that the club supported the town's views. All these associations had overlapping memberships and largely congruent aims. In public statements, they were careful to articulate and justify their positions; when crowds took to the streets, they favored symbolic actions that were clearly and explicitly linked with their political intentions.[31]

By the mid-1760s, Boston had achieved a greater degree of concord and cooperation between radicals and moderates, and had proceeded farther in mobilizing public action against imperial intrusions, than any other Anglo-American town. Three newspapers—the *Boston Evening-Post,* edited by Thomas Fleet Jr. and John Fleet; the *Boston-Gazette and Evening Journal,* under the joint editorship of John Gill and Benjamin Edes; and John Green and Joseph Russell's *Massa-chusetts Gazette and Boston Weekly News-Letter*—served as mouth-pieces for the movement, giving coherent and sustained attention to radical concerns. And the web of local associations meant that Bos-tonians were especially well equipped to organize crowd actions when it suited their purposes.

HUTCHINSON'S PREDECESSOR, Governor Francis Bernard, feared this network of clubs and associations, with its capacity to bring crowds into the Boston streets. Bernard was not one of those gov-ernors with local roots: educated at Oxford, he practiced law in

Lincolnshire for two decades before entering the colonial service in middle age. His principal interest in doing so was to gain a patrimony for his large family. He had married Amelia Offley, daughter of a sheriff and, more important for the Bernard family fortunes, cousin to the perennial officeholder and current secretary at war William Barrington, second Viscount Barrington, whose connections were instrumental in gaining Bernard a colonial governorship. Posted first to New Jersey in 1758, he arrived in Massachusetts Bay in August 1760, as the Seven Years' War in North America was approaching its successful conclusion. His early experiences were generally favorable, but the Stamp Act riots in the fall of 1765 profoundly alarmed him; from that point forward, he feared that Boston had fallen under the sway of a "faction"—a term he used repeatedly in his correspondence— that made the town dangerously incendiary. For Bernard, the riots highlighted the constitutional weakness of the crown in Britain's North American colonies—a weakness that exposed his vulnerability and aroused his fears.[32]

The Stamp Act, which presumed Parliament's right to impose taxes on its North American colonies, was widely opposed in British North America. Most colonists believed that they enjoyed the rights of Englishmen, and that chief among those rights was the consent to taxation. Since they had no representatives in Parliament, only their individual assemblies had the power to tax them. Parliament, by contrast, claimed supreme legislative authority, not only in Britain, but in its colonies as well—and that authority extended to the taxing power. Word arrived in Boston in late May 1765 that the Stamp Act had passed; Andrew Oliver, one of the town's wealthiest merchants and brother-in-law to Thomas Hutchinson (their wives, Mary and Margaret Sanford, were sisters), was appointed stamp distributor. The statute was scheduled to take effect on November 1. On the morning of August 14, an effigy marked "A.O." was suspended by a noose from an ancient elm tree located on Orange (now Washington)

Street, near the intersection with Essex. It remained all day, the sheriff having concluded that it would not be safe to remove it. Then, "just at dark" that evening, "an amazing mob" cut down the effigy and paraded it toward the waterfront; along the way, it passed through the ground floor of the Town House while Bernard's council was meeting upstairs. The group of townspeople proceeded to Oliver's wharf, on Kilby Street, where Oliver had recently erected a small building. "In a few minutes," Hutchinson wrote, "the building was level with the ground."[33]

Next the group brought its message home to Oliver himself. It carried the effigy two blocks south, to the summit of Fort Hill, and lit a bonfire in sight of Oliver's home. Then members of the crowd charged downhill to begin an assault on his house, breaking windows and window frames where they were exposed and battering shutters until they were smashed; finally they burst inside. Hutchinson had arrived at Oliver's house ahead of the mob along with several other friends; now, he wrote, "we tho't it time to withdraw." He sought out Joseph Jackson, colonel of Boston's militia company, and urged him to raise an alarm, but Jackson feared that a drummer who tried to drum up the unit would be set upon—and the attempt was likely to be futile in any case, he mused, since "probably all the drummers of the Regiment were in the Mob." Instead Hutchinson rounded up the sheriff, Stephen Greenleaf, and returned to Oliver's house, hoping that the sight of the two of them would cause the crowd to disperse. Instead they were met with "a volley of stones & bricks." Eventually, Hutchinson fled—suffering only minor injuries—and the crowd dispersed.[34]

The next evening at about 9 o'clock, a crowd of several hundred people approached Hutchinson's home. Anticipating trouble, Hutchinson had already sent his children to his sister's house; he took refuge upstairs. The crowd forced its way through his gate and banged on the door, demanding that he come out to talk with them. Hutchinson stayed put as his windows began to shatter. A neighbor leaned out of his house to shout that he thought Hutchinson was out of town. As the destruction of property was about to escalate, a member of the crowd—a "grave elderly tradesman" who was "a noted speaker in town meetings"—intervened and claimed the crowd's attention. He argued that it was wrong to assume that Hutchinson favored the Stamp Act; had Hutchinson been at home, the orator continued, he would surely have appeared to account for himself to the crowd. Eventually he persuaded them to disperse. The "siege," as Hutchinson called it, had lasted about an hour. The next day, he gathered his children and decamped to the family's country house in Milton.[35]

But for Hutchinson, the worst was still to come. After more than a week in Milton, he returned home on August 26. That night, a crowd set upon the houses of Benjamin Hallowell and Charles Paxton, both customs collectors, and William Story, a vice admiralty court judge, but its real fury was reserved for Hutchinson. Though he had never advocated for the Stamp Act, Hutchinson was a conspicuous local symbol of royal authority, and the sentiments of many Bostonians were turning sharply against him. On the night of the twenty-sixth, Hutchinson's family home—a three-story brick Palladian built by his grandfather in the late seventeenth century in the now-unfashionable North End—bore the brunt of their passions. The "hellish crew," Hutchinson wrote, "fell upon my house with the Rage of devils & in a moment with axes split down the door & entred." They tore hangings and wainscoting off the walls, splintered the doors, and beat down interior walls; cut down the cupola and removed slate tiles and boards from the roof; flattened fences and trees in the yard; plundered the house of its silver plate, furniture, clothing, and £900 in cash; and left "not a single book or paper in it & have scattered or destroyed all the manuscripts & other papers I have been collecting for 30 years together besides a great number of publick papers in my custody." Working all night, the destructive crew left the scene only with the

THE HUTCHINSON HOUSE.

Built by Thomas Hutchinson's grandfather, John Foster, Hutchinson's family home stood on Garden Court Street in the North End. His primary residence during all the years he lived in Boston, it was extensively damaged in the riot of August 26, 1765.

approaching light of the following day. Hutchinson estimated his loss to be between £2,000 and £3,000 — an amount roughly comparable to $300,000 to $450,000 today. "Some gentlemen say they have seen towns sacked," he wrote to a friend, "but never saw an instance of such hellish rage as was expressed here."[36]

Bernard observed these events with horror, even as he noted similar occurrences in New York and Connecticut. In truth, the Stamp Act generated unprecedented forms of resistance throughout Britain's North American colonies. What struck Bernard with such force in the fall of 1765 was not simply the willingness of colonists to intimidate officers of the crown: of much greater concern was the inability of royal authorities to respond. The governor and his allies constituted an embattled minority, powerless in the face of a community that closed ranks behind its rioters in the way that Boston did. "The Fact was this," Bernard wrote to the Board of Trade. "Between 30 or 40 of the lowest of the people worked at the demolishing the Lieut Governors house for 4 or 5 hours together. At that time the Magistrates & Civil Officers were 3 to one the Military Corps 30 to one the fighting Men of the Town 100 to one of the Mob: And yet the whole Town acquiesced in the procedure."[37]

Nor did town leaders moderate their position in the months that followed. "At present," Bernard wrote in January 1766, "the Leaders of the Faction, from which All present evils proceed, are concerting to oppose the Kings Power in Massachusetts Bay" by compelling the colony's royal officeholders to "do their business without stamps." His correspondent was Henry Seymour Conway, the secretary of state responsible for colonial affairs. "It would give me the greatest pleasure imaginable to be able to restore peace & tranquillity to this Province by lenient Methods," Bernard concluded. "But I must own, that there is little or no prospect of this at present. The persons who originated these mischeifs & now preside over & direct the Opposition to Great Britain are so wicked & desperate, & the common people, whom they have poisoned are so mad & infatuated, that I fear there will [be] no submission untill there is a subjection."[38]

THIS IDEA — THAT there would be "no submission untill there is a subjection"— became Bernard's guiding conviction. "Whenever the parliament have determined what submission they require, & expressed their resolution to enforce it; The taking possession of 2 or 3 principal Towns & Ports will determine the contest." The scenario he imagined required sustained, energetic action from Parliament, supported by men in arms. But Parliament in these years was in continual flux, and Bernard could never be sure whom he was taking orders from. The government passed to the Rockingham Whigs, who repealed the Stamp Act in March. Soon William Pitt (now the Earl of Chatham) replaced Rockingham as prime minister, while William Petty, the Earl of Shelburne, became the secretary of state for the Southern Department, with responsibility for colonial affairs. In a long series of letters, Bernard sought to educate Shelburne, while Shelburne urged patience and moderation. "Upon this Occasion," he admonished Bernard, "it is proper to observe in general, that the Ease & Honor of His Majesty's Government in America, will greatly depend on the Temper and Wisdom of those who are entrusted with the Administration there." Only "temperate conduct" from the officers of the crown, in Shelburne's view, could put relations with the colonies back on track.[39]

For a time Shelburne's approach appeared to work, but in 1767 Parliament adopted another set of revenue measures for the colonies. Crafted by Charles Townshend, the new revenue act taxed colonial imports, including tea, lead, glass, paper, and painters' colors. At the same time, Parliament created a new administrative body, the American Customs Board, to oversee revenue collection and act more aggressively against smugglers. Five commissioners were appointed to the board and took up residence in Boston in November 1767. Two of them — Henry Hulton, the senior commissioner, and William Burch — were new to Boston. A third, Charles Paxton, was a Boston native who returned home with Hulton and Burch. Arriving on the same vessel, which sailed into Boston Harbor on November 4, were numerous other officials, including Samuel Venner, who would serve as the board's secretary; John Porter, the comptroller general; and John Williams, inspector general.[40]

The other two commissioners were already resident in the colonies. One was John Robinson, collector of customs at Newport, Rhode

Island, an energetic official of like mind with Hulton and the others. The fifth commissioner, John Temple, stands apart. A Boston native who had been serving as the surveyor general of the Northern Customs District until that office was abolished by the creation of the Customs Board, Temple resented the loss of his earlier office and quickly made enemies among the other commissioners. Hulton and the others considered themselves to be vigorous imperial reformers. Temple, however, was closely associated with the Boston faction that Bernard so despised. His wife, Elizabeth, was the daughter of James Bowdoin, a "Man of large property" who "had great influence with the People"; Bowdoin's brother-in-law, John Erving Jr., was perhaps the town's leading smuggler of illicit European goods. As long as Temple enjoyed sole responsibility for revenue collection in Massachusetts, tax receipts languished while smugglers went about their business with impunity.[41]

Ominously, Hulton and his party disembarked on the evening of November 5. In Britain this was Guy Fawkes Day; in Boston, where the holiday was called Pope's Day, it was celebrated with bonfires and brawling — or, as Bernard would have had it, "with great Licentiousness & Disorder among the lower people." Nevertheless, Bernard noted with some surprise, the commissioners wound their way through town "& even passed by one of the bonfires without receiving Any affront whatsoever."[42] Against the governor's expectation, the good fortune of their first night in Boston persisted for several months to come.

CHAPTER 3

Smugglers and Mobs

IN TRUTH, the arrival of the customs commissioners in Boston did not go unnoticed. As they prepared to disembark, the commissioners could see that the waterfront was crowded with people celebrating Pope's Day with bonfires, banners, and effigies. And the crowd was certainly expecting them: when they made their way from the docks into town, they found themselves in a crush of people carrying "twenty Devils, Popes, & Pretenders, thro the Streets, with Labels on their breasts, Liberty & Property & no Commissioners." This was a pointed message, and possibly a threatening one. But the crowd was good-natured. Henry Hulton reported to his family that he joined the locals in laughing at the effigies, and the Bostonians were content to let his party make its way to its lodgings. Reflecting on the night's events, Hutchinson later reported that there was a rumor circulating ahead of time that the commissioners would not be allowed to land, but that town leaders "determined that there should be no mobs or riots."[1]

Subsequent events seemed to confirm Hutchinson's view. At a town meeting shortly after the commissioners' arrival, James Otis Jr. argued that Bostonians should resist the new customs duties but must respect the customs commissioners and avoid "private tumults and disorders." The *Boston Gazette* reminded its readers, "No Mobs and Tumults, let the Person and Properties of our most inveterate Enemies be safe." A few months later, "Populus" (whom Harbottle Dorr identified as Samuel Adams) praised the *Gazette* for "calling upon all to be quiet. . . . NO MOBBS — NO CONFUSIONS — NO TUMULTS. . . . Let this be the language of ALL."[2] These exhortations were consistent with the image that Boston's leaders hoped to project to outside audiences: that Boston was not a "mobbish" town, but a virtuous commonwealth, united in purpose and singular in identity. To secure this impression, town leaders sought to act as the mouthpiece for a unified populace. Boston would express its unhappiness with the new revenue measures, but it would not appear disorderly or lawless.

To Governor Bernard and other royal officials, the leaders of the town meeting spoke not for all of Boston, but for a "faction" that sought to undermine loyal attachment to the crown. This was the town's "popular party," a phrase the Massachusetts governor used disparagingly. From the perspective of James Otis Jr. and the town's other prominent spokesmen, the label was apt: they did indeed represent Boston's "popular party" — its party of the people. They were no faction; they spoke for the community as a whole against the encroachments of crown officers and placemen. Their legitimacy was demonstrated by the town's single-minded unity of purpose.

Crowd action bore a complex relationship to this desired unity. When mob activities were carefully orchestrated to give symbolic expression to community concerns, they powerfully demonstrated the depth and strength of Boston's collective will. But when they veered away from purposeful acts toward apparently atavistic outbursts of violence, they could undermine unity and distract attention from the shared intentions of the town. For this reason, town leaders had a long history of disparaging crowd actions after the fact, even when they helped to achieve broadly shared goals. Crowds were not like armies, with clearly defined personnel and unambiguous chains of command. Every crowd that gathered in Boston during the 1760s and 1770s had its own unique constitution. Participants and purposes varied widely.

Sometimes crowd actions were carefully planned; at other times, crowds formed spontaneously, without direction. Even when they were called into being intentionally, no one could control or orchestrate their actions with any degree of precision. When Boston's crowds were yoked to the aims of town leaders, their activities could be decisive. But whatever the intentions of their leaders, crowds were diverse and chaotic by nature. Crowd action was a protean force, and no one ever had a sure command of its outcomes.

BOSTON'S POPULAR PARTY coalesced in the mid-1760s around the united interests of three distinct groups. The first was composed of local merchants, who were unhappy with Parliament's new revenue acts. By themselves, new taxes were only one source of concern. They were made much more threatening by Parliament's determination to reform the customs service, tighten tax collection, and curtail smuggling. In his study of 439 Boston merchants of the 1760s and 1770s, John Tyler found that he could document smuggling activities for 23 — about 7 percent of the whole. Given the secrecy surrounding illicit trade, it is likely that this substantially understates the proportion of Boston merchants who were involved in smuggling. (To take one example: Thomas Hancock, uncle of John and the source of his mercantile fortune, is a documented smuggler, while John is not, but it is almost certain that the younger Hancock persisted in his uncle's business practices.) As Tyler notes, the twenty-three smugglers were especially prominent in Boston, and several were important leaders of the patriot movement. William Cooper served as secretary for the Boston town meeting, while Edward Payne was secretary of the Boston Society for Encouraging Trade and Commerce; Solomon Davis and William Molineux were closely identified with crowd activities. Boston's merchants opposed Parliament's new tax policies almost unanimously, but those who relied on evading or bribing tax collectors were especially keen to resist them.[3]

As Boston merchants sought to articulate their grievances, they made common cause with a second group: leading figures in the town meeting who resisted the expansion of imperial oversight at the expense of local and provincial prerogatives. The town meeting had bred in its leaders a deep sense of local autonomy, and men like Samuel Adams reveled in the opportunity to articulate the principles that supported their views. Finally, these two groups yoked their resistance efforts to the power of a third—the Boston crowd—by instigating public demonstrations that dramatized their critiques of British policy. Local artisans and workingmen, including many apprentices and other boys and young men, participated in a series of riots and crowd actions that struck fear into Boston's royally appointed officials; observers claimed that gentlemen also took part in at least some of them. In the high-water years of 1765 and 1766, Boston's united front successfully agitated against the Stamp Act and the Revenue Act of 1766 and, in response to the latter, formulated a petition that outlined a comprehensive view of the appropriate limits of trade regulations. In the process, they also moved toward a common understanding of their community's proper relationship to Parliament and the British Empire.[4]

Nothing illustrated the town's unity as fully as the series of riots and public demonstrations protesting the Stamp Act that culminated on the night of August 26, 1765, when a large crowd took to the streets of Boston. At the home of William Story, deputy commissioner of the Vice-Admiralty Court, members of the crowd broke open the door and burned his files. At customs collector Benjamin Hallowell's house, the crowd broke windows, smashed china, and broke into his desk. Rioters then proceeded to Thomas Hutchinson's house and tore it apart. Again, they made a particular target of Hutchinson's papers. There is good reason to believe that prominent local merchants chose these targets carefully: they had been persuaded that their extensive involvement in smuggling was documented in the collections of papers destroyed that night. The sheriff, William Greenleaf, arrested

Ebenezer McIntosh but was promptly persuaded by "a number of merchants, and other persons of property and character," to release him. A handful of others were arrested as well, but before their trial a group of townspeople visited the jailkeeper in the night, took his keys, and secured their release. As Hutchinson later remarked, "There was no authority, which thought it advisable to make any inquiry after them." According to Hutchinson, the wealthy smuggler-merchant John Rowe later admitted that the crowd had acted at his behest.[5] This coordinated and unified attempt to impose its will by force is the epitome of a town united in common cause and shared action.

But by 1767 cracks had appeared in Boston's united front. On the one hand, after the Stamp Act riots patriot leaders tried to distance themselves from crowd actions. Though crowds had induced Andrew Oliver to resign his commission as stamp tax collector, such actions by crowds were controversial. In London, Boston gained a reputation among leading ministers as a disorderly and dangerous town. However useful the destruction of August 26 may have been, Boston leaders, concerned for the town's reputation, later disavowed the violence. The Loyal Nine—the small circle of radical leaders who worked with artisans, laborers, and apprentices to organize the anti–Stamp Act protests—evolved into the Sons of Liberty, a much larger and less focused patriot organization. While that group became what Dirk Hoerder has rather derisively labeled a "Middle-Class Dining Club," artisan leaders like Ebenezer McIntosh fell into relative obscurity. In their efforts to secure the appearance of order and unity, town leaders discouraged the Boston crowd from asserting itself.[6]

On the other hand, the merchant community—which had come together in common cause in 1765 and 1766—began to fracture in its response to the Townshend Duties of 1767. Nonimportation was the issue that divided them. The Townshend Duties placed new taxes on an array of colonial imports, including lead, five types of glass, painters' colors, sixty-three grades of paper, and tea. To protest those duties, some Boston merchants advocated for a policy of nonimportation — but others objected to the idea. Crown officials believed that the nonimportation movement was a self-interested ploy on the part of larger and more established merchants to drive their competitors out of business. British traders had been extending generous credit to small shopkeepers, while others had even sent their own factors to Boston, so the number of people dealing British goods in town had expanded dramatically during the 1760s. Nonimportation would help large dry-goods merchants to reduce their stocks of merchandise in a time of economic stagnation, while it would also drive many newer and smaller-scale merchants and retailers out of business. As John Hancock wrote, "Our trade must be in fewer hands, or it will not be worth my pursuit." Whatever the motive for nonimportation, many merchant firms resisted the pressure to sign an agreement — especially firms that were less well established and less well stocked. It would take months before the merchant community could agree on a course of action.[7]

In the meantime, the customs commissioners came to town. Though local leaders did not want to concede the taxing power to Parliament, their position was precarious. Hoping to disguise the fissures in the merchant community while projecting an image of unity and good order, men like James Otis Jr. and Samuel Adams lobbied behind the scenes to orchestrate nonconsumption and nonimportation agreements at the same time that they labored to present the appearance of a united front and to ensure the personal safety of the crown officers in their midst.

CROWD ACTIVITIES were nothing new in eighteenth-century Boston. In Britain and throughout western Europe in the early modern era, out-of-doors action was a central feature of political systems in which the vast majority of a kingdom's subjects were disenfranchised and had no formal role. Yet surviving accounts of crowd actions were almost always penned by powerful men who were targeted, threatened, or inconvenienced by them. Nearly every eighteenth-century description of politically motivated crowds acting out of doors disparaged them. Such gatherings were never characterized in neutral or sympathetic or favorable terms. They were called a "rabble" or a "mob." The etymology of these words is instructive. "Rabble," according to the *Oxford English Dictionary*, first came into use in the fifteenth century and had a rich array of closely related meanings in the early modern era: as a verb it meant "to speak or read aloud in a rapid and incoherent way," and also "to attack or assail (a person or his or her property) as, along with, or by means of, a rabble; to mob." As a noun, "rabble" referred both to a pack or swarm of animals and to a disorderly and unruly crowd.

"Mob" was a more recent coinage. The earliest use of the term to mean "a disorderly or riotous crowd," according to the *OED,* appeared in 1688 — coincidentally, the year of the Glorious Revolution, which not only deposed a king but also set the stage for a new kind of partisan politics. Use of the word became ubiquitous in the course of the eighteenth century. Though Henry Fielding wrote that "mob" could be used to refer to "Persons without Virtue, or Sense, in all Stations" of life, in practice it was almost always used by men of a higher station to characterize the behavior of their social inferiors. It was a shortened form of the phrase *mobile vulgus* (roughly translated, the fickle crowd).[8] Writers sometimes expanded the term to refer to the "mobility," which could be humorously contrasted with the nobility as a separate order of the political classes, or to the "mobocracy," which had a similar connotation. The mob was urban, and it came to occupy a distinct place in the imaginations of eighteenth-century gentlemen: it referred to the capacity of large groups of ordinary people to assert themselves in public. While mobs were often characterized as senseless, in fact mob actions were generally purposeful, even if they were disorderly. At times — as in the Stamp Act riots in Boston — gentlemen would join a mob; but in that case they disguised themselves and tried to blend in. Their presence constituted an affirmation of the mob's purposes and activities, while the disguise allowed them to obscure or deny their involvement.

In the nineteenth and twentieth centuries, the term "crowd" largely replaced "mob." In the work of scholars like the French sociologist Gustave Le Bon (reflecting on the French Revolution) and the Bulgarian-born writer Elias Canetti (reacting to the rise of Nazism), the crowd came to be seen as an anonymous, irrational, and violent force in modern life.[9] More recently, scholars have begun to look favorably upon early modern crowd activities as legitimate expressions of the popular will. George Rudé, a pioneering figure in this process of reexamination, argued that the term "mob" had loaded political connotations, and — overlooking the legacy of Le Bon and Canetti — used the term "crowd" because he considered it to be more neutral.[10] Historians have generally followed Rudé's advice and preferred "crowd" to "mob" for much of the past half century.

Yet it is worthwhile to recover the eighteenth-century sense of these two terms. A crowd, in the early modern era, had no distinctive character; it referred merely to a crush of people massed together. A mob, by contrast, had character and purpose. Its actions might be chaotic or threatening, but they were also pointed and purposeful.[11] It was precisely this quality of mobs that made gentlemen — especially government officials — fear them and refer to them so disparagingly. When writers humorously contrasted "the mobility" with "the nobility," they were acknowledging what many eighteenth-century members of the political classes were loath to admit: that large numbers of people, acting out of doors, could take on the character of a separate, independent estate in politics.

As THE END OF 1767 approached, Governor Bernard was optimistic that Boston's mobs had been neutralized and that the worst had passed. With the date for implementing the Townshend Duties only a week away, he expressed no concern about an impending public protest. "The Apprehension of tumults which was so threatning [for the past] 2 or 3 Months," he wrote, "has been gradually dying away for sevral Weeks past [and] is now entirely over." The Boston town meeting was pushing a nonconsumption agreement among the general populace to discourage the use of expensive imported goods, but that effort had been "so genuinely rejected & discountenanced by the principal Gentlemen of the Town, that It can have no effect." The town's efforts to propagate a nonimportation agreement had been even less successful. "The Country," he concluded, "is generally dissatisfied with the late proceedings of the Boston Faction, & begin to open their Eyes to the imposition which has been put upon the province by these Seditious men."[12]

But Bernard soon concluded that the appearance of calm was illusory. Three months later, events in Boston had begun to panic him, and he wrote a series of letters intended to communicate his fears to government officials in London. The first, sent to his cousin Lord Barrington, the secretary at war, suggested that violence was looming in Boston and raised the possibility of sending troops to town. He reported that Boston's merchants had finally reached an agreement on nonimportation, and worried that the town was about to erupt. Merchants refused to let customs officials board their ships; one — Daniel Malcom, a Boston smuggler-merchant — had unloaded a cargo of wine in the night without entering it at the Custom House. Riots had twice been threatened in recent days, and "violent methods of Opposition are every Day expected." The customs commissioners, he reported, had "asked me what Support I can give them, if there should be an Insurrection; I answer none at all." He told them that he could not request troops without the support of the Governor's Council, which it would never offer. "Indeed I no more dare apply for Troops than the Council dare advise me to do it." He wanted to let the secretary at war know that troops would be welcome in Boston, but also "to be able to say, and swear to, if the Sons of Liberty should require it, that I have never applied for Troops. And therefore, my Lord, I beg that Nothing I now write may be considered as such an Application."[13]

At the same time that Bernard sought to alarm the secretary at war, he also wrote again to the Earl of Shelburne, this time to alert him that the Massachusetts Assembly was guilty of libel and sedition. In February it sent a circular letter to the assemblies of Britain's other North American colonies. Its aim was to ensure that the colonies' responses to Parliament's new round of taxes "should harmonize with each other." The letter's sentiments were not new, but it articulated the argument against the validity of parliamentary taxation more fully and forcefully than any previous text prepared by a formal governmental body had done. Then a "Virulent Libell" appeared in the *Boston Gazette* that disparaged Bernard and "concluded with a blasphemous abuse of Kingly Government itself." Bernard—who was certain that the piece had been written by Adams and Otis—tried to persuade the General Court to bring a libel suit against Edes and Gill, the editors of the *Gazette,* but he was unable to convince either the assembly or the council to support the effort. To Richard Jackson, former agent for the colony and a member of Parliament, Bernard wrote, "Every Things here is running into Confusion; People here are ready to refuse to submit to any Laws of Trade imposing Duties; the Officers are threatened; Mobbs are expected; the Commissioners are frightned; the Government is defenceless; &c. &c. These are the Effects of America (or rather Boston) being left to Right itself."[14]

Bernard's flurry of correspondence coincided with another change in leadership in London. Shelburne, who had always tried to moderate Bernard's fears and steer a middle course in colonial policy, was eclipsed by the appointment of Wills Hill, the Earl of Hillsborough, to the newly created position of secretary of state for the American colonies. Shelburne would almost certainly have downplayed Bernard's concerns, but Hillsborough was a different case. Like Bernard, he tended to judge American affairs with alarm. The seeds of panic scattered through Bernard's correspondence would find fertile ground in Hillsborough's temperament and inclinations.

THE BOSTON WATERFRONT WAS HOME to most of the town's productive labor. Here, merchants, ship captains, mariners, longshoremen, carters, warehousemen, and day laborers worked in concert to load, unload, and provision ships, while coopers, joiners, carpenters, woodcutters, and others plied their trades along the docks. Some of these workers were longtime residents of Boston; others were transient, shipping out as mariners for a time, working as laborers while they were ashore. With wharves fanning out from Boston's center in every direction, every neighborhood was oriented to the harbor, and most of the work done in town was done along its docks, which were lined with warehouses, shops, ropewalks, and manufactories. Well-to-do merchants and ship captains employed skilled and unskilled laborers in a variety of tasks, creating a sense of communal solidarity and interdependency that transcended class lines and shaped local attitudes and loyalties.

For decades, customs officers trod lightly on Boston's waterfront. Customs collector Benjamin Barons and surveyor general of customs John Temple had been reluctant to seize cargoes and had ingratiated themselves with the merchant community; the new Customs Commission was intended to reverse the tide and challenge the long-standing pattern of lax oversight. The commissioners—especially Hulton, Burch, and Paxton, newly arrived from Britain—cast a shadow across local business practices and threatened the livelihoods

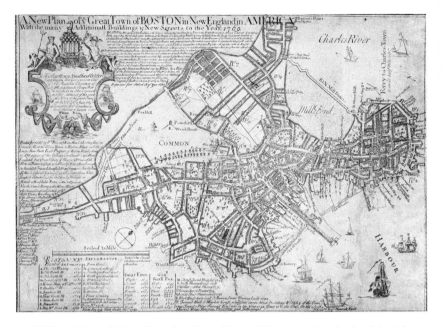

William Price, *A New Plan of ye Great Town of Boston in New England* (1769). Price's extraordinarily detailed map of Boston, based on the famous John Bonner map of 1722 but updated to reflect recent development, illustrates the way that the waterfront dominated the town.

of laborers, mariners, captains, and merchants alike. Though leaders of the town meeting continued to urge restraint, the intrusive new practices of customs collectors rubbed everyone the wrong way.[15]

John Hancock was among the most outspoken of those who objected to the commissioners' interference. The son of a Braintree minister, he became the ward of his uncle, Thomas Hancock, after his father's death. The elder Hancock was one of Boston's most substantial merchants by midcentury, and he augmented his wealth considerably as one of Boston's principal wartime contractors during the Seven Years' War. Like Samuel Adams, young John Hancock attended Boston Latin School and then Harvard College before entering his uncle's counting house. When Thomas Hancock died in 1764, John inherited the business and became one of Boston's most substantial traders. In the spring of 1768, he made it known in town that he intended to bar customs officials from boarding any of his vessels.[16]

In April revenue officers boarded Hancock's vessel *Lydia* and then, in violation of the law, proceeded below decks. A month later, on the evening of May 9, Hancock's sloop *Liberty* arrived at his Boston wharf, having sailed from Madeira. When customs officials inspected the ship the next day, they found twenty-five pipes of wine—only a fraction of its carrying capacity. Hancock paid the assessed duties; Boston's customs commissioners presumed that he had unloaded the lion's share of the *Liberty*'s cargo overnight, but they could not prove it. A month later, however, they decided to act against Hancock. They had written in the meantime to Commodore Samuel Hood in Halifax to request naval support in their enforcement efforts; in response, on May 17 the British frigate HMS *Romney,* a fifty-gun man-of-war—the largest Royal Navy warship in American waters—anchored in Boston Harbor.[17]

While he awaited further instructions, the *Romney*'s commanding officer, Captain John Corner, took action to press additional sailors into service on his short-handed vessel. On Sunday, June 5, he dispatched a press gang to scour the wharves for able seamen. The shoreline was crowded with people—strolling or lounging, not working, on the Sabbath—who quickly became aware of what was happening. As the gang's boats approached the wharf, sailors and laborers on the waterfront reacted so furiously—throwing stones and brickbats while they massed along the shore—that Corner's men were forced to turn around without landing. In the coming days, Corner succeeded in pressing three sailors. An angry crowd managed to free one of them, but the other two remained on board the *Romney.*

Thus, Bostonians were already on edge when Joseph Harrison, the town's customs collector, finally got the evidence he needed to charge Hancock with unlawfully unloading the *Liberty*'s cargo. On June 10, Harrison and Benjamin Hallowell, the comptroller, called upon the *Romney* to tow the *Liberty* into custody. A party of sailors came ashore, claimed the *Liberty,* and hastily unmoored it from the wharf before the locals could stop them. An outraged crowd of five hundred to a thousand townspeople responded by setting upon Harrison, Hallowell, and their sons, injuring both of the older men (they were "so violently hurt" that Harrison was "confined to his Bed" and Hallowell "to his House") and burning a barge that belonged to Harrison. The commissioners, their families, and the other customs employees, fearing for their safety, fled to the *Romney* and, from there, to Castle William in the harbor. Numbering sixty-seven people in all, they remained on Castle Island for nearly five months.[18]

In the wake of the *Liberty* incident, Governor Bernard concluded that Boston was ungovernable after all. The customs commissioners too acquired a deep-seated fear of Boston's mobs. Henry Hulton's sister Anne, who had joined her brother in Boston and fled with him to Castle Island, shared her impressions with a friend in Liverpool. She noted that mobs in Boston had a stronger sense of purpose, greater determination to act, and a deeper proclivity to destruction and violence than those she had known in Britain:

We soon found that the Mobs here are very different from those in O[ld] England where a few lights put into the Windows will pacify, or the interposition of a Magistrate restrain them, but here they act from principle & under Countenance, no person daring or willing to suppress their Outrages, or to punish the most notorious Offenders for any Crimes whatever, These Sons of Voilence [*sic*] after attacking Houses, break[in]g Window, beating, Stoning & bruising several Gentlemen belong[in]g to the Customs, the Collector mortally, & burning his boat, They consult[e]d what was to be done next, & it was agreed to retire for the night, All was ended w[i]th a Speech from one of the Leaders, conclud[in]g thus, "We will defend our Liberties & property, by the Strength of our Arm & the help of our God, to your Tents O Israel." This is a specimen of the Sons of Liberty, of whom no doubt you have heard, and will hear more.[19]

WHEN WORD of the *Liberty* riot reached Thomas Gage, the commander in chief of British forces in North America, he immediately contacted Governor Bernard. "It gives me concern to hear," he wrote, "that there has been some fresh Commotions in Boston. I have received a Letter from the Commissioners of the Customs to acquaint me, that the Collector, Comptroller, and other Officers, had been beat and abused in the Execution of their Duty." Well aware of the long-standing English principle that troops could be employed in peace-keeping operations only at the invitation of local magistrates, Gage now reminded Bernard that he had to decide whether armed force was needed to restore order in Boston. "You must be the best Judge of the Situation of Affairs in Your Government, and whether the Aid of Troops is wanted to enforce the Laws, and to preserve Peace and Tranquility in the City. The Moment you shall Judge it convenient to apply to me for the Assistance of the King's Forces, I shall Order such a Number to March as you shall have Occasion for."[20]

Bernard — not uncharacteristically — was of two minds. "The State of Affairs in Boston is full as bad as the reports you have received can make it," he acknowledged. "All real power is in the hands of the people of the lowest class; Civil Authority can do nothing but what they will allow." Yet no one on the council would support Bernard in requesting military aid to suppress a riot. And anyway, Bernard noted, if he were to issue such a request in the event of a riot, the episode would be past long before the troops arrived. (To drive home the point, he noted that a riot had occurred "last fryday which was quitted without any mischief done; I am just told that there will be one tonight which will not be so easily quelled.") Wouldn't it be better for Gage simply to station a regiment or two in Boston, where they could be garrisoned and therefore near at hand if the need for them arose?[21]

Bernard's dithering frustrated Gage, who continued to insist that he could act only in response to a clear request from the civil authority for military support. But then Gage received orders from Hillsborough instructing him to station troops in Boston, just as Bernard had requested. Here was the time lag in transatlantic communications at work: five months earlier, in February, the Speaker of the Massachusetts Assembly had sent a circular letter to the assemblies of Britain's other North American colonies that Hillsborough and the Board of Trade considered "extraordinary & seditious." In March, Bernard had peppered his London correspondents with alarming letters, and the customs commissioners had joined in as well. Gage was just now receiving Hillsborough's response to those letters. Hillsborough instructed Gage to send a regiment, "or such force as you shall think necessary, to Boston, to be Quartered in that Town, and to give every legal assistance to the Civil Magistrate in the Preservation of the Public Peace."[22]

Gage wrote in turn to Bernard to ask whether he thought one regiment would be enough, or whether he should send a second as well. Fearful that the Boston faction might catch wind of the plan, Gage sent his letter by personal courier in the care of Captain William Shirreff, his aide de camp, who pretended to be in town on personal business. ("You may rely on his Discretion, Prudence, and Secresy," Gage assured Bernard.) Shirreff carried orders for the 14th Regiment to leave Halifax for Boston; Gage also "left a Blank in the Letter, for Captain Shireff to fill up with the like Order for the 29th Regt., in case you shall judge it proper."[23] Bernard opted for both regiments, and Gage ordered Lieutenant Colonel William Dalrymple to move the 14th and 29th Regiments from Halifax to Boston.

In the meantime, word of June's "great riots and disturbances" in Boston had reached the ears of the king. Concerned about the "dangerous Spirit of Opposition to the Authority of the Laws of this Kingdom" he observed in North America, he concluded that "the Hands of Government in His Colonies should be further strengthened by the Addition of Two Regiments from Ireland," and he ordered the 64th and 65th Regiments of Foot to leave Cork for Boston "with all possible dispatch."[24]

Four regiments of foot—some two thousand men—were now ordered to Boston. But the escalation of concern, and of military resources, was not yet complete. Gage soon heard reports of a town meeting that seemed to threaten sedition and armed resistance. Having gotten word that troops were on the way, the town meeting declared its objection to a standing army in peacetime and pointedly voted to ensure that every militiaman and householder was supplied "with a well fixed Fire Lock Musket" so that residents would "be prepared in case of sudden danger." In response, Gage wrote to Hillsborough to note that the "Mutinous Behavior" of the citizens of Boston was continuing, now manifested in a set of "Treasonable and desperate Resolves." These were no longer the respectful protests of loyal subjects; instead, he wrote, the Bostonians "have now delivered their Sentiments in a Manner not to be Misunderstood, and in the Stile of a ruling and Sovereign Nation, who acknowledges no Dependence." Gage was resolute. "Whilst Laws are in force, I shall pay the obedience that is due to them, and in my Military Capacity confine Myself Solely to the granting Such Aids to the Civil Power, as shall be required of me," he avowed; "but if open and declared Rebellion makes it's Appearance, I mean to use all the Powers lodged in my Hands, to make Head against it." Expecting the worst, Gage added a detachment of the Royal Regiment of Artillery to the complement of troops bound for the mutinous little seaport town.[25]

By late September, Governor Bernard and General Gage had begun to think about the deployment of troops to Boston in very different ways. Bernard continued to plan for a peacekeeping force, and he fretted over the best way to fulfill the terms of the Quartering Act. Both the selectmen of Boston and the Governor's Council insisted that there was a barracks in Boston, which could be fitted up to accommodate the troops: the barracks on Castle Island in Boston Harbor. They argued that the barracks was large enough to hold the two regiments from Halifax; "as for the two regiments from Ireland, it would be time enough to provide for them when they came." Bernard, on the other hand, was persuaded that Castle Island was too far from Boston (three miles by sea and seven by land) for the troops to fulfill their intended purpose.[26]

But this was no simple matter. Noting that "there are no barracks at Boston," Bernard worried that "if the soldiers were quartered in public houses & thereby intermixed with the Townspeople in the humour they are at present, it would occasion perpetual feuds & affrays." Presciently, he predicted that dispersing the troops through town "would also occasion frequent desertion." Moreover, in a show of solidarity in opposition to the troops, Boston's innkeepers had declared their intention to give up their licenses rather than house the soldiers. Boston's public houses, in short, appeared to offer no useful solution to the problem. Bernard proposed, instead, to "fit up" public buildings as barracks. He had his eye on one in particular: the Manufactory House, a workhouse built to support local textile production that had fallen into disuse. The council refused to support his intention to appropriate the building and fit it for a barracks. Nevertheless, Bernard was determined. He assured Gage that he would claim the building for the troops' use on his own authority, but had no money to outfit it. "When I have done this, which will make a clamour," he dolefully concluded, "I have done all I can. . . . There will then remain difficulties on every side."[27]

Gage would have to reckon eventually with the issues that worried Bernard so much, but in late September he was not focused on the quartering of troops. He was preparing for the possibility of war, and his correspondence with commanding officers mapped a strategy for the invasion of Boston. Castle William, whose barracks were thought to be so unsatisfactory as a base of operations for a peacekeeping mission, now appeared to be a vital strategic target if the city was to be taken by force. Gage learned that there was a company of provincial soldiers garrisoning the castle. If a "Body of Rebels" wanted to oppose the landing of British troops in Boston, Gage reasoned, they might gain "Possession of the Castle, thro' the Treachery of the Garrison, before the Troops arrive." In that case, Gage was confident that his warships would "soon be able to drive them out of it. . . . I can no longer be tender of putting the King's Troops in Garrison in the Castle, and Fortifying it as well as we can." His orders to Lieutenant Colonel William Dalrymple, the senior officer in charge of the 14th and 29th Regiments, mapped out the contingencies. "What opposition may be made to your Landing the Reg[imen]ts under your Command Ordered to Boston, time must discover," he wrote, "but I think should any considerable Number of Rebels appear in Arms to oppose you, they can never Prevent your Taking Possession of Castle William."[28]

As an addendum to Dalrymple's general orders, Gage offered one last instruction. "As attempts may be made to Debauch your Men and Encourage them to Desert" once they arrived in Boston, "you may throw out hints amongst them, that the King will Reward his Officers and Soldiers with the Estates of the Rebels. The Hopes of Estates may keep them."[29] This contingency—planning for the confiscation and redistribution of rebel estates—highlights how far Gage had gone, by the end of September, in conceiving of Boston as a town in rebellion.

CHAPTER 4

Imperial Spaces

THOMAS GAGE'S preparations for the conquest of Boston made up one small part of a vast geopolitical reorientation. It had been decades in the making, but the Seven Years' War accelerated changes in North America and forced officers like Gage to contemplate new realities and address unprecedented challenges. The empires of Europe had been sending tentacles into the Atlantic and Indian Ocean worlds for 250 years, but in the eighteenth century administrators and officers of empire began to conceive of their imperial projects in more comprehensive ways. The primary engine of this change was war: between 1689 and 1763, Britain fought in five major wars with its European rivals, and as they progressed the fighting spilled over, more and more, into colonial territories. In the Seven Years' War, many of the most critical battles and all of the most decisive outcomes occurred in the Americas.

Boston, like the other long-established communities of British North America, had deeply established local traditions and prerogatives that residents valued highly. After 1763 Gage and other crown officials in the colonies attempted to smooth the semi-independent communities of British North America into a new, more uniform and undifferentiated kind of imperial landscape. In the diverse, variegated polities of eastern North America, Gage and his associates were attempting to exercise British authority in a way that was principled, consistent, and effective. In the process, they trampled on local privileges and triggered waves of resistance in communities across the eastern half of the continent. It was Gage's job — as it was the job of imperial officers and administrators everywhere in North America — to persevere against all opposition in the name of the crown.

One striking aspect of this process of imperial aggrandizement was the way that European empires alternately competed with each other and cooperated in a larger effort to secure and defend their control over distant territories. Times of war were, of course, times of fierce competition; and even in peacetime, European rivals eyed each other warily and angled for advantage. But the empires of Europe also respected one another's claims to sovereign power. They supported efforts to impose imperial authority on recalcitrant local populations, and they shared the need to master American spaces, especially in the form of large-scale cartographic projects. They upheld the idea of a law of nations that applied to all of them and that they hoped to extend, wherever possible, into new imperial spaces. They saw themselves, collectively, as agents of civilization and progress in a massive effort to rationalize and improve distant parts of the globe.[1]

The residents of Boston were not accustomed to thinking of themselves as uncivilized or backward. But in their resistance to trade regulation and their reluctance to pay parliamentary taxes, they resembled other colonial populations whose shoulders had not yet been yoked to the plow of empire. After 1763 Boston's own urban spaces — its waterfront, its public buildings, its streets and warehouses — became battlegrounds where imperial authority competed with local autonomy.

EUROPEAN INTRUSIONS INTO DISTANT lands and oceans had been under way for two and a half centuries by the end of the Seven Years'

War, but the result was nothing like a mastery of vast stretches of the globe. Instead, Europeans had carved out "corridors and enclaves" of influence in key places, which led in turn to a wide array of imperial anomalies—"imperfect geographies and . . . variegated spaces with an uncertain relation to imperial power," in Lauren Benton's evocative account of the phenomenon.[2] Boston, with its long history of mercantile innovation, Puritan Congregationalism, and local self-rule, was just one of many such places that were formally subject to a distant European authority but, in actuality, largely self-created and self-sustaining.[3]

Europe's eighteenth-century wars generated strenuous new efforts in Britain, France, and Spain to extend and rationalize imperial power in the Americas. One dimension of this process was played out in warfare, where the contest for American territory and influence became ever more important to imperial administrators. From its entry into the War of the League of Augsburg in 1689 until the battle of Waterloo in 1815, Britain was at war with its principal European rivals more or less continuously.[4] The twenty-six years from 1713 to 1739 constituted the longest interruption in an era of profound militarization. Beginning with the War of Jenkins' Ear in 1739 and continuing through the War of the Austrian Succession, the Seven Years' War, and the American Revolution, European combatants came to see the strategic value of North American landscapes in ever more compelling terms, and invested correspondingly more resources in the effort to strengthen and extend their claims there. Borderland zones grew more hotly contested. Increasingly ambitious mapping projects illustrate the corresponding desire to overcome the depths of European "geographical ignorance" and arrive at a more complete and systematic image of the Americas.[5]

At the same time, Spain and Britain sought to implement reforms in colonial administration that would strengthen the hands of metropolitan authorities in the affairs of distant American colonies. The

Bourbon reforms in Spanish America created new viceroyalties, introduced the office of intendant to bolster the crown and improve revenue collection, and reduced the autonomy and authority of local officials throughout Spanish America. Beginning in 1748, when George Montagu-Dunk, the second Earl of Halifax, became president of the Board of Trade, Great Britain undertook a similar pattern of reforms, which gained momentum after the Seven Years' War. Halifax and his successors aimed to increase the power of the king-in-Parliament in colonial affairs, make royally appointed governors and other officers more independent of local influence, and, after 1763, enhance revenue collection in the colonies.[6]

As the commander in chief of British armed forces in North America, Thomas Gage was a foot soldier in these processes. Born into a prominent Sussex family in 1719 or 1720, Gage purchased a commission as lieutenant in 1741 and served in Flanders during the War of the Austrian Succession and under the Duke of Cumberland at Culloden in 1746. From 1748 to 1755 his regiment was stationed in Ireland; in the latter year, at the beginning of the Seven Years' War, it was sent to North America. Gage served as a lieutenant colonel in the disastrous Braddock campaign of 1755, then rose steadily in the ranks during the course of the war. He replaced Jeffery Amherst as commander in chief of British forces in North America in 1763. Initially serving in an interim capacity, in the end he remained in that position for thirteen years.[7]

Gage assumed the role at an auspicious moment. The Treaty of Paris of 1763, which ended the Seven Years' War, brought vast changes to the shape of European power on the continent. France ceded all of its claims east of the Mississippi River to Great Britain, while Spain ceded East and West Florida to Britain as well. For Great Britain, acquiring something like half a billion acres of new territory in North America utterly transformed the nature of its American enterprise. Its colonies began as maritime commercial undertakings, with very little centralized direction or control. Though a weak imperial apparatus emerged fitfully to coordinate trade policy and oversee royal colonies, in 1763 Britain's imperial system remained largely unreformed—and poorly adapted to the new challenges the Treaty of Paris imposed.[8]

To begin with, the new territories ceded by France and Spain were maintained through a web of forts, more than three dozen in all, that secured the St. Lawrence, spanned the Great Lakes, descended the Illinois and Mississippi Rivers, and flanked the Gulf coast. Their principal function was to sustain networks of trade and alliance with a large number of Native American nations who remained almost entirely unknown to Britons in 1763. These forts demanded a new, more centralized imperial apparatus to oversee diplomatic and commercial relations with Native American polities. Only a military force—a peacetime standing army—could effectively sustain the complex networks Britain had inherited in the continental interior.

Standing armies had been anathema to Englishmen since at least the early seventeenth century, and even in the mid-eighteenth century opposition to them remained an article of faith for many traditionally minded critics. They regarded peacetime armies as expensive and unnecessary; more important, they considered them to be an indispensable support of arbitrary government. Standing armies, they believed, threatened popular liberties wherever they appeared and were the tools of ambitious kings who sought to expand royal prerogatives at the expense of the people. Standing armies, as John Trenchard wrote in 1697, "are the instruments of tyranny and their country's ruin."[9]

Nevertheless, as Britain embarked on a series of wars after 1689, a permanent military establishment came to be seen as essential to the national defense. It was simply too costly to demobilize an army at the end of every war, only to remobilize it again in a few years' time. With the end of each eighteenth-century war, the peacetime establishment grew. In 1763, anticipating that renewed warfare was likely to be imminent, the ministry proposed to retain some forty-five thousand troops in half-strength regiments. Of the seventy-eight battalions of foot active in 1764, fifteen were stationed in England itself, five were in Scotland, twenty-three in Ireland, fifteen in North America, eight in the West Indies, and six each in Gibraltar and Minorca.[10]

The North American troops were thus a small part of a large, complex military organism that presented novel challenges to Great Britain in the post–Glorious Revolution era. In peacetime there was no code of military justice in force, nor was there any provision for allocating funds to the army. In 1689 Parliament addressed both these issues when it passed the Mutiny Act, which allowed the army to hold courts-martial during times of peace and which also provided it with funds. Because the Bill of Rights of 1689 specified that a peacetime standing army was illegal except with Parliament's approval, passing a new Mutiny Bill became an annual ritual that allowed Parliament to exercise ongoing oversight and hold officers accountable for their expenses and actions. Under the terms of successive Mutiny Bills, a peacetime standing army became a fact of life in Britain during the course of the eighteenth century.

Billeting—one of the most controversial army practices even in wartime—became a pressing concern in times of peace. Traditionally, armies claimed shelter and sustenance where they could find them. On the move under urgent circumstances, early modern armies expected the support of loyal communities and subjects. In practice this meant that, as soldiers passed through, resident civilians often opened their homes, especially to officers, and even more often opened their larders to feed troops. As the size of armed forces increased during the seventeenth century, such ad hoc practices became increasingly controversial. Both the Petition of Right of 1628 and the Bill of Rights of 1689 made the billeting of troops one of the principal objections to a standing army, and the Mutiny Acts routinely prohibited quartering troops in private homes.[11]

In search of an alternative to the haphazard practice of billeting in private homes, in 1685 King James II decreed that, in order to be licensed, keepers of inns and public houses had to accommodate troops on the march. The War Office conducted a census of public accommodations and soon had a comprehensive list of all the beds available to soldiers in England.[12] Astonishingly, though James was deposed in the Glorious Revolution only three years later, his solution to the problem of billeting remained in force throughout the eighteenth century. English innkeepers regularly provided lodgings to troops on the march, and just as regularly complained that they were not paid enough to do so.

In Ireland, the problem of accommodating troops in peacetime led to a more comprehensive and innovative solution: the development of a barracks system. The first Irish barracks were built in the last years of the seventeenth century as the best means available to house, feed, supply, and train soldiers in peacetime. The Irish Parliament devoted nearly £100,000 to the construction of permanent housing for soldiers between 1698 and 1700, and thereafter established an annual fund to maintain and expand them. (Set at £13,336 10s. per annum in 1704, the fund remained in force until the 1760s and was chronically overspent.) By 1713, 102 barracks had been built in Ireland, and a wave of new construction was about to begin. Irish members of Parliament, landholders, and communities supported barracks because they brought economic benefits in the form of building and supply contracts, rent, and demand for local goods and services. Along with the new emphasis on barracks came a new management system for housing, training, and disciplining troops. As the British army moved into new imperial spaces, the barracks system offered an ideal model for maintaining order among troops far from home.[13]

From the perspective of Britain's Parliament, the logic of the Irish establishment was less strategic than fiscal. Since local communities housed, supplied, and victualed the troops stationed in their midst, the Irish establishment was a way for Parliament to economize in its support of a peacetime army. In 1769 British troops in Ireland occupied barracks in sixty-five communities, stretching from Belfast in the northeast to Dingle in the southwest. A few of Ireland's largest towns housed substantial numbers of soldiers. Dublin was home to seven regiments of foot, while Limerick, Cork, and Galway housed two each. The rest of the Irish troops were dispersed in barracks that housed a third of a regiment or less; given the reduced size of peacetime forces, this would amount to fewer than a hundred men. By the 1760s military reformers had begun to complain that the barracks were often ramshackle and that discipline was hard to maintain, but for soldiers and the communities that supported them, the dispersed pattern of quartering offered both stability and a degree of freedom. Officer absenteeism, drunkenness among the rank and file, and various other forms of indiscipline and malingering were considered to be chronic features of the Irish establishment.[14] Nevertheless, in peacetime Ireland was an especially useful place to park troops: this accounts for the fact that some 30 percent of Britain's battalions of foot and 42 percent of its regiments of horse were stationed there in 1764.

Despite its obvious benefits, the barracks system was a solution that would never fly in England itself. As a corollary to the deep antipathy of the English to standing armies, barracks were anathema to them. Because they concentrated soldiers in one place and separated them from the civilian population, they were considered dangerous to the body politic. "The people of this Kingdom," commented Field Marshal George Wade, "have been taught to associate the idea of barracks and slavery so closely together that, like darkness and the devil, though there be no connection between them, yet they cannot separate them, nor think of the one without at the same time of the other." Instead, most soldiers were dispersed unevenly through the island and were often on the march. In the mid-1760s, cavalry forces stationed in England spent half their time either assisting civil powers in peacekeeping efforts, on coastal duty, or marching through the countryside; infantry units in the same period spent just over a third of their time in these activities. They either occupied beds in inns and public houses, or they set up temporary encampments; especially in the summer, British soldiers in England could often be found living in tents for months at a time. In either case, soldiers' lodgings were impermanent, their training haphazard, and their interactions with civilian populations often fraught with the potential for conflict.[15]

Elsewhere, troops were accommodated in a variety of ways. In Scotland, where Jacobite sympathies had led to open rebellions in 1715 and again in 1745 and were a persistent feature of Highlands political culture, British troops were concentrated in and near castles and forts that commanded strategic sites and transportation routes. By themselves, castles and forts could accommodate relatively few soldiers; after the 1715 rebellion, the army added fortified barracks to its complement of structures in Scotland. In the foreign ports of Gibraltar and Minorca, which were granted to Britain by Spain in the Treaty of Utrecht in 1713, British soldiers were an occupying force. In Minorca, soldiers rented rooms or homes in dilapidated neighborhoods near the fort they manned. Some barracks had been built by 1718, but accommodations were an ongoing source of conflict between local authorities and British officials. At Gibraltar, soldiers accounted for half the community, while their wives and families accounted for another quarter of it. They lived alongside a small mixed population of Jewish, Genoese, and Spanish residents. As in Ireland, the troops were housed in barracks (most of them converted convents). Gibraltar thus stood alongside Ireland as Britain's most "modern" site of military accommodation and discipline in peacetime. As in Ireland, however, the limits of eighteenth-century military discipline were clear. Soldiers, like civilian subjects of the crown, knew their rights and demanded a degree of autonomy in their everyday lives.[16]

The British army maintained a small peacetime presence in North America and the West Indies during the eighteenth century as well. After 1713 it posted independent companies in Nova Scotia and Newfoundland, which had just been acquired from France by the terms of the Treaty of Utrecht, and also in New York, Jamaica, and Bermuda. The colony of Jamaica began to build residential barracks for soldiers in the 1730s, but elsewhere these companies were too small to require separate housing arrangements.[17]

For most of Britain's mainland colonies, soldiers were an intermittent presence that appeared, if at all, only in wartime. In Massachusetts, engagement with the crown's expanding military initiatives began in the War of the League of Augsburg (1689–1697), which included two expeditions against Canada mounted from Massachusetts, and the War of the Spanish Succession (1701–1714), which gave rise to a series of raids in the borderlands of New England and New France, as well as two more attempts to conquer Canada.

The emergence of imperial warfare caused residents to reassess the state of Boston's defenses. It was during the second of those wars that Wolfgang William Romer, a Dutch military engineer, spent two years supervising the construction of a stone fort on Castle Island in Boston Harbor. A small earthen fort had been built there in the seventeenth century, but given Boston's proximity to French Canada, the new era of war called for a more substantial structure. Named Fort William to honor Britain's recently deceased Protestant monarch, Romer's edifice was a substantial square, one hundred feet on a side, with bastions at each corner. The island commanded the channel leading to Boston from Nantasket Road and the sea lanes of the Atlantic. Any ship entering the harbor had to navigate a three-mile approach, during which time its bow would point toward the island (leaving the ship unable to discharge its cannons) while it would be vulnerable to bombardment. Romer designed two batteries, each intended to house fifty guns, to defend the island's approaches from the south and east and to control this channel.[18]

When war resumed in the middle of the century after twenty-six years of peace, the town of Boston and the Massachusetts Bay Colony were especially supportive of British military initiatives. Massachusetts soldiers volunteered in large numbers for the British campaign against Cartagena in 1741, and the colony's soldiers, sailors, and ships were essential to the capture of Louisbourg during the War of the Austrian Succession in 1745. In the Seven Years' War, in recognition of his role in the capture of Louisbourg, Massachusetts governor William Shirley was enlisted by General Edward Braddock to organize an expedition to capture the French fort at Niagara; upon Braddock's death, Shirley was temporarily named commander in chief of British forces in North America. Nearly eight thousand Massachusetts men enlisted in military service in 1755, and thousands volunteered for the Crown Point expedition in the following year. More than seven thousand were mobilized in a three-day period to assist with the relief of Fort William Henry in 1757. In 1758 more than ten thousand Massachusetts men served in one capacity or another in the British service, and in 1759 — despite the strain the war was placing on the colony — it provided five thousand to the summer's campaign. Another four thousand fought in the final year of fighting. In all, something like

Boston, Its Environs and Harbour (1775). Boston sat on a peninsula that was almost an island. This image of the harbor illustrates its setting and shows the two navigable channels approaching the town, which converged at Castle Island. Beginning at Nantasket Road in the lower right corner of the map, they ran on either side of Long Island and Spectacle Island before joining in front of Fort William and following the single, narrow channel that led the rest of the way to Boston's wharves. Castle Island is situated so that any approaching vessel would have to approach its defenses head on.

half of Massachusetts's men of military age served in the provincial forces during the course of the Seven Years' War.[19]

Defensive preparations were as important as these offensive campaigns. Boston was the colony's most strategically important and vulnerable site, and Castle Island held the key to its defense. Building on Romer's foundation, Governor Shirley and his successor, Thomas Pownall, shored up and expanded the island's capacity. By 1758 the island's defenses included the stone fort, which contained officers' barracks and a governor's state room; the battery designed by Romer, which was known as the Royal Battery; an additional battery — called Shirley's Battery in honor of the governor — that commanded the island's southeast approach; a long breastwork and ditch built by the Dorchester and Weymouth militias; two additional gunners' batteries; a barracks suitable for a thousand men; and an older barracks that had been converted into a hospital. Pownall's 1758 description enumerates a total of ninety guns overlooking the channel, including twenty-three forty-two-pounders and nineteen thirty-two-pounders.[20] In its inception, improvement, and use, Castle Island — like the rest of the war effort — was a joint venture between colony and crown.

The military partnership between empire and colony was also embodied in the expenditure of crown funds. Merchants who won the contracts to supply Britain's military campaigns made enormous profits: the crown expended £200,000 for the Louisbourg expedition alone, much of it paid to Boston traders. By war's end, as Gary Nash has noted, "the three wealthiest men in Boston — [Thomas] Hancock, Charles Apthorp, and John Erving — were the town's three largest war contractors." They benefited from the free-spending ways of Governor Shirley, who approved many of those contracts in his capacity as a military commander. To accommodate the soldiers of the 50th and 51st Regiments, the Massachusetts General Court built barracks on Castle Island, while Shirley spent crown funds on beds, firewood, and other necessities.[21]

In 1763 the partnership between Great Britain and its North American colonies was at its apogee, and Massachusetts Bay had invested more in the military dimension of that partnership than any other colony. Despite early setbacks in the war, Britain persevered in a stunning triumph against its French and Spanish adversaries, and

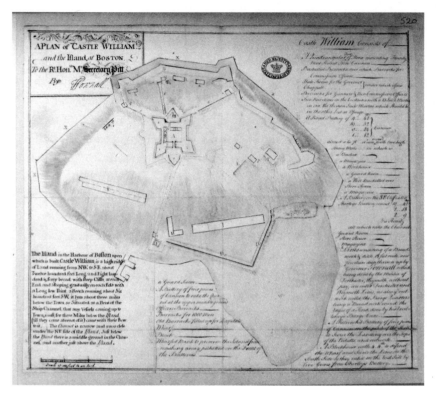

Thomas Pownall, "A Plan of Castle William and the Island at Boston" (1758). Though Pownall lacked the training of an engineer, his carefully drafted plan of Castle Island shows the state of its defenses in the closing years of the Seven Years' War. The fort commanded the channel approaching Boston. The island, wrote Pownall, was "so Situated at a Bent of the Ship Channel, that any Vessels coming up to Town, must, for three Miles below the *Island,* (till they come abreast of it) come with their Bow to it. The *Channel* is narrow and runs close under the NE side of the *Island.*"

nowhere was the victory more decisive than in the Americas. The Treaty of Paris remade the map of North America; it remained to be seen how Britain would convert its new territories into useful imperial spaces.

AS COMMANDER IN CHIEF, it was Thomas Gage's responsibility to manage the logistics of Britain's North American army after 1763. The details were daunting. In 1766 it had soldiers stationed at thirty-seven different posts, with forces ranging in size from a company of 40 men to a battalion of about 350.[22] They stretched from St. John's in Newfoundland to Fort Bute on the lower Mississippi, some thirty-three hundred miles distant from each other (or approximately the distance separating London from Jeddah, the ancient port city on the Red Sea). Many were accessible only by long overland marches or circuitous water routes interrupted by daunting portages. Viewed from its headquarters in New York — the army's nerve center of transatlantic communication — the network of posts included Halifax, which anchored the British fisheries in the northeast; Niagara, Detroit, and Michilimackinac, occupying the strategic choke points on the Great Lakes; Forts Pitt and Chartres, at opposite ends of the Ohio valley, which linked the Great Lakes to the Mississippi; and Apalachee, Pensacola, and Mobile, strung along the Gulf coast. Simply to take in the strategic significance of all these posts, to appreciate the ways in which climate and geography made them different from one another, and to grasp how Native American nations largely determined their capacity for effective action could require a lifetime of study and reflection.

The challenges of managing Britain's army in North America were legion, and only uncommon administrative acumen could make it work. Fortunately, Gage was an unusually competent administrator, with an extraordinary capacity for patience and good humor given the impossible demands of his job. From his headquarters in New York, he maintained an intricate web of correspondence, with lines stretching outward to dozens of American outposts. Incoming letters from the hinterland detailed the dilapidated state of British fortifications and facilities, the challenges of creating diplomatic relationships with dozens of Native American nations previously unknown to the British, and conflicts between officers and merchants, among a thousand other things. At the same time, he was, of necessity, in close and continual contact with the Treasury, the War Office, and the Board of Trade. Gage knew the North American setting well enough to be sympathetic to the colonists' interests, but only to the point where they intruded on the capacity of the empire to function. He was, above all, a pragmatist — a busy pragmatist — with little patience for the sensitivity colonial radicals were beginning to display toward questions of constitution, law, and right.[23]

A letter sent by Gage to Lord Barrington, the secretary at war, in October 1766 is worth quoting at length to convey the scope of the challenges he faced in managing deployments in North America:

Since My last Letter by the September Mail, Three Companys of His Majesty's Seventeenth Regiment have Marched into this Town [New York] from the Detroit and Niagara. Two More Company's of said Regiment are expected here from Michilimakinak, but not yet arrived, tho' the relieving Garrison Marched from Albany early in June — The remaining four Companys of the Seventeenth Regiment are posted, Two at Crown-Point, and Ticonderoga, one at Albany, and one divided between Fort Stanwix and Fort George. Upon the Approach of the above Company's to this Place, the whole of the 28th Regiment went to the Province of New Jersey, and are quartered, five Company's at Amboy, and four at Elizabeth Town, The Royal Highland Regiment which has been some time dispersed in the Province of Pennsylvania, have been more collected, and are now quartered Six Company's at Philadelphia, and three at Fort Pitt. The Assembly of Pennsylvania has lately voted the Sum of four Thousands Pounds for the Purposes of quartering and providing His Majesty's Troops according to Act of Parliament, and the Soldiers in the Province are in general in comfortable Quarters.[24]

One challenge represented in this passage is the simple problem of distance. To get from Michilimackinac to New York, the two companies of the 17th Regiment whose arrival Gage awaited first had to travel by bateaus (flat-bottomed transport barges that became ubiquitous in the North American interior during the Seven Years' War) from the northwestern extremity of Lake Huron nearly three hundred miles to its southern end. There they would have entered the St. Clair River, then Lake St. Clair, and then the Detroit River, which empties into Lake Erie. They would next have crossed Lake Erie from west to east — another 250 miles — to arrive at the Niagara River. Their watercraft could go no farther; given the size of the Niagara Falls and the scale of the portage, the western Great Lakes required their own shipyard and fleet.[25] From the bottom of the falls, they would have followed the Niagara River into Lake Ontario; after crossing the lake — another 150 miles or so — they would have begun the descent down the St. Lawrence River to Montreal, which lay perhaps 180 miles distant. Thirty miles beyond Montreal, the troops' transports would have entered the Richelieu River; now traveling upstream, they would have portaged around the rapids at Fort Chambly and then continued southward into and across Lake Champlain, past Crown Point to Ticonderoga. The most likely route from there was to enter Wood Creek at the southern end of the lake and follow it to Fort Anne, where a portage of about ten miles would have brought the troops, finally, into the Hudson River, which would carry them past Albany on their way to the city. In all, this was a journey of more

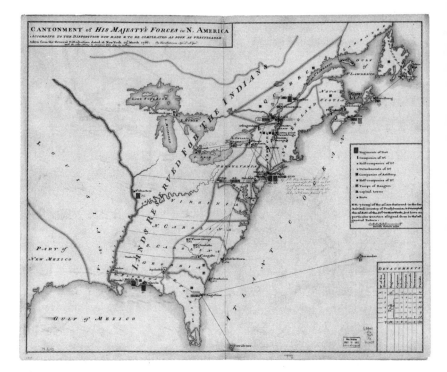

This map, executed by Daniel Paterson in 1766 and updated in 1767, captures a critical moment in Britain's effort to manage its North American territory. It illustrates the vast expanses separating post from post and suggests how difficult it must have been to oversee the army's affairs. It also highlights the difficulty of capturing troops in motion. Titled *Cantonment of His Majesty's Forces in N. America According to the Disposition Now Made & To Be Compleated as Soon as Practicable, taken from the General Distribution dated at New York 29th March 1766,* it was subsequently updated: "with the alterations to Summer 1767 done in yellow." (In this grayscale reproduction, the yellow appears as light gray boxes and text alongside the darker script.)

than twelve hundred miles, with four major portages, through country that was controlled along almost the entire route by Native American nations. All things considered, it is not surprising that four months was not enough time for two companies to make the trip to Michili-mackinac northwest from Albany (traveling upstream on every river but the Richelieu), and two others to complete the return trip to New York.

Despite the challenges, the British army was committed to the principle that troops should rotate during peacetime. In part, the idea that every unit should return periodically from distant stations to its regimental headquarters was conceived as a way to replace men who had been lost to desertion or had died in service. In part, too — influenced by the practices of the Duke of Cumberland — British administrators and army officers came to see troop rotation as an essential bulwark to troop discipline. When they spent long periods of time in remote settings, soldiers were more likely to seek work and make lives for themselves away from quarters; they were also more likely to desert their units altogether. It was easier to maintain order among troops who were regularly on the move. The process of moving was itself a form of drill that instilled discipline and encouraged regiments to develop and maintain a distinct sense of identity and purpose.[26]

But the geographic scale of North America — the distance from station to station, as well as the distance to regimental headquarters across the Atlantic — made the principle of rotation difficult to sustain. And the vast distances involved in North American deployments were only one aspect of the challenge faced by Gage's army. A second point highlighted in Gage's letter is the variety of circumstances in which troops were housed and provisioned. At the Great Lakes posts, they occupied fortifications that stood alongside trading communities. As the jumping-off point for troops bound for Montreal, Quebec, and the Great Lakes, Albany functioned as a way station where troops massed before departing, and where the quartermaster periodically had to devise means to house, feed, and transport large numbers of them. In New Jersey, troops were the object of frequent complaints during the war, when they commandeered houses and wreaked havoc. But after the colony built barracks at Perth Amboy, Burlington, Trenton, New Brunswick, and Elizabeth Town—a pattern that provided housing for the soldiers while preventing too many of them from collecting in one place—those conflicts had subsided. In New York City, a new barracks structure some 350 feet long spanned the width of the town common, where it shared space with the jail and workhouse. Pennsylvania had experienced few problems with its troops, whether they were dispersed in the countryside or concentrated at Fort Pitt and Philadelphia. Given its pacifist roots, the Pennsylvania Assembly had traditionally supported military ventures only indirectly. In that spirit, it was willing to assist in the quartering of troops both during and after the war. For much of the war, the biggest problem faced by the army in that friendly, prosperous colony was widespread desertion; if anything, Gage might have said that Pennsylvanians were too welcoming to the soldiers in their midst.[27]

Two issues gave General Gage particular cause for worry. The first, illustrated by the army's experience in Pennsylvania, was desertion; the second was billeting. In Britain, Parliament's annual Mutiny Bill regulated both concerns, but it was never clear whether its provisions applied to North America. As Gage noted in January 1765, "It is declared generaly, that the Mutiny Act, does not extend to America, but in such Clauses only where it is particularly Specified to extend to the Plantations, or to His Majesty's Dominions beyond the Seas." As a result, colonists in North America harbored deserters with impunity and refused to provide quarters for troops. "It will soon be difficult in the present Situation, to keep Soldiers in the Service; or possible to March and quarter them where the Service shall require, or however urgent the Occasion, without Numberless Prosecutions, or perhaps worse Consequences." The proper remedy, Gage believed, was to amend the Mutiny Act to extend its provisions explicitly to North America.[28]

His plea received immediate attention in London, where the Grenville ministry set to work on a solution. The eventual result was the Quartering Act of 1765. One of the principal difficulties it had to address was the general shortage of inns and public houses in the colonies. Today, Americans commonly believe that this law required that troops be housed in private homes when other accommodations were unavailable. In fact, the opposite is the case: during the war, troops had been quartered in private homes from time to time. But the Quartering Act of 1765, which was drafted by Thomas Pownall with the assistance of Benjamin Franklin, specifically protected private homes—as they had been protected in Britain itself since 1689. Instead, the new law required local officials to make military barracks available for soldiers' use; where those did not exist, they were expected to secure lodgings in livery stables, inns, public houses, and the like. Where such accommodations were inadequate, they should use "uninhabited houses, outhouses, barns, or other buildings, as . . . necessary." To make them habitable, local officials were also required to furnish firewood, bedding, candles, salt, vinegar, cooking utensils, and a daily ration of liquor.

The Quartering Act of 1765 was, from one point of view, an important validation of colonial rights. It extended to North America the same safeguards against quartering soldiers in private homes that had existed in Britain for decades. At the same time, though, it clarified the obligations of colonies and local magistrates in their relations with the army. Appearing at about the same time as the Stamp Act, the Quartering Act—with its requirement that soldiers be provided with lodging and food at local expense—could be interpreted as yet another tax imposed by Parliament on the colonies without their consent. In fact, as John Shy has noted, the Quartering Act failed to address "the problem which had been uppermost in Gage's mind — troops on the march — and instead required the colonies to help support troops on *station,* a burden borne largely by the Crown in the past." This was not an accident: given the size of the peacetime army after 1763, the crown intended to offload expenses on its subordinate territories in North America, just as it had done for three-quarters of a century in the case of the Irish establishment.[29] In better times colonists might not have taken umbrage so easily, but in 1765 the law offered one more example of Parliament usurping local prerogatives. .

At the same time, however, the Quartering Act unintentionally granted the colonies a powerful weapon in the emerging conflict with parliamentary authority. Like the Stamp Act and the Townshend Duties, it effectively imposed a tax on the colonies that their assemblies had not approved. But unlike those other statutes, which were primarily contested by ordinary citizens acting out of doors, the Quartering Act required provincial legislatures to appropriate funds for the support of the army. In moments of conflict, nothing would be easier than to withhold that support; when a province chose to do so, there was little a commanding officer could do to force the issue. Thus, when New York's assembly refused to acknowledge the terms of the Quartering Act, Gage had little choice but to accept the partial support it did offer and direct his complaints to London. In response, Parliament passed the New York Restraining Act, which prorogued the assembly until it complied with the Quartering Act. The result was a stalemate that satisfied no one.[30]

GREAT BRITAIN WAS not the only imperial power scrambling to adjust to the new realities in North America after 1763. Though Spain had lost East and West Florida to Britain in 1763, it had regained Havana, just offshore, and taken possession of New Orleans. Havana had been a Spanish stronghold in the Caribbean for nearly two hundred years when it fell to an invading British army in 1762. By the terms of the Treaty of Paris, Britain returned Cuba to Spain in exchange for the Floridas. France granted Spain that portion of Louisiana that lay west of the Mississippi River, since — with its principal holdings in North America now forfeited to Britain — it made little sense to hang onto the few remaining posts strung along the west bank of the river. New Orleans — still home to a small, fiercely independent community of French traders who had sustained Louisiana's commerce with France and its Caribbean colonies for decades — was the most important of the outposts on the Mississippi that now passed into Spanish hands.

Antonio de Ulloa was appointed Louisiana's first Spanish governor and captain general in May 1765. After assembling a small expeditionary force of ninety men in Havana, he sailed to New Orleans the following spring. The Spanish Empire in the Americas was a vast, sprawling assemblage, and although the Spanish crown appreciated the strategic importance of Louisiana — which served as a buffer between New Mexico, to the southwest, and Britain's expansive new territories to the east — it was hard pressed to devote the resources necessary to secure it. Ulloa hoped that, rather than diverting Spanish soldiers to Louisiana, he could persuade the French troops already stationed there to enlist in service to the Spanish crown. He was disappointed to learn that they preferred to return to France rather than serve in the new Spanish colony.[31]

Ulloa needed men because he intended to establish a string of new forts that could defend Louisiana against the British strongholds to the east — putting him in the odd position of fortifying Spanish territory against what had been, until 1763, Spanish territory. East and West Florida were anchored by three principal settlements strung from the Atlantic across the Gulf coast: St. Augustine, Pensacola, and Mobile. Supported by that axis, Britain manned smaller posts along the Mississippi, including Fort Bute, at the junction of the Iberville, and Fort Panmure (formerly Fort Rosalie), near present-day Natchez, Louisiana. To shore up Spain's position, Ulloa ordered the construction of four new outposts: Fort El Príncipe de Asturias at the mouth of the Missouri; San Gabriel, in the Iberville district; San Luis de Natchez, opposite Fort Panmure; and Isla Real Católica de San Carlos, on a small island at the mouth of the Mississippi. This was an ambitious plan, even for a commanding officer whose mission was well funded and sufficiently manned. Spanish Louisiana was neither, and Ulloa's correspondence with his superiors included persistent requests for money and manpower.

With funds in short supply, Ulloa had to turn to the New Orleans merchant community to request provisions on credit. Ulloa was on thin ice with them. When he first arrived, his force was so weak that he chose not to take official possession of the city, since that would have required him to present his instructions to the Superior Council— and thereby impose new regulations, which he knew he was unable to enforce. Instead, he waited for more troops and spent as little time in New Orleans as possible. Eventually, however—recognizing that support from Spain was not forthcoming—he issued a new set of commercial regulations, the gist of which was to curb trade with France in order to drive Louisiana's commerce into the sphere of the Spanish Empire.

The merchants of New Orleans strongly opposed Spain's new regulatory regime. In this respect, they bore a close resemblance to Boston's merchant community, for whom a new imperial commitment to commercial oversight was also disrupting established trading patterns. Like Governor Bernard, Ulloa felt the need for military support to assist him in enforcing the dictates of a distant crown. In other ways, though, the circumstances of New Orleans contrasted sharply with those of Boston. The hinterland of New Orleans, for example, could not support it, and the city therefore relied on British traders for provisions. Ulloa tried to maintain the illusion that they operated only at his sufferance. The "independence of the English merchant vessels, which arrive with flour, meat, and other provisions for this city," vexed Ulloa. He required all such vessels to gain his permission before entering New Orleans, but British captains resisted because they did not want to pay anchorage and piloting fees. "They also wish to avoid the inspection which I have ordered made of all vessels before departures, in order to prevent the desertion of seamen and troops," Ulloa wrote. He had no choice but "to order the captain of His Majesty's packet *Volante* to fire on any which may tie up on the opposite bank without first present[ing] permission in writing from me."[32]

But even as Ulloa tried to regulate British traders, he worked to accommodate the interests of the British crown. In the Treaty of Paris, Spain and Britain had agreed to share the right of passage on the Mississippi River, without which Britain could not supply Fort Chartres, upriver in the Illinois country. Thus, his instructions relating to British traders did "not apply to war vessels nor those freighted for account of the British King." Similarly, when a British naval officer arrived in New Orleans with a hydrographer, "engaged in making a map of all the coast of Florida and of this region," they proceeded with Ulloa's blessing.[33]

Ulloa's plan to build a string of forts to defend Louisiana against British encroachments belied this spirit of cooperation. Despite the formal peace between Spain and Great Britain, New Orleans was isolated and vulnerable, and the embattled governor knew it. It was with considerable relief, therefore, that he reported "important news" from General Frederick Haldimand, the commanding officer at Pensacola. Haldimand informed him that Britain intended to withdraw its troops from Fort Bute on the Iberville and Fort Panmure at Natchez, "demolishing the first and abandoning the second." Ulloa also learned that Britain intended to reduce the forces at Pensacola and Mobile to a minimum. "This indicates," he concluded, "that the English have been undecided about the value of these possessions, and that the expense occasioned England is not repaid by the profit taken from them." The implications for Ulloa's own defensive scheme were clear. "Formerly," he wrote, "800 men were not sufficient to garrison" Louisiana, but "now on account of our not being faced by forts or troops of another nation," 400 would be enough to support the colony.[34]

As Haldimand's letter to Ulloa suggests, Boston was only one small piece of the puzzle General Gage was trying to solve in the summer of 1768. In June, at the same time he was corresponding with Bernard about the *Liberty* riot, he received orders to consolidate Britain's forces in North America. They came from the Earl of Hillsborough, whose new office of secretary of state for the colonies was created to centralize colonial administration. Hillsborough had not yet learned of the Boston riot, but he had seen the panicky letters Bernard had written in March. Moreover, he had long been wary of Britain's extensive post–Seven Years' War commitments in the trans-Appalachian West. Now he succeeded in persuading King George that, in order to economize, as many western posts as possible should be abandoned; that those which remained essential should be managed, wherever possible, by small detachments; and that the remainder of the troops stationed in North America should be massed in four locations: Quebec, Nova Scotia, East Florida, and "the middle Colonies." This would dramatically reduce expenses while keeping the army "so united, and in such a State of Discipline, as that it may be complete & effectual to answer any Exigency, and so situated, that it may be transported to whatever Places may require It's Service, with as little Trouble and Expence as possible." With these instructions in hand, Gage ordered the garrisons at Forts Louisbourg and Amherst to Halifax; troops from Bermuda, New Providence, St. Marks, and Pensacola, as well as Forts Bute and Panmure, were ordered to St. Augustine; and the frontier posts of Fort Frederica, South Carolina, and Fort Augusta, Georgia, were abandoned and their garrisons transferred northward.[35] Ulloa soon received shadowy intelligence about events in Boston, and passed that along as well. Two visitors reported that "the troubles in New England continue to spread. The people have compelled Governor General Don Thomas Gage to flee from the capital and retire to the fort, where it is said they have him besieged." Ulloa's informants identified Boston as the center of the "troubles and conspiracies" that Gage was contending with. "The inhabitants there," he concluded, "are determined on total independence from old England."[36]

Ulloa's intelligence was not entirely accurate, of course. It was the customs commissioners stationed in Boston who had fled to Castle William, not Gage; he remained in his headquarters in New York. He was not besieged: at least, not literally.

CHAPTER 5

Settling In

A FTER THEIR ARREST in the early hours of March 6, 1770, Captain Thomas Preston and his eight men settled into Boston's Queen Street jail, where they would spend the next seven months. The jail was only a few years old. Rebuilt in 1766 to replace an older structure on the same site — a "most shocking loathsome Place," in Hutchinson's view — the new jail was built of granite, two stories high with eighteen rooms. A persistent tradition suggests that Governor Bernard himself, who had a reputation as a gentleman architect, supplied the design.[1] While Boston's populace was understandably aggrieved and outraged by the events of the previous evening, Preston and his men had had a harrowing experience of their own. Though they were the ones with firearms in their hands, the violence in King Street fulfilled the worst fears of British soldiers posted to watch over a civilian population. After the shootings, Preston initially feared for his life. "I am, though perfectly innocent," he wrote, "under most unhappy circumstances, having nothing in reason to expect but the loss of life in a very ignominious manner without the interposition of His Majesty's royal goodness."[2] He had good reason to be afraid: Britons everywhere hated soldiers in their midst. Preston was in precarious circumstances, and he knew it well. The jail's walls were thick, but jailers had surrendered their keys to mobs before; there was no reason to believe it couldn't happen again.

WHEN TROOPS BEGAN TO arrive in Boston in late September 1768, Colonel William Dalrymple first acted, as Gage had instructed, to secure Castle Island. The 14th and 29th Regiments came in full force from Halifax, along with a detachment of the 59th Regiment and a company of the Royal Regiment of Artillery, commanded by a Captain Carter, carrying five six-pound cannons and two three-pounders. It was Governor Bernard's wish that one of the regiments would be quartered in town, while the other soldiers occupied the barracks on Castle Island. Since "Rebels" had not taken over the island in arms, as Gage feared they might, Bernard left the fort itself in the hands of the company of provincial troops that commanded it. The barracks intended for the British soldiers stood outside the fort, "and close to it, surrounded by a Line of Pickets which joins to the Covered-way of the Fort." Here, a British regiment could be quartered without challenging the colony's control of the fort itself. Because Bernard had been unable to persuade the town selectmen or the Governor's Council to supply the barracks, Dalrymple brought bedding with him from Halifax.[3]

Gage continued to think about the occupation of Boston as a military operation, not a peacekeeping one. He contravened Bernard's intention to leave Castle William in the hands of provincial soldiers and ordered Dalrymple to take possession of it, "as it belongs to the crown." He sent Captain John Montresor, an engineer in the 48th Regiment who was stationed in New York, to Boston to meet with Dalrymple. Engineers were scarce and highly valued, both for their ability to oversee major construction and repair projects and for their skill as surveyors and draftsmen. Gage had heard that the fort on Castle Island was in disrepair, and he instructed Montresor to "set out for Boston with all Expedition" in order "to assist Lieut. Colonel Dalrymple in fortifying and Repairing of Castle William, and such other works as the Exigency of the service may require." Gage also ordered Montresor to cast a critical eye on the approaches to Boston and the situation of the town. He told the engineer to "take a Transitory sketch of the country you pass through," with

remarks on the Rivers and Creeks you shall pass, of their Fords, Ferrys and Banks, as well as the number and kind of Craft to be found thereon.

It is necessary likewise, that you should remark the Hills, Mountains, Woods and difficult Passes in the Course of your Journey, together with the Roads, Situation of the Towns and Villages, what advantages of Defence or attack they afford, the Distances from one to the other, and the Different Roads that lead to them.

When you arrive at Boston you will after some time have leizure to take a more particular sketch of that Town and the Circumjacent Country, remarking how the City is supplied as well by land as Water, and what Posts may be taken to cut off their supplies.

Wherever you perceive a strong and advantageous camp may be taken, that the Flanks are covered by Rivers, Woods, Mountains Villages &ca. and that it will at the same time Cover the Country from whence the Supplies are received, you will not fail to be as particular as you have time to be in your Remarks thereon. . . . As for Castle William you will send me a Draught of that Fort and Island with Remarks on the State of its Fortifications, Artillery, &ca.[4]

In short, Gage asked Montresor to provide him with all the intelligence he would need to besiege or attack the town.

The Halifax fleet arrived at Castle Island on Wednesday, September 28. Bernard and the council traveled to the island to meet with Dalrymple on the following day. The council urged him to house both the 14th and the 29th Regiments in the island's barracks; Dalrymple insisted that he would obey his orders and place one of the regiments in Boston proper. Bernard asked the council to support him in claiming the Manufactory House and fitting it up as a barracks. When the council insisted that it had no money, Bernard assured its members that the work could be done at the expense of the crown. Still, the council refused to approve the plan. Bernard and the council had been dancing around each other in this fashion for a long time, and were accustomed to it, but for Dalrymple, who was caught in the middle of their exchange, it was an outrageous spectacle. "My surprize was infinite," he wrote, when he learned that no quarters had been prepared for his troops. The council's argument that Castle Island was within the town of Boston he called "idle and futile," and he "endeavoured to stimulate the Governor to exert his authority but in vain." The day ended without any resolution to Dalrymple's quandary.[5]

Montresor arrived on September 30 with additional orders in hand from Gage. Based on those directives, the three men "immediately resolved to land both regiments at Boston the next day." Dalrymple, relieved to have clear instructions at last, planned to "take quarters on the Common untill some provision should be made for us." Once

A View of Part of the Town of Boston in New-England and Brittish Ships of War Landing Their Troops, 1768, engraved and printed by Paul Revere [1770] *(opposite).* Paul Revere's famous engraving of the occupation of Boston highlights the aggressive character of the troops' arrival. Note the warships, positioned broadside; the boats transporting soldiers; and the ranks forming up on Long Wharf, preparing to march up King Street and into the center of town. Based on a watercolor executed by Christian Remick in October 1769, the Revere print was dedicated to the Earl of Hillsborough and was first offered for sale in April 1770, a month after the shootings in King Street.

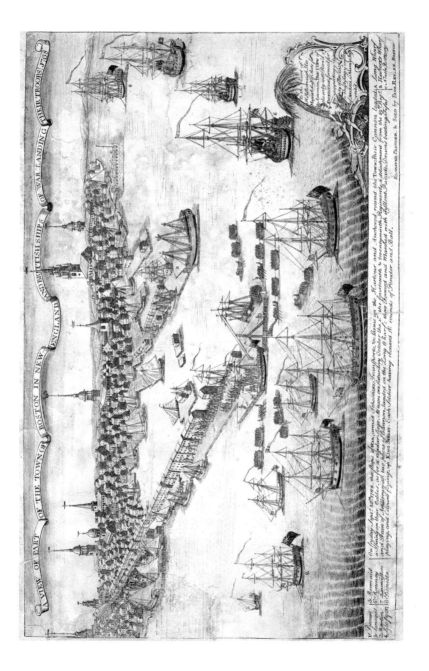

A VIEW OF PART OF THE TOWN OF BOSTON IN NEW ENGLAND AND BRITISH SHIPS OF WAR LANDING THEIR TROOPS, 1768

the decision was made, the Halifax fleet — one ship of the line, seven frigates, and two tenders — weighed anchor and sailed toward Boston's wharves, where it "formed a line round & within musquet shot of the Town, in order to facilitate the Disembarkation of the Troops."[6]

The troops began to come ashore at noon on October 1. Paul Revere captured their arrival in a famous engraving that emphasized the hostile character of the proceedings. The text beneath the image lays particular stress on the ships' preparation for war. "On fryday Sept[embe]r 30th 1768," it notes, "the Ships of WAR, armed Schooners, Transports, &c." anchored in Boston Harbor. Eight vessels are identified by name: the *Beaver, Senegal, Martin, Glasgow, Mermaid, Romney, Launceston,* and *Bonetta.* Their cannons were loaded, and they had "a spring on their Cables, as for a regular siege." This was an important detail: these vessels were not simply acting as transports to deliver soldiers. Arrayed broadside, with loaded cannons pointed toward town, they were prepared to cannonade Boston if necessary. They were held at anchor by cables attached near their bows. A "spring" was a second, slack cable attached near the stern. By hauling on the spring and slackening the anchor cable simultaneously, it was possible to swing the ships around nearly 180 degrees — thus doubling the firing capacity of each vessel. The most imposing of them was HMS *Romney* (the same fifty-gun warship that had towed Hancock's *Liberty* into custody in June), with its cannons arrayed in two tiers along each of its broadsides; in the Revere print, each cannon is carefully delineated and colored red to catch the viewer's eye. HMS *Launceston* was nearly as formidable, with forty guns in two tiers. Even with the ships at repose, several dozen armed cannons were directed toward Boston's shoreline. The springs on their cables doubled the vessels' firing capacity. "So that we now behold Boston surrounded at a time of profound peace," one observer wrote, "with about 14 ships of war, with springs on their cables, and their broadsides to the town!"[7]

The cartouche of Revere's 1770 print shows a reclining figure symbolizing the American colonies, armed with a bow and arrow, with one foot placed squarely on the chest of a disarmed and prostrate soldier of the 29th Regiment. Engraved in the aftermath of the King Street shootings, this detail symbolized the reversal of fortunes that resulted from the actions of members of the 29th.

Revere's print first appeared for sale in April 1770, after the shootings in King Street. An important detail highlights the antagonism that had developed between Bostonians and redcoats. Decorating the cartouche in the lower right-hand corner is the half-reclining figure of an American Indian — by 1770 a common symbol of American identity — with a bow in one hand and an arrow in the other. It is easy to overlook a second figure lying beneath the Indian's feet, but one foot is pressing down on the throat of a British grenadier. His cap identifies him as a member of the 29th Regiment.[8]

The regiments disembarked, formed up on Long Wharf, and marched down King Street "with insolent Parade, Drums beating, Fifes playing, and Colours flying." No one knew what to expect. Revere noted that each soldier had been supplied with sixteen rounds of powder and ball. That was a lot of firepower, but it may not have been enough. Rumors suggested that town leaders had enlisted militia units from neighboring towns to "Surprise" the troops when they arrived. Samuel Adams had reportedly urged Bostonians to "behave like men" and "take up Arms immediately," and predicted that thirty thousand men would join them from the countryside. The soldiers of the 14th and 29th must have disembarked with great trepidation, but at the end of the day, Dalrymple could report with considerable relief that "all the threatnings of opposition vanished, [and] I marched immediately to the Common."[9]

Gage's worst fears having gone unrealized, Bernard's more prosaic worries came to the fore. Once they had disembarked, it was unclear where the soldiers should go. By nightfall, the men of the 29th Regiment had pitched their tents on the Common, while the 14th crowded into temporary lodgings in Faneuil Hall. The next day, Bernard arranged to make the ground floor of the Town House available to the 14th as well. "We now behold the Representatives' Chamber, Court-House, and Faneuil-Hall, those seats of freedom and justice occupied with troops, and guards placed at the doors," one correspondent wrote; "the Common covered with tents, and alive with soldiers; marching and countermarchings to relieve the guards, in short the town is now a perfect garrison."[10] Massed as the soldiers were in the town's most important public spaces, the symbolism was unmistakable: they had infringed on Boston's local prerogatives and created new imperial spaces in the literal and metaphorical center of town life.

Dalrymple, acting on Bernard's suggestion, initially set his sights on the Manufactory House as a suitable barracks. Originally built by the province to encourage local industry, the manufactory was no longer in operation as a public enterprise, but several Bostonians were living and working there as tenants, among them its former superintendent, John Brown. For three weeks Brown parried every attempt to clear the building. On October 1 an officer of the 14th Regiment brought an order from the governor instructing the tenants to vacate within two hours. Instead they barred the doors. Dalrymple and Bernard continued to hope that the building would be made available to the troops, but they could make no headway with the council. On October 18, anticipating the arrival of the 64th and 65th, the council finally endorsed Bernard's order to clear the tenants from the Manufactory House. Still they refused to budge. When the sheriff arrived to serve a warrant, Brown argued that he was a tenant at will of the province, and therefore only the General Court could require him to leave. Bernard had prorogued the assembly at the end of June, and Brown refused to accept the authority of the governor and council acting on their own. The sheriff forced his way into the cellar and posted sentries in an effort to claim the building, but the tenants still refused to leave. On Saturday, October 22, after a long standoff, the sheriff finally "raised the siege," and the idea of using the Manufactory House as a barracks was abandoned. Gage had recommended that Boston's "workhouse & Poorhouse" might also serve, but these buildings — owned by the town rather than the province and already occupied — were never considered. Alternatively, Gage suggested, "if the Proposal of running up Slight Barracks in a hurry cannot be avoided," perhaps they could be "Erected on some advantageous spot for Defence or Offence," such as Fort Hill or Beacon Hill.[11]

It soon became clear that there was no building large enough to house the troops, and neither the town nor the council would approve the construction of a new barracks that might house them all. Despite Bernard's conviction that the soldiers should not be dispersed through town, that was the only remaining option. Only by negotiating a variety of rental agreements with local storekeepers and merchants was Dalrymple able to find accommodations for all his men. Divided company by company, they occupied stores and warehouses in Brattle Street, Green's Lane, and New Boston, on Griffin's Wharf and Wheelwright's Wharf. Many others — principally officers and enlisted men who arrived with their families — rented rooms or houses in town. In the end, unwilling to prolong the controversy with the town over expenses, Gage defrayed the cost of maintaining the troops.[12]

The occupation of Boston highlights the unresolved contradictions in British attitudes toward peacetime armies. The Governor's Council embodied the attitudes of Englishmen who regarded the army as an illegitimate presence unless it had been summoned for a specific peacekeeping purpose — as it had not been in this case. In England, where barracks were considered anathema, troops spent much of their time on the march, and officers had to be carefully attuned to local sensibilities. When troops were required for peacekeeping efforts, local magistrates issued a request for deployment, the troops received orders from a secretary of state, and in most cases they were deployed on the fly. Wherever they went to serve as a police force, they left as quickly as possible.

But for Gage, expectations that derived from English practice bore little relationship to the reality of military deployments in North America. As he oversaw the movements of thousands of troops, he expected support and cooperation from magistrates and assemblies. The cautious interplay between Bernard and his council was maddening to Gage and his subordinate officers. Especially when the Massachusetts Assembly and the Boston town meeting were issuing outrageous statements challenging the authority of Parliament and the legitimacy of the army's presence, he was inclined to treat the posting of troops as a military operation, not a police action.

However frustrating he found the situation, though, Gage was as constrained as anyone by the long-standing expectation, grounded in English precedent, that in any confrontation between soldiers and subjects, the presumption of right was on the side of the subjects. The occupation of Boston defied normal English practice in a way that caused profound uncertainty about its purpose. Bernard had never formally requested the troops — they came partly on Gage's authority and partly on that of King George III himself — and they arrived, not in response to a crisis, but anticipating the possibility of one. And they stayed indefinitely, forcing townspeople to confront the hard material reality of troops — their uniforms and arms, fifes, drums, and colors, not to mention the simple problem of urban crowding — everywhere they turned. In the initial battle over quartering, the town could claim at least a partial victory. It remained to be seen who would win the war of attrition Gage had set in motion.

SOLDIERS — TO BEGIN with the most basic fact — were recruited to fight wars. The army's constitution, organization, and operation were dictated by the demands of war. At the time of recruitment, most soldiers were young men; to take one sample, of fourteen thousand troops serving in North America in 1757, 34.5 percent were twenty years old or younger; another 26.5 percent were between twenty and twenty-five. Only 10 percent were over forty — and that tabulation includes commissioned and noncommissioned officers as well as rank and file (approximately 10 percent of the whole consisted of officers). Common soldiers in the British army were not well paid; with an estimated annual income of £14 per year, they ranked just below unskilled laborers in income. As a group, in fact, soldiers had much in common with unskilled workers; the most frequent occupation claimed by soldiers upon enlistment was "husbandman / labourer." Recruits came predominantly from the British Isles, especially from Ireland and Scotland. In the 1757 sample of troops serving in North America, 55 percent were either Scots or Irish, while English and

Welsh accounted for another 30 percent; the remaining 15 percent were recruited in North America or on the continent.[13]

Commissioned officers differed in many ways from the rank and file. About two-thirds of British officers purchased their commissions, while the other third received them on the basis of merit. Despite the prevalence of the purchase system, scholars generally agree that British officers were mostly capable men who served for long periods of time and brought considerable experience to their posts. In the era of the Seven Years' War, officers were even more likely to be Scottish or Irish than the soldiers who served under them: of those serving in North America in 1757, 31.5 percent were Scots, 31 percent Irish, and 24.5 percent English or Welsh. Fraternization between officers and their men was all but unheard of, and officers disciplined soldiers harshly for all kinds of transgressions. But officers and their men took great pride in functioning together effectively in the field, and they were connected by strong bonds of loyalty and common interest.[14]

A peacetime army was an aging army. As Britain mobilized for war, recruiters brought thousands of young men into military service; with demobilization, recruiting slowed dramatically, and the men who remained began to grow old in service. Consequently, the soldiers deployed to Boston in the fall of 1768 were seasoned veterans.[15] Both the 14th and the 29th Regiments were headquartered in Ireland. The 14th spent all of the Seven Years' War there before being transferred to Halifax in 1765; at the time of the transfer the regiment consisted of nine companies, with two sergeants, two corporals, a drummer, and forty-seven privates in each. (This was a fairly typical peacetime composition; regiments were at half strength, with a notional size of about five hundred soldiers.) The service of the 29th had been more varied. In 1745 it was mobilized against the Pretender, and it served in the following year at Culloden. It was deployed on the Sussex coast in 1751 and in Gibraltar for seven years beginning in 1752. From 1759 until 1766 it served in England again, where three of its companies were assigned to Windsor and Hampton Court. In recognition for that service, George III had a new figure — a white horse, with the motto *Nec aspera terrent* (roughly, "Scared of nothing") — emblazoned on the black bearskin caps of the regiment's grenadiers. The 29th embarked for North America in 1766, where it, too, was headquartered in Nova Scotia. The other regiments that came to Boston in 1768 — a detachment of the 59th, along with the 64th and 65th — were all newly created during the Seven Years' War. The 59th was raised in Nottinghamshire in 1755 for service in Ireland and transferred to Halifax in 1763; the 64th and 65th each originated as battalions in older regiments in 1756 and were then established as separate regiments two years later.[16]

Command of the troops in Boston fell to three men in succession. Dalrymple, a Scottish colonel of the 14th Regiment, was the ranking officer among the first arrivals. When the 64th and 65th Regiments arrived in the last week of November, Colonel John Pomeroy of the 64th, as the senior officer, became brigadier-general. It was a temporary assignment, intended to last only until the arrival of Colonel Alexander Mackay of the 65th. But Mackay, sailing separately, was blown off course after departing from Ireland. He finally arrived in Boston on April 31, 1769, after a six-month odyssey, to assume the rank of major general. When the 64th and 65th Regiments left Boston that summer, Mackay and Pomeroy left with them, and Dalrymple became the town's commanding officer once again.

None of the three relished the task. All were acutely aware of the precariousness of their command, and all repeatedly importuned Gage to send them home. Dalrymple was the most engaged and assiduous of them, and his long tenure gave him the opportunity to develop strong opinions about military-civilian relations in Boston. As the occupation dragged on, he had many occasions to express his misgivings to Gage. "I consider myself to be without support," he wrote in October 1769; "government here is in the hands of the multitude, and I am sure something very unpleasant is at hand. . . . I dispair of being able to stand against such a complication of artifices and violencies, tho no attention shall be wanting, nor temper." In Dalrymple's view, he and the troops he commanded had been abused by Boston's radicals, ill served by the colony's crown-appointed officers, and abandoned by Parliament. "I hope Sir," he concluded, "you will make our condition known[. It would be] better [to] have no troops here than [to] abandone them to the will of the people."[17]

Though Dalrymple considered his situation dire, it would have been familiar to many British officers assigned to police civilian populations. The army was an unpopular institution in England, and everything it did was constrained by law and custom. The Riot Act of 1714 offers a good illustration of those constraints. Before it was passed, when a crowd gathered, its members were not committing a felony unless they undertook some violent act. Once they did commit a felony, under common law anyone — a civilian or a soldier — could use any means to stop them, up to and including shooting into the crowd. The problem arose when a crowd had gathered but had not committed any act of violence. This is what the Riot Act was for. Once the text of the law was read in front of a crowd, its members had one hour to disperse. If they did not do so, they became felons and could be dealt with accordingly, whether or not they had committed any other crime. But although the original intent of the Riot Act was to criminalize crowd behavior and thereby strengthen the hands of magistrates and soldiers, its meaning was gradually inverted. As soldiers came to be used more often for civilian police functions in peacetime, courts in Britain interpreted the Riot Act to mean that soldiers could not act against a crowd, whatever it was doing, unless they were explicitly instructed to do so by local officials. In 1765 the War Office instructed soldiers not to use any force in dealing with a crowd "unless in case of absolute necessity and being thereunto required by the civil magistrates."[18]

Soldiers who overstepped those limits were often tried in local courts, and almost as often found guilty. If that happened, their only recourse was to seek a pardon from the crown. They were likely to receive it, but even then their fates were uncertain. The outcome that commanding officers everywhere feared most was the one suffered by John Porteous, a captain of the City Guard in Edinburgh whose men fired into a raucous crowd as it tried to prevent a hanging on April 14, 1736. Six members of the crowd were killed, and Porteous was subsequently convicted of murder in a local court. When his execution was delayed on appeal, a crowd stormed the prison and lynched him. A few years later, an army colonel who was asked to restore order in Bristol wrote, "Captain Porteous's unhappy fate was too fresh in my memory not to make me act with the utmost caution and security." Another officer charged with suppressing a riot in Henley mused on his dilemma. "What would be any of our fates had we the misfortune of killing any of these people in our own defence?" he wondered. "They will not quarter enough of us in one town, for were we more together we might with sticks and other weapons turn out against a mob, and get the better of them, whereas our small numbers with firearms, which they know we dare not use, only makes us appear more despicable, and more liable to have our brains beat out."[19]

WHATEVER THOUGHTS DALRYMPLE and his men entertained as they took up residence in Boston, they could not have worried that they were too few in number. In 1765 Boston's adult male inhabitants, black and white, amounted to fewer than thirty-five hundred. The town had 1,676 houses and just over two thousand families.[20] After the 64th and 65th Regiments arrived in November, Dalrymple could have assigned one soldier to oversee each family in town. Nor could the troops have been more conspicuous. They paraded on the Common, in Brattle Square—wherever the cramped city afforded them the space. Only five days after the arrival of the first occupying troops, a whipping was staged on the Common. "To behold," a contemporary chronicler wrote, "Britons scourg'd by Negro drummers, was a new and very disagreeable spectacle." A few weeks later, Richard Ames, a private of the 14th Regiment who had tried to desert but was caught, was publicly executed by a firing squad. Bostonians could not escape the sights and sounds of military spectacle and discipline, which caused them to view soldiers as a people set apart but could also arouse sympathy and compassion for their plight.[21]

As the troops settled into their routines, Pomeroy complained that townspeople were "very ready on the most trivial occasions to promote disputes." Soldiers established checkpoints throughout Boston that inflamed hostility. "Though the people had been used to answer to the call of the town watch in the night," Hutchinson wrote some years later, "yet they did not like to answer to the frequent calls of the centinels posted at the barracks, and at the gates of the principal officers, in different quarters of the town." Instead, Pomeroy noted, "they generally at night refuse to answer our Centrys, & when they do, it is often in the most abusive Language." Complaints of *"ill usage of some respectable inhabitants"* made their way to the governor. Pomeroy appealed to Bernard to request help in getting Bostonians to cooperate; Bernard laid the request before the council. Council members argued "that particular Instances of refusing to answer, could not be understood as a general Practice, or a Design to make a Quarrel with the Soldiers." Moreover, "they had on the other Hand heard complaints of ill usage of some respectable Inhabitants of the Town by the Military," and the controversy was making its way into the local court. Since "there were actions now depending in the Law" that would soon adjudicate such disputes, the council decided "it would be improper for them to interfere." Six weeks later, a Private Dukesberry of the 29th Regiment appeared in court, charged with assault for challenging a townsman as he passed a checkpoint. Justice of the

Peace Richard Dana advised the jury "not to submit" to such challenges because, once they did, other impositions would proceed "by degrees so as at last to reduce them to a state of Slavery and make them subservient even to these Soldiers."[22]

Gage responded in a spirit of exasperated resignation. "Tho' the Council might have used their Endeavors to conciliate the people to the Practice of being Challenged, it would have availed but very little," he wrote to Pomeroy. In Gage's eyes, the council was only the tip of the iceberg. "You may depend upon it, that the soldiers would only be answered with abuse, & Fellows set on purposely to irritate them to strike, or to seize them in order to give rise to prosecutions, and Complaints against the Military." He believed that ordinary Bostonians, even more than the council, had it out for the troops. "And if a Tryal Ensues, You must not Expect that a Boston Jury will either decide by the rules of Justice, Law, or Equity, or trouble themselves about what is right or wrong." In a legal contest, he presumed that no soldier could expect a fair outcome. Instead, he privately instructed the captain of the Main Guard to discontinue the practice of challenging passersby.[23]

While Gage and Pomeroy strained to accept the constraints placed on their operations in Boston, officers, soldiers, and townspeople gradually settled into a new set of routines. Officers had extensive contacts with Boston residents. They rented houses or rooms from local property owners, they had more freedom of movement than enlisted men, and they were especially likely to socialize with prominent Bostonians. To facilitate social intercourse with Boston's most prominent residents, Pomeroy and his officers initiated an assembly. The assembly was an eighteenth-century institution that allowed men and women to interact according to genteel standards of behavior. Dancing was generally the central activity of an assembly. "Last night," Pomeroy reported happily to Gage, "our assembly began which was Brilliant, & promises to be more so."[24]

John Rowe was one of the Bostonians who took advantage of every opportunity to interact with the soldiers in town. A merchant who was born in England but had spent his adulthood in Boston, Rowe held moderate political views and had a wide range of social contacts, including radicals like William Molineux, John Hancock, and Samuel Adams, as well as future loyalists like Ralph Inman (his brother-in-law) and Thomas Hutchinson. When the troops arrived he began angling for their supply contract. His diary offers a glimpse of the social world inhabited by merchants, lawyers, colony officials, and military officers during the months of occupation. Rowe interacted cordially with General Gage while the latter was in town and described Colonel James Robertson as "a Gentleman of Great Abilities & very cool & dispassionate." When John Forbes, chaplain of the 29th Regiment, conducted a service in Trinity Church in March 1769, Rowe noted, "Mr Forbes of the 29th Regiment preached a most excellent discourse[.] This Mr Forbes is a most delightful & charming preacher." Social occasions often brought Rowe in contact with officers; on March 5, 1769, for example, he recorded that he "Spent the evening at the Assembly with the Governour, Commodore, General, Colo. Kerr Colo. Lesly, Major Furlong, Major Fleming, Major Fordyce. A Great Number of Officers of the Navy & Army & Gentlemen & Ladies of the Town, that it was a Brilliant Assembly & very Good Dancing."[25]

Rowe apparently enjoyed the officers' company and appreciated the luster and refinement they brought to town. Rowe and his wife were childless, but their niece Susanna Inman (nicknamed Sucky) lived with them. Born in 1754, she was fifteen when the troops first came to town and seems to have enjoyed the connection with British officers as much as her guardians did. One visitor to the Rowes' home was John Linzee, a captain in the Royal Navy and commander of the British warship *Beaver*. He first called on the Rowes in 1769, and made a point of visiting thereafter whenever he was in town. In 1772, when Sucky was eighteen, she married him. It was a match that apparently pleased the elder Rowes as much as it did their niece.[26] Officers' attentions were not always so favorably regarded by the fathers of Boston girls. On the day the 14th and 29th Regiments first marched into town, their route took them past the home of William Sheafe, a deputy collector of customs for the port of Boston. Family legend has it that his daughters, hearing the commotion, went out on the balcony to watch the soldiers pass by. Captain Ponsonby Molesworth—the fifth son of a prominent Irish family—spotted the oldest daughter, fourteen-year-old Susannah, and fell in love. A short time later, when she had just turned fifteen, Molesworth asked her father for her hand. Thinking Susannah too young, Sheafe refused. But Molesworth and Susannah were determined, and with the help of a sympathetic governess who served as a witness, they eloped and returned a few days later as a married couple. Against all odds, the marriage prospered. Their first child—a boy named William—was baptized in Trinity Church in February 1770. Eventually they settled in England, where, according to family lore, "their married life proved uncommonly happy."[27]

Romantic tales like the story of Ponsonby Molesworth and Susannah Sheafe tend to overshadow the more prosaic, and much more common, realities of family life for many of the soldiers stationed in Boston. Even in wartime and even when they were on the march, women accompanied early modern armies everywhere. In peacetime the army became an even more complex social organism. Many soldiers were married and had children; for the men of the 14th and 29th Regiments, stationed in North America for a period of four years or more, sustaining their families often required that their wives and children accompany them on their deployments. Though the army kept no official record of the presence of soldiers' families, anecdotal evidence allows us to sketch a broad outline of the patterns they formed.[28]

Many soldiers — enlisted men as well as officers — rented rooms in town rather than living in the makeshift barracks that had been set aside for them. Many also developed friendships with Bostonians, as depositions taken after the March 5 shootings make clear. A soldier of the 29th Regiment named Charles Malone visited the home of Amos Thayer the evening before the shootings to warn Thayer to stay indoors for a couple of days. He had an inkling that trouble was brewing, and he explained that he had "a greater regard" for Thayer "than anyone in Boston." A week or so earlier, four or five soldiers were visiting the home of John and Sarah Wilme, along with a Bostonian named David Cockran. At least one of the soldiers' wives was present as well. Richard Ward worked with Patrick Dines of the 29th Regiment in John Piemont's peruke maker's shop and visited Dines in the rooms he rented in town. At least two other soldiers of the 29th Regiment rented lodgings for their families: James Hartegan and his wife Elizabeth rented in King Street, and Hugh Montgomery rented a house from Royall Tyler in the North End where he lived with his wife Isabella and their children Mary and William. Hartegan and Montgomery were two of the soldiers accused of firing into the crowd on March 5, 1770. After they were jailed, their families, left without support, were warned out of town.[29]

Soldiers and Bostonians shared many experiences in common during the seventeen months of the occupation. None, for example, could escape the possibility that they or their family members might fall ill. Smallpox plagued the town in the summer and fall of 1769. Though its incidence was limited enough that it should probably be called an outbreak rather than an epidemic, at least forty-one people can be identified as victims. Many were initially hospitalized in town, but most were quarantined to the "pest house" on Rainsford's Island in Boston Harbor. The first case, reported on June 11, involved a private who "had the Small Pox broke out upon him in the Regimental Hospital." General Alexander Mackay assured local officials that his was the only case among the soldiers in town. Two weeks later, Joseph Tyler's wife fell ill in Orange Street, then Edward Craft's wife and daughter near the Liberty Tree—all in the South End. From there the contagion spread; a ship's captain recently arrived from Philadelphia fell ill in late July, and the selectmen suspected that he brought his case with him from that city. Quick action and widely shared information helped to keep the disease in check, but residents fell ill at a steady pace throughout the summer and fall, until the arrival of colder weather finally slowed its progress.[30]

It is striking that although the first reported case of smallpox involved a soldier, Bostonians accepted General Mackay's assurances and did not blame the soldiers for the illness. And in fact, the next nineteen victims were civilians. But on August 22, the child of a soldier named Matthew Chambers fell ill. The child was living "near the Orange Tree" on Hanover Street; he and his mother were sent to Rainsford's Island on August 30. Of the last twenty-one victims identified in the records, either eight or nine were soldiers' children and three were soldiers' wives. Town records identify the victims' neighborhoods, but because barracks were scattered through town it is usually impossible to tell whether these soldiers' families were living in rented rooms or in barracks. One victim is explicitly identified with the "Sugar House Barracks [in] New Boston"; three others are identified with Wheelwright's, which almost certainly refers to the barracks on Wheelwright's Wharf. The others were living either in West Boston or New Boston, whether in barracks or rented rooms is impossible to tell. In either case, it is striking how many wives and children of soldiers appear; in the end, more than 25 percent of those who fell ill were soldiers' family members. They were not among the first cases, but they were disproportionately affected once the illness was established among them. This suggests the possibility that their living quarters were especially close—and it also highlights the fact that Boston's barracks were not tightly regulated homosocial spaces, but instead functioned as makeshift lodgings for soldiers and their dependents alike.[31]

All these forms of interaction and shared experience make it clear that, during the seventeen months of Boston's military occupation, soldiers and townspeople were not sealed off from one another, either physically or psychically. The traditional English sensitivity to standing armies had resulted in two dominant patterns in the quartering of soldiers in peacetime: in Ireland and Gibraltar, and to a lesser extent in Scotland, they were generally concentrated in barracks; in England, they were dispersed and mobile. The North American setting placed new demands on the peacetime army that made it difficult to maintain either pattern. Gage's decision to crowd as many as two thousand troops onto Boston's tiny peninsula and leave them there indefinitely — in retrospect, an obviously ill-considered idea — violated English norms but failed to replicate Irish ones. It forced soldiers and townspeople to accommodate themselves to one another to a degree without precedent in early modern Britain.

ONE KEY TO THE SUCCESS OF IRELAND'S experiment with a network of military barracks was the opportunity it created to spread money around. Bostonians may have initially resisted the plan to quarter troops in their midst, but that did not prevent them from capitalizing on the costs of provisioning and supply. The British army spent a great deal of money in the colonies, a large percentage of it in Boston during the months of the occupation. John Shy has offered the most comprehensive estimates of military spending in the period between the Seven Years' War and the American Revolution. He identifies four principal categories of spending: provisioning, extraordinary expenses, soldiers' pay, and the expenses associated with artillery battalions and ordnance. On average in the interwar years, Shy estimates that the army spent £314,000 per year in North America.[32] Extraordinary expenses account for £94,000 of that total; provisioning, £90,000; pay, £90,000 (nearly three-quarters of that amount was paid to officers); and £40,000 for artillery battalions and ordnance.[33] Army expenditures in Boston were at their highest between November 1768, when most of four regiments had arrived, and July 1769, when the 64th and 65th sailed for Halifax. In that eight-month period, nearly two thousand troops—more than a quarter of the soldiers serving in North America—crowded into Boston, with all the demands for provisioning and extraordinary expenses that number implied. Thereafter, from August 1769 until March 1770, the number of troops fell to seven or eight hundred.[34]

A very large funding stream flowed through the pockets of local inhabitants in the first eight months of the occupation. If pay for the soldiers brought £90,000 per annum to North America, then during the course of 1769 the share of that money paid to men in Boston would have been—conservatively—some £18,000. A comparable sum would have been spent on provisioning (that is, rations) during the course of the year.[35]

Extraordinary expenses covered the additional costs of housing soldiers, beyond bare provisioning. Two men accounted for the lion's share of this spending in Boston. The first was Lieutenant Colonel James Robertson, Gage's barrack-master general for the northern posts in North America. It was Robertson's responsibility to furnish the barracks with firewood, candles, fresh straw for beds and bolsters, brooms, and furniture; to pay for sweeping the chimneys; and to cover miscellaneous costs. Between October 1, 1768, and June 17, 1769, he spent £4,530 5s. 1d. on these expenses. The most expensive item was firewood—more than three thousand cords of it. Robertson paid not only for the wood itself, but also for carting, scaling, wharfage, cording, and piling. He also bought more than six thousand pounds of candles and oil, paid an allowance for "finding Bowls & Platters &ca," and purchased "Barrack Furniture such as Beds, Blanketts, Potts, Trammells, &ca."[36]

These expenses were paid to local tradesmen and merchants. Other funds were directed to Boston property owners: in the same eight-and-a-half-month period, Robertson spent more than £1,000 on rent, presumably for the buildings that were converted into the town's makeshift barracks. Officers who chose not to be quartered in barracks but instead to rent lodgings on their own received an allowance of "Quarter Money" to help defray their costs; Robertson paid out more than £300 for that purpose.

To put these costs in perspective, consider a roughly simultaneous accounting of expenses for seventeen other military outposts. Robertson submitted a receipt for a total of £9,936 12s. 2d. for supplying those posts over varying periods of time, ranging from 12 months to 38 months and averaging 28.4 months.[37] That is about £350 per month to supply all seventeen. In the first nine months of its occupation, Boston cost more than £500 per month — more than all seventeen of the other posts for which Robertson was responsible combined. As unlikely as this seems, it highlights the extraordinary character of Boston's occupation. Soldiers were farmed out through town in a way that maximized cost and minimized efficiency; not only did Robertson have to pay rent to various Boston property owners, but he also had to provide firewood, candles, and the like to makeshift barracks all over town, rather than having to supply only one or two large structures. And Boston was an especially expensive town in which to provision. Firewood was not available near at hand; it was cut at a distance, principally along the coast to the north, and then shipped to town. Food, too, came from farther away and was generally more expensive than in port towns like New York and Philadelphia. Even frontier forts like Detroit and Fort Pitt were more easily provisioned from local suppliers than Boston was. In acknowledgment of its distinct status from a barrack-master's point of view, Robertson kept his Boston accounts separate from his accounts for the rest of the barracks he oversaw.

The other officer with substantial discretionary spending power in Boston was John Montresor, the engineer Gage sent to Boston to help shore up Fort William. After the troops moved from Castle Island into town, it was Montresor's job to ensure that the town could absorb the troops. This was not simply a matter of confirming that the barracks buildings were structurally sound, though that was one of his concerns. In the statement of expenses he submitted to Gage, he enumerated the tasks he had overseen:

> The Repairs of Officers and Soldiers Barracks, for Three Regiments, 14th, 29th, and 64th: One Company of Artillery, and Detachment of 59th Regiment, Hospital, Artillery Magazine, Main, Neck, and Barrack Guard Rooms, & Houses; Centry Boxes, Pumps & Wells, Grates & Cranes, Tables, Chairs, Forms, Coal Boxes, Births & Cradles, Racks for Arms, fixing the several Stores, Cartage, Materials & Laborers work, together with the Expences of fitting up the Coal and Wood Yard for the Barrack Master General.[38]

In making Boston ready to receive the troops, Montresor's greatest expense was to pay fourteen property owners to make their buildings available to the army. The list of those property owners suggests that Boston was a community in which opportunism was not generally interpreted as a sign of hypocrisy. Its most accommodating landlord was William Molineux, the merchant and radical Whig, who was paid more than £500 to make four buildings available as barracks. It is striking to see Molineux profiting so handsomely from his adopted town's military occupation, but perhaps he was able to convince his political allies that he was doing good by fleecing the crown, rather than enriching himself at the town's expense. Samuel Drake, a nineteenth-century Boston historian, claimed that Molineux was not renting his own buildings but instead acting as agent for Charles Ward Apthorp, one of Boston's leading property owners. Montresor paid thirteen other landlords sums ranging from approximately £20 (Samuel Waterhouse, for a building to be used for the Main Guard) to about £160 (Jeremiah Green, for a warehouse to be used as a barracks). In addition, Montresor employed many of the town's artisans for jobs large and small. He paid hardware and lumber dealers, masons and carpenters, blacksmiths, locksmiths, pump makers, glaziers, and tinmen; he hired carters, bought gravel, and paid for casual labor. In all, between October 1 and November 23, 1768, Montresor spent £2,049 7s. 10s. on these projects; from the end of November until the following June, he spent an additional £486 19s. 7d.[39]

Even when troops left Boston, local merchants profited. When the 59th, 64th, and 65th Regiments left town in the summer of 1769, they departed not on vessels belonging to the army or the Royal Navy, but on private ships. The army hired and fitted six sloops, a schooner, and a brig to do the job, and paid local laborers and craftsmen to measure the ships, supply water casks, and carry supplies to them in the harbor. The total cost of this partial evacuation was £410 11s. 11d.[40]

Laborers, tradesmen, merchants, and landlords profited handsomely from the town's occupation — but they did so selectively. Soldiers and officers were paid in specie (probably Spanish dollars), as were most of the local laborers, tradesmen, and landlords who did business with the army. Larger merchants would have been paid in bills of exchange rather than cash, a form of paper money that was vitally important to their overseas trade. Money had been in short supply in Boston since the end of the Seven Years' War, and the rising tide of cash must have been a welcome change. But its effects were felt unevenly: money flowed into the pockets of those who

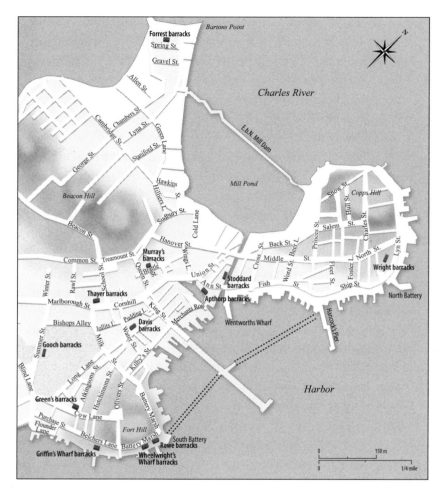

Barracks in Boston, 1768. The locations on this map are approximate and in most cases conjectural, based on the known property holdings of the men identified as landlords who leased barracks space to the army. Despite the lack of precision, it provides a sense of the way barracks were distributed through town.

were willing to do business with the army, while anyone who refused to work for the soldiers or who was shut out of army contracting would have suffered by comparison. Among merchants, for example, John Rowe profited handsomely from his connections with the army, while John Hancock, who received no such preferment and perhaps would have refused it, gained nothing.

As the army settled in, townspeople felt its effects in a variety of ways. The town meeting considered it to be an affront to local prerogatives and an insult to the character of the city, and many residents were deeply affected by the sights and sounds of military discipline. But in an economically stagnant community, the army also brought opportunity in the form of supply contracts, rental income, and periodic demand for casual and artisanal labor. Over time, personal connections among soldiers, their families, and local residents deepened. But resentments grew as well, eventually leading to orchestrated confrontations with soldiers on duty. As time wore on, Gage and his subordinates in Boston faced an escalating series of provocations that challenged their capacity to respond.

CHAPTER 6

Provocations

DURING THE SEVENTEEN MONTHS of Boston's occupation, soldiers and townspeople spun competing narratives about their interactions. Two clearly defined points of view were articulated, one by British military officers and crown officials, the other by Boston opinion leaders: spokesmen for the town meeting, members of the Governor's Council, and radical printers, in particular. Each sought to denigrate the other with charges of malfeasance while defending their own efforts to uphold good order and the rule of law. The town began immediately to employ the press to broadcast its concerns about military occupation; the local courts also instigated proceedings against soldiers accused of malfeasance. As it usually was when troops were stationed in desirable locales with large hinterlands, desertion was a continuous headache for British officers—and a source of gleeful pride for many townspeople. Throughout the occupation, Gage and his subordinate officers blamed townspeople for tempting their soldiers away from their duties and vacillated on the best way to discourage the practice. At other times, soldiers found themselves before local justices of the peace, where—in the opinion of their commanding officers—they could rarely expect to receive justice. At times, confrontations between soldiers and townspeople turned violent. Throughout these prolonged interactions, town leaders, military officers, and crown officials competed for the attention of the ministry and leading members of Parliament, each group retailing its own narratives of order and disorder, legitimacy and misrule.

The town's initial strategy in dealing with the soldiers was to broadcast accounts of the indignities its residents suffered. The most audacious and effective example of the attempt to publicize their plight was the Journal of the Times, a regular series of reports from Boston distributed for printing in New York, Philadelphia, and elsewhere. The authorship of the Journal has always been a mystery, but—in the same way that so many other affairs of the town were orchestrated—a small circle apparently composed the text of the Journal and sent it to John Holt, a New York printer with radical sympathies, on a regular basis. It consisted of daily entries, sometimes a single short paragraph, at other times several columns. Beginning on September 28, 1768—three days before the troops disembarked—and running until August 1, 1769, an entry was written almost every day. A week's worth or more would appear in Holt's *New York Journal,* generally on Thursday; the same material was reprinted in William Goddard's *Pennsylvania Chronicle* on Saturday; finally, it would surface in the *Boston Evening-Post,* published by John and Thomas Fleet. Many items were picked up in other newspapers, both in the colonies and in Britain, and most of the entries were collected and published as a pamphlet in England as well.[1]

This was an extraordinarily effective way for the town to circulate its grievances. The Journal of the Times detailed episodes of conflict between soldiers and civilians to dramatize the corrosive effect of military occupation on the town; it cast aspersions on key figures of authority, including the customs commissioners, Bernard, and Hillsborough; and it explored various legal questions associated with the occupation in detail. It highlighted bad behavior by soldiers—assaulting townspeople in the streets, encouraging slaves to "ill-treat and abuse their masters," harassing women, attempting rape—but also stressed the savage punishments soldiers suffered at the hands of their officers. It included resolutions of the town meeting and messages of support from outlying communities. Much to Bernard's aggravation, the Journal periodically reported on deliberations of the council, suggesting that some member of that body was supplying information to the authors. In myriad ways, it sought to dramatize the alien and unfamiliar qualities of the occupation. When Gage visited town in October to review the troops, the Journal described his reception: "This afternoon the troops were drawn up, on the Common, on the appearance of General Gage; at sunset there was 17 discharges from the field cannon; he passed the front of the battalion in his charriot, preceded by a number of aid de camps on horseback."[2] A general in a charriot, a seventeen-gun salute: here, the Journal seemed to suggest, were the trappings of an empire that had lost touch with its republican roots.

Though the Journal included long passages detailing various controversies and grievances, its most effective entries were often its briefest. Throughout its run, the Journal stressed Boston's dual devotion to religion and commerce. The entry for November 6 sharply contrasted the moral tenor of Boston with the martial values of the soldiers. "This being [the] Lord's day," it reported, "the minds of serious people at public worship were greatly disturbed with drums beating and fifes playing, unheard of before in this land—*What an unhappy influence must this have upon the minds of children and others, in eradicating the sentiments of morality and religion, which a due regard to that day has a natural tendency to cultivate and keep alive.*" A few days later, the Journal's author wrote:

What an appearance does Boston now make! One of the first commercial towns in America, has now several regiments of soldiers quartered in the midst of it, and even the Merchants Exchange is picquetted, and made the spot where the main guard is placed and paraded, and their cannon mounted; so that instead of our merchants and trading people transacting their business, we see it filled with red coats, and have our ears dinn'd with the music of drum and fife. — *How would the merchants of London be startled if they should behold their exchange thus metamorphosed*[?][3]

These were the concerns of honest gentlemen, not a disorderly rabble, and they were crafted to resonate with men and women of sense throughout the British Atlantic world. Even members of Parliament — especially members of Parliament — could appreciate this kind of appeal to the values that connected England to its Atlantic outposts.

Bernard complained bitterly about the Journal's inaccuracy. "It is composed by [Samuel] Adams and his Assistants," he wrote, "among whom there must be some, one at least, of the Council. . . . But if the Devil himself was of the Party, as he virtually is, there could not have been got together a greater Collection of impudent virulent and seditious Lies Perversions of Truth and Misrepresentations than are to be found in this Publication." Some items, he wrote, were "entirely invented," while others were "founded on Fact but so perverted as to be the direct contrary of the Truth." Pomeroy, the senior officer in Boston, had a similar reaction. "I find the journal of Boston occurrences published in Mr Holts paper — at New York — makes very free with officers as well as soldiers," he wrote to Gage; "however it is with pleasure I can acquaint you that I have not had one complaint made to me against an officer since I commanded here — nor one against a soldier except on the subject of challenging, & that above six weeks ago."[4] Perhaps Bernard and Pomeroy were correct to suggest that some of the Journal's items were fabricated or exaggerated. It is impossible to verify many of the anecdotes it reported. Any soldier accused of assault or rape should have appeared before a justice of the peace, for example, but none of the cases reported in the Journal made their way into Boston courts.

Nevertheless, both the substance and the tone of the Journal made it persuasive and believable. Carefully modulated, generally sober rather than hyperbolic, the Journal convinces its readers that soldiers did not belong in Boston, and that the decision to post them there could only lead to trouble. When the Journal's authors describe public deliberations or seek to explain a matter of principle, they are scrupulous in their attention to accuracy and detail. Violent interactions are described without sensationalism, as matters of fact. To an audience reading it at a distance, the Journal appeared to be a fair account of events in an aggrieved and embattled town.

As the Journal of the Times broadcast Boston's plight to a wide readership, the Boston town meeting issued sustained protests against the occupation. In the months leading up to the troops' arrival, Bernard and the customs commissioners had largely controlled the flow of information to London, creating a sustained narrative about Boston as a town on the verge of rebellion. The challenge for town leadership was to establish a counternarrative that objected to the presence of the troops on principle without verging into behavior that could be interpreted as rebellious or anarchic.

In February it crafted an address to the governor that challenged his version of the past year's events. When "artful & mischievous Men" have inspired divisions in the empire and broken the bond of trust between Britain and its American colonies, they began, "the Selectmen of this Metropolis cannot be the unconcerned or silent spectators of the Calamities, which in consequence thereof have already fallen upon its inhabitants." It bore all the earmarks of town meeting rhetoric, echoing the cadences of Samuel Adams and James Otis Jr. Adams had been peppering the *Boston Gazette* with essays on military power, civilians' rights, and the dangers of standing armies for months; now, the address continued, "to behold this Town surrounded with Ships of War; and military Troops even in a time of peace; quarter[e]d in its very Bowels: Exercising a Discipline with all the severity which is used in a Garrison, and in a state of actual War, is truly alarming to a free people."[5]

The substance of the address was to blame crown officers, and especially Bernard, for misrepresenting the character of the town. Troops had been called to aid the civil power when no such aid was needed. "Loyalty to the Sovereign; and an inflexible Zeal for the support of his Majestys Authority and the happy Constitution is its Just character," the citizens of Boston insisted. "And we may appeal to the impartial World, that Peace and order were better maintained in the Town, before it was ever rumoured that his Majestys Troops were to be quarter[e]d among us, then they have been since."[6]

Bernard answered the town's address by insisting that he had not misrepresented the events of the past year, nor was the character of Boston misunderstood in London. The town replied to Bernard's reply; Bernard replied again in turn. Having reached an impasse, the town meeting again used the press to amplify its concerns: it ordered the entire exchange to be printed in the newspaper.[7]

At the same time, members of the Governor's Council were working behind the scenes to discredit Bernard more decisively. Hillsborough had been deeply impressed by Bernard's letters, which he laid before Parliament as it began, once again, to reconsider its colonial policy. As Samuel Danforth, James Bowdoin, and other members of Bernard's council became aware of the importance of the governor's correspondence, they scrambled to get their hands on his letters. In the spring of 1769, they succeeded in getting copies and having them printed. The result was to put enormous pressure on Bernard. He had been hoping for months to be recalled or reassigned; the flap over his letters finally made that wish a reality. In April, Hillsborough informed him that he was to return to Great Britain to report on the state of affairs in Massachusetts to the king. He also told Bernard that George III was "conferring upon you the Dignity of a Baronet" in recognition of his service to the crown.[8]

Though it would be several months before Bernard finally left Boston — with a raucous crowd cheering wildly for his departure — his recall signaled the final failure of his administration. The hard line he had so strongly advocated, and that Hillsborough had so vigorously pursued, was now discredited. Parliament was backing away from a punitive colonial policy: a policy of which the troops stationed in Boston were the most conspicuous symbol. It remained to be seen, now that Bernard was going home, what would become of the soldiers crowded into Boston's streets.

DESERTION WAS THE GREATEST plague of early modern armies, and officers punished it ferociously to discourage soldiers — often serving for life and poorly paid and provisioned — from considering their options. Accused deserters who faced courts-martial were less likely to be acquitted and more likely to be executed than those accused of any other offense; those who were not sentenced to death were often flogged to within an inch of it. Deserters were always trickling away from the ranks of the British army in the eighteenth century, but in certain times and places it became an epidemic. In North America, the most notorious example was the flight of troops from the 60th, or Royal American, Regiment at the end of the Seven Years' War. Stationed in the Pennsylvania countryside in the winter and spring of 1763–1764 — when the prospect of an impending campaign in the Ohio country to quell Pontiac's War perhaps gave them an extra incentive — men from several companies of the 60th deserted in such large numbers that by July, as John Shy has written, the regiment "had all but vanished." It was in large part to prevent mass desertion that the troops in Boston established checkpoints throughout town and a fortified guardhouse at the Boston Neck, where a single road connected the peninsula to the mainland.[9]

Desertion highlighted the tension at the heart of the military occupation of Boston — a tension that operated as the mainspring of interactions between townspeople and soldiers. In officers' eyes, soldiers were a clearly distinct population, set apart from Bostonians by a high wall that was maintained by discipline, honor, and the belief that military personnel were essentially different from the population they were assigned to police. But in reality, soldiers and colonists were very much alike. Sometimes their commonalities drew them together, while at other times they brought them into conflict; but in either case, they often saw their similarities clearly. Like colonists, soldiers were laborers. Labor was scarce in the colonies and much more highly valued than in the British Isles. Soldiers also stood, like colonists, in a problematic relationship to the British crown. They were subjects of that crown, but with diminished rights, beholden to the disciplinary apparatus of the British state. In this, too, they shared a fundamental similarity with their host population. While Gage and his subordinate officers worked to maintain the soldiers' sense of identification with the British military and its surveillance and policing mission, townspeople recognized a different, but equally compelling, kinship with the soldiers in their midst.

Despite the threat of harsh reprisals, and notwithstanding the precautions taken by commanding officers, desertions began as soon as troops arrived. Like so much else about the occupation of Boston, the issue of desertion starkly highlighted the contrast between military and civilian values and priorities. Most deserters fled to the countryside, where their prospects of employment were favorable and it would be hard to track them down. "Hundreds of the Troops station'd here have already deserted," wrote Samuel Cooper less than five months after the arrival of the 14th and 29th Regiments, "delighted with the Country, and mixing with its Inhabitants, carrying useful Arts and Trades as well as military Skill, wherever they go."[10]

In response, Boston's commanding officers periodically sent parties into the countryside to round up deserters. Thus Sergeant William Henderson and three privates of the 14th Regiment traveled to Londonderry, New Hampshire, in January 1769 to pursue a deserter named Sherwood. Passing by a farmhouse, they spotted Sherwood working outside. Henderson arrested him and they started back toward Boston. After they had traveled five or six miles, Sherwood told Henderson that they were near a house where another deserter — named Darnby — was employed. They stopped and Henderson made a second arrest. The group of soldiers, now six in number, continued on toward Haverhill, Massachusetts. But they didn't get there. Near sunset, a party of fifty armed men overtook them, called out to the deserters, and fired at Henderson's party. The soldiers stopped and were quickly surrounded. The armed men freed the deserters, leaving Henderson and his men to return to Boston empty-handed.[11]

After hearing this tale, Pomeroy wrote to John Wentworth, governor of New Hampshire, to request his aid in recapturing Sherwood and Darnby. Wentworth soon wrote to inform Pomeroy that Sherwood "was brought to my House, and is now safely confined in the Goal in this Town, to wait your further Orders." But he also urged Pomeroy to treat Sherwood with leniency. He had "most sincerely repented" for abandoning his regiment, according to Wentworth; moreover, he had not chosen to escape from Henderson's party but was "instantly compelled" to do it. Wentworth argued at length that Sherwood should be pardoned for deserting. A pardon, he wrote, "will have the most undoubted good tendency to regain all the others, that have escaped from their Duty." Not only would deserters be more likely to return to their posts, but the New Englanders who shielded them would be more willing to give them up if they knew that the escaped soldiers would not be prosecuted upon their return. "If Hopes of pardon might be given," Wentworth predicted, "within Twenty Days, every Deserter in New England, would be driven by the Inhabitants, thro' Portsmouth to receive the Kings Mercy at their Regiments."[12]

Gage was initially unreceptive to the idea of a pardon. When he first learned what happened to Henderson's party, he urged Pomeroy to "send out Stronger Partys" in the future, "and again acquaint the Soldiers, that no Deserter in these critical times must hope for Mercy." Wentworth's reasoning did nothing to persuade Gage. "The Desertion of the Troops hurts me at such a time as this," he admitted to Pomeroy, "when they should exert themselves in demonstrating Principles of Duty and Loyalty to their King and Country: And I observe with Concern in the return you sent me, that the soldiers continue to Desert." Nevertheless, he believed that the threat of punishment, not the promise of leniency, was the best way to keep soldiers in the service. "I am determined to pardon no Soldier who shall be Convicted and Condemned for Desertion during the present Crisis of affairs; And if you find it necessary, you will inform the Troops in Publick orders, how much is expected from their Loyalty and affection to their King and country, and that no Deserter must expect mercy."[13]

Yet within a few weeks, Gage's view of the Sherwood case had grown more circumspect. He granted Pomeroy the authority to pardon the deserter: "I am certain you will do what is proper in it." Should he choose to pardon Sherwood, Gage advised Pomeroy to attribute his decision to Sherwood's "good Behavior for giving Evidence against those concerned in the Rescue."[14] In this case, as in every other decision related to desertion, Gage's dilemma was familiar to commanding officers everywhere. It was standard practice to punish deserters ferociously, but it was also common to offer either individual pardons or general amnesties from time to time. During the occupation of Boston, Gage would have ample opportunity to reconsider his position. The essential, imponderable question, on the one hand, was whether deserters commonly regretted their decision once they had gotten away. Were deserters likely to return to the ranks, given the opportunity? And, on the other hand, how effective was ferocious punishment as a deterrent to those who had not deserted? It was a numbers game, and Gage corresponded with every commanding officer in Boston on the subject.

Pardons and amnesties were appealing, in part, because Gage and his officers sympathized with their men and blamed colonists for the soldiers' decisions to desert. "The Town, and Country People," according to Colonel Maurice Carr, "use[d] all methods to perswade, and Inveigle" the soldiers "by promises which they never mean to perform." The result was that deserters were enticed away from their posts, but then came to regret their decision. Most soon grew "quite tyr'd" of their new employers, "as they never give them, anything for their Work, but what they think proper." Gage echoed Carr's views. "I have long since been persuaded that both the Town & Country People have encouraged the soldiers to Desert," he wrote, "and I don't wonder that after having been some time with them they should be desirous of returning again to their Duty for they keep them under[,] work them hard, Pay them nothing, and upon any Complaint, threaten them with delivering them up to their Regiment." Though Gage's first instinct was to take a hard line, even he could be persuaded to sympathize with the plight of his deluded, exploited subordinates.[15]

As the occupation of Boston dragged on, Gage's approach to pardons and amnesties became more flexible. A few weeks after the confrontation in Londonderry, Pomeroy reported that as many as twenty deserters from the 29th Regiment "wish to surrender, provided they would be pardoned." The prospect of recovering so many men caused Gage to grant Pomeroy whatever leeway he needed, though he still resisted the idea of a general pardon. Gage suggested instead to "try it privately to get them in as it were voluntarily, and then apply for their Pardon." But, as he continued to stress, "it is impossible after what has happened to publish a general Pardon for Deserters to come in and surrender."[16]

But the possibility of a general pardon could not be dismissed so easily. On the same day that Gage was writing from New York to rule it out, Pomeroy put pen to paper in Boston to report that he had "called the officers Commanding the different Regiments together" to consider the best way "to put a Stop to desertion." They concluded that the best remedy was a general pardon. "As we daily receive accounts that numbers of them are willing to come in provided they get their pardon," he wrote, "the Gentlemen were of opinion if your Excellency would order a pardon to be published for those men who have deserted from hence, provided they return at a limited time, that it would have a good effect." If Pomeroy's information was correct, the idea of a general pardon was gaining currency among the rank and file, and even among the deserters themselves. Oddly, this led to the argument that desertions had increased in anticipation of such a pardon. Colonel Carr explained the logic of this phenomenon: "I am likewise inform[e]d," he wrote, "that the soldiers all here, have it amongst themselves, that there will be a General Pardon very soon for all Deserters, which I believe induces them sometimes to take that step, in order to avoid being brought to a court martial for any crime they may have [previously] committed."[17] However improbable it seems that men who feared being court-martialed for some crime would desert in order to receive the benefit of an amnesty, Carr's argument was one strand in the skein of rationalizations used by officers to understand the mutinous actions of a large number of their men.

As the catalogue of desertions grew, Gage eventually capitulated. When Major General Alexander Mackay finally arrived on the last day of April 1769 to assume command of the forces in Boston, Gage saw his opportunity. Their earliest exchange of letters was filled with news of deserters, some of whom had been caught, some who had turned themselves in, and some who remained at large. After discussing particular cases at length, Gage concluded, "As for the other Deserters who are still out, if you shall be of Opinion they would return on a Promise of Pardon, You have now the best pretence for an Act of Grace, from your first entering your Command, which You Choose to begin with shewing mercy." Though he stopped short of instructing Mackay to issue a general amnesty, Gage granted his permission to "act in this Matter as you shall judge the most Expedient for the Service, and I shall confirm what you shall be pleased to do in it." Mackay soon reported that he had published a general amnesty to anyone who turned himself in before the end of June 1769.[18]

These evolving responses to desertion highlight the tangled calculus of effective command during the occupation of Boston. Ever the model officer, Gage knew that the harshest discipline was the appropriate reaction to desertion—which was, after all, a mutinous act. To pursue a court-martial against a deserter was to uphold an officer's responsibility to the crown and to maintain discipline in the ranks. But such an approach presumed that the army was a closed system, with high walls that sustained a collective sense of identity and purpose and gave the threat of punishment, even execution, its force. In Boston, the army was nothing like a closed system with high walls. It was a force whose purpose was unclear, even to those who commanded it, with exceptionally porous boundaries that made the distinction between soldiers and civilians impossible to police and, often, difficult even to see. Harsh discipline was one way to shore up the collapsing boundary between colonists and men in arms; paradoxically, Mackay's general amnesty in May and June 1769 was another attempt to achieve the same end.

But leniency proved no more effective than harshness, and by fall Gage and his subordinate officers had come full circle in their approach. On September 10, Gage ordered the resumption of courts-martial. "The Desertion is indeed intolerable amongst the Troops at Boston,"

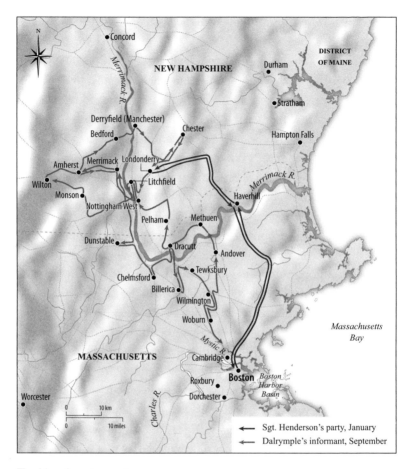

Tracking deserters, 1769.

he wrote, "and I fear nothing but severity will stop it." Dalrymple, once again in command, was grateful to resume courts-martial. "I am much embarrassed by the numbers of prisoners in our Guard rooms for desertion," he reported, "and I could wish they were brought to trial, people begin to wonder at their long confinement and to doubt my powers." Nevertheless, Dalrymple entertained no illusions that the renewed threat of punishment would deter soldiers from deserting when they had the chance. "The encouragement they receive from the inhabitants, as well as the high wages, are inducements too forcible to be withstood," he observed. In addition, Dalrymple believed, "their long continuation here naturally created intimacies with the people ruinous to the service."[19]

With the prospect of appropriate punishments restored, Dalrymple redoubled his efforts to identify and capture deserters. He dispatched a subordinate to scour the countryside between Boston and southern New Hampshire for intelligence. Following a circuitous 205-mile route, Dalrymple's informant visited twenty-two towns and described the activities of dozens of runaway soldiers. In Merrimack, for example, "one whose name is Page, a Weaver by trade[,] work'd with one Cliney all winter, & now moves about to work." In Billerica, he noted "a Stout Young Man" who had exchanged his uniform for civilian clothing, and another, "James Fox a Shoemaker," living with his shoemaker employer. In New Plymouth, New Hampshire, he found "at least six" deserters, including three laborers, a mason, a tailor, and another shoemaker. Arrest parties followed soon after. On October 22, Richard Eames, a private of the 14th Regiment, was convicted of desertion by a court-martial; a week later, Gage issued the order to bring him before a firing squad.[20]

By June 1769, Gage had concluded that the occupation was futile. He ordered the 64th and 65th Regiments and the Royal Artillery Company to prepare to sail for Halifax, and asked Bernard whether he would allow Gage to withdraw the rest as well. Characteristically, Bernard—though he had already been recalled to London and was beginning to plan for his departure—overreacted. "It is impossible to express my surprise at this proposition," he burbled to Hillsborough in a subsequent letter. He accepted Gage's plan to send the 64th and

65th to Halifax, but contended that the idea of removing all the troops from Boston caused "a general Consternation among the civil Officers of Government, the friends of it & the importers of goods contrary to the combination, who are Many." Bernard insisted that both the 14th and the 29th Regiments should remain.[21]

Though Bernard was convinced that the soldiers would help preserve order in Boston, Gage and his officers doubted it. At the same time that he wrote to Bernard, Gage also asked Mackay for his opinion. Mackay observed the same dynamics at work in Boston that Bernard had noted. The town — "those who have the Popular sway here" — opposed "every Government measure." They especially resented the customs commissioners and the merchants "who wou[l]d not agree to the Resolution of not importing Goods from Great Britain, but who on the Contrary have continued to Commission & import Goods." If the troops were withdrawn, Mackay acknowledged, there was no telling how the town might act on that resentment. But — unlike Bernard — Mackay was attuned to the essential dilemma that hamstrung the Boston regiments. As long as they remained in town, "the Bulk of their Men will be Seduced to Desert." Those who attempted to do their duty would be harassed with "Imprisonment & fines" for nonexistent offenses. Yet — if the occasion arose when troops were needed to keep the peace — not "one Civill Majestrate wou[l]d step forth & act." The troops would be useless. And "I may ad[d]," he concluded, "as I have often been told it, that this is as much owing to the fear of not being supported from home, as the fear of the Mob here."[22]

Here was a point upon which Britain's military leadership and its crown appointees in Boston could all agree: their essential problem was the lack of support in Parliament. Bernard, Gage, and the customs commissioners longed to hear that Parliament was taking a hard line at last against Boston's rebellious leaders. Every day they awaited word that Parliament had revoked or altered the Massachusetts Bay charter. Such news would surely provoke the Boston radicals to respond, perhaps with violence. "Boston is threatened hard at home," Gage wrote to Pomeroy in February. It was vital that Pomeroy be "ready to oppose any Insurrection of the People which such news might Occasion on a Sudden. The Arms are in Faneuil Hall, a Battery on Castle Hill, and a small one on Beacon Hill, would command the town, if you find them resolved to Revolt."[23] Just as he had done during the occupation in the fall, Gage continued to plan for the possibility of a full-scale military response to insurrection in Boston. He seemed almost to wish for it. As terrible as such a crisis would be, it would at least justify an unambiguous response. As long as the soldiers served only to support local magistrates, Gage knew as well as anyone that they would never be called upon. But in a case of open revolt he could bring the full force of arms to bear on the problem that Boston had become.

Pomeroy clearly hoped to avoid the kind of crisis his commander envisioned. He was "much obliged to you for the hints you are so kind to give me, & shall duly attend to them in case necessity require it," he wrote, "which I hope will not happen, as every thing here is at present quiet." Pomeroy was acutely aware that the town's armaments were close at hand in Faneuil Hall, where townspeople could arm themselves in no time. "I have long wished [they] were deposited in some safer place," he wrote, but if he tried to commandeer them without provocation, "you are sencible what a handle the Province would make of it." For the time being, he would await the outcome of events. "However if I find the least suspicion of intention to oppose his Majesties troops—they shall, no doubt, claim my just attention."[24]

Bernard had long advocated that the Massachusetts Bay charter should be revoked or revised to replace the elected council with an appointed one, and more generally to strengthen the hand of the crown in the colony's affairs. If such a change provoked rebellion,

Gage and his subordinate officers knew how to respond. But they did not know how to act in the face of Boston's maddening legalisms, its constant attention to the rights and privileges of citizens, which it used to blunt the power of armed authority. Rebellion would be bad, but the uncertainties and ambiguities of ill-defined imperial power were worse. "That there is a very turbulent & seditious spirit in this Province at present, I think is but too evident," Mackay noted, "but I am so much persuaded of their averseness to serious opposition that I am convinced, they will allways prefer the Weapons they are most expert at, abuse, falsehoods, & scribbling, to that of Powder & Balls."[25]

By the summer of 1769, Gage and his officers were ready to give up on the occupation of Boston. But Bernard would not hear of it, and the 14th and 29th Regiments remained. Much of the summer of 1769 was taken up with preparations to send the 64th, the 65th, and the Royal Artillery unit back to Halifax; then, in August, Bernard himself left the colony for good. Lieutenant Governor Thomas Hutchinson became acting governor; the remaining regiments consolidated their quarters; and, with the departure of Mackay and Pomeroy, Dalrymple once again became the ranking officer in Boston.

IN THE FALL AND WINTER OF 1769–1770, a series of violent episodes in the streets of Boston gave new life and urgency to the question of whether troops might be called upon to assist the civil power. The politics of nonimportation—a source of divisions in the town since 1767—collided with the hostility that many townspeople felt toward both the customs commissioners and the troops who had been sent to protect them. The result was a series of altercations and riots. In no case were troops called to assist in peacekeeping; instead, Gage and Dalrymple expressed relief whenever troops were not themselves implicated in the proceedings. Throughout the fall and winter, troops were more likely to be victims of provocation and violence than they were to prevent it. Only in policing their own — in the ongoing efforts to curb and punish desertion — were Dalrymple and Gage able to act decisively. Without stronger support from Boston officials, they were helpless either to assist in peacekeeping efforts or to defend themselves against the provocations they faced.[26]

The violence afflicting Boston in the fall and winter took various forms. In early September, James Otis Jr. attacked customs commissioner John Robinson in the British Coffee House, triggering a brawl that spilled into the streets. When Dalrymple reported the event to Gage, he noted that "the town has been in an uproar ever since," but expressed relief that "no military person is charged with any part of the disorder." Gage responded, "It gives me very great pleasure, that you say none of the Military were concerned in the Fray," though he noted that soldiers were nevertheless being blamed in the New York papers. In early October, Dalrymple reported "endeavours . . . to terrifie" two traders believed to be violating the nonimportation agreement. On October 28 the printers John Mein and John Fleeming — whose *Boston Chronicle* had been accusing the merchants supporting nonimportation of hypocrisy for several months — were attacked by a crowd of several dozen people. The same night, a much larger Boston mob tarred and feathered a sailor named George Gailer, who was believed to be an informer. On November 3 Dalrymple reported rumors of an impending riot; though he told Gage that the troops were ready to help, both men knew that they would never be called upon. In January 1770 the town meeting acted against merchants who intended to sell British goods in violation of the nonimportation agreement, and throughout January and February, Dalrymple reported, there were "many and various attempts made to render the Importers odious."[27]

Throughout this period of intermittent violence and disorder, the troops were unable to act. Dalrymple and Gage repeatedly noted that the troops had restrained themselves, despite the many provocations they received. In February, Dalrymple wrote, Bostonians had "begun to ill treat the troops," noting that "they lay in wait in the streets and knock them down." He observed that although "this has caused much ill blood, I have however forbid them to retaliate so I hope nothing material will ensue."[28] Here was the folly of Boston's occupation in a nutshell: even with fights, riots, and demonstrations erupting periodically, the troops made no contribution to local peace-keeping. Instead, they became another target of local leaders and Boston crowds who sought new ways to dramatize their frustration with parliamentary policy.

AMONG ALL THE PROVOCATIONS townspeople visited on the troops, none aggravated their officers more than the use of law to challenge their behavior. Beginning in June 1769, correspondence between officers in Boston and New York was peppered with references to "vexatious lawsuits": proceedings instituted against soldiers merely, in the opinions of Gage and his subordinates, to harass their men and prevent them from carrying out their responsibilities. Soldiers faced proceedings for assault, for debt, for disturbing the peace or provoking disorder. Here was the ultimate indignity, and the irony, of Boston's occupation: the soldiers' greatest antagonists were the same magistrates whom they were supposedly there to serve.[29]

The image of Boston that shines through officers' correspondence is an obverse of the one presented in the Journal of the Times. Soldiers, not townspeople, were assaulted in the streets, and it was essential that they maintain their discipline or they would face the consequences. "The situation here is most disagreeable," Mackay wrote; "our soldiers are Insulted & struck when on their post, without the smallest provocation given." In one case, a soldier was assaulted by a man in the street. Mackay applied to a justice of the peace for redress, but the justice refused to act because the soldier had subsequently retaliated and struck the man back. In another case, a Boston resident spat in the face of one of Mackay's soldiers. The soldier "push[e]d the man from him with his firelock." In response, a justice of the peace jailed the soldier and imposed a fine on him. "If this is Liberty, happy they who live under it," Mackay concluded with wry sarcasm; "& We are in a pleasing Situation, who are order[e]d here to Aid & assist the Civill Magistrate in preserving the peace & protecting his Majestys Subjects, when those very Magistrates are our oppressors."[30]

But it was not always that simple. Officers like Mackay imagined the military in Boston as a single body, united in purpose and sharing a single set of interests. But soldiers interacted with townspeople in a variety of ways. Legal proceedings, like desertions, sometimes highlighted the bonds that ordinary soldiers shared with ordinary townspeople. The experience of John Moise, a private of the 14th Regiment, offers a case in point. Moise was arrested and charged with theft in May 1769. In the company of five Boston laborers, Moise allegedly broke into a shop and stole money and goods worth more than £26. Two of the six were arrested. The other arrestee was acquitted, but Moise was convicted and sentenced to twenty lashes and treble damages. Since Moise was unable to pay damages amounting to more than £78, the court empowered the shopkeeper to sell him as an indentured servant for a term of three years.[31]

Mackay and Gage were outraged at Moise's treatment. Mackay wrote that the court had "indented him as a Slave." Gage considered Moise's fate to be one more example of the "Oppression and Tyranny" being "exercised over the Troops by the Civil Magistrates. . . . The Selling of a Soldier like a Negro for a Slave is beyond Comprehension." The case presented a legal conundrum. The crown's lawyers considered it absurd that a soldier, engaged for life in His Majesty's service, could be "made the property of a subject." Nevertheless, the law did not seem to offer a remedy; in this case, it appeared, "a partial

Colony statute defeats the spirit and entention of a British Act of Parliament." Seeing no way to institute a legally binding procedure to free Moise, Gage instead recommended a more expedient solution. His advice to Mackay was to get Moise safely on board one of the transports in the harbor, where he could be carried to Halifax and beyond the reach of his onerous indenture. "I do not know anything else can be done in it, unless the man can make his Escape. Such an infamous piece of Tyranny, savours more of the Meridian of Turkey, than a British Province."[32]

But outrage soon gave way to uncertainty, and then indignation of a different sort. Mackay explained to Gage that their efforts to rescue Moise had come to nothing. "The greatest Difficulty," he wrote, "is that the Soldier is a thorow Rascall." As it turned out, Moise was conspiring with the man who held his indenture "in order to secure him his Discharge or in other words a sort of Legall Dismission from the Reg[imen]t." To avoid being rescued by a party of soldiers, Moise stayed away from his regimental barracks and rarely appeared in the streets. If a party of soldiers spotted him, he would duck into his master's house, where they could not pursue him without violating the law. "If the soldier sold for a slave, is in Collusion with the Fellow to whom he is made over," Gage wearily admitted in reply, "it may be difficult to get him."[33] With the assistance of Boston's court, Moise had exchanged a lifetime of service to the crown for a three-year indenture in a colony where his prospects were bright. Evidently, he considered it a good trade.

In other cases, however, townspeople employed law and precedent to challenge the soldiers' claims to public space in Boston. One focus of local concern was the location of the Main Guard, which stood just southeast of the Town House, where the Massachusetts General Court sat. In the eyes of many assembly members, having sentries posted almost at the door of the Town House was an affront to the civil power. They "complain[e]d of the noise of the Drums disturbing them when on business" and requested that the Main Guard move to another location, farther from the center of town. Mackay replied that he would do so if the town would "provide a proper guard house in any centreall open place of the Town, without putting the government to any expence." Failing such an accommodation, he refused to act. Neither the assembly nor the town was interested in providing another space for the Main Guard; instead, in an effort to assuage the concern, Bernard prorogued the General Court to Cambridge and asked that they resume their normal business. This was an unprecedented act that colony officials regarded as a violation of the charter; the legislature protested the move and continued to refuse to do business. Hutchinson attempted a compromise by suggesting that the quarters of the Main Guard be converted to a barracks, allowing the Main Guard to occupy the vacated barracks. Dalrymple argued that it was beyond his power to comply, so Hutchinson carried the practice of assembling the General Court in Cambridge into the spring of 1770. By that time, their complaints were the least of his worries. "I have met with but little trouble from the Assembly compared with what I meet with from the Town of Boston," he wrote.[34]

Having lost the battle over the Main Guard, private citizens in Boston made a concerted effort to displace another hated symbol of military occupation: the guard house on Boston Neck, which controlled the flow of traffic onto and off of Boston's peninsula. Erected shortly after the troops' arrival, the Neck Guard was one of the places where soldiers routinely challenged townspeople as they came and went, a practice that from the beginning was considered especially burdensome. But it did not come in for special attention until the fall of 1769, when Boston merchant Robert Pierpoint instituted a legal challenge to its presence. The town's selectmen had leased him the land it stood on. Now he intended to build a house of his own on the site, for which purpose he insisted that the Neck Guard house be removed. Dalrymple permitted some structures on the site to be torn down, but he refused to cede the guard station itself, and a standoff ensued.[35]

After the failure to eject the Neck Guard through a legal remedy, the site became a focus for crowd agitation. On Tuesday, October 24, Pierpoint visited the guardhouse and accused Ensign John Ness of the 14th Regiment, the officer in charge of the Neck Guard that day, of stealing his lumber. Pierpoint was not alone; a crowd of people had followed along. When Ness turned Pierpoint away, the crowd stayed and began harassing Ness's men. Local blacksmith Obadiah Whiston punched a soldier in the face, causing Sergeant James Hickman to push him away with his halberd. A short time later, Ness's company was relieved and they began to march in formation back toward town. The crowd followed and set upon the soldiers; they shouted insults, threw stones, and "attempted to break in upon the Guard." The soldiers pushed the townspeople away with their firelocks and regrouped. One soldier fired his gun; the bullet struck a nearby blacksmith's shop. Ness immediately "gave positive orders for no soldier to load, or strike any of the Mob." The crowd gave way but continued to harass the soldiers, one of whom was struck in the head with a rock, while another was punched in the face.[36]

When the Neck Guard approached the lodgings of Captain Ponsonby Molesworth, who was serving as captain of the day, he rushed forward to investigate. Observing the men's distress, he instructed them to close their ranks and avoid striking any civilians unless they struck first. But if someone did strike, Molesworth said, "put [your] Bayonet through him." The guard regrouped once again, marched to their barracks, and were dismissed.[37]

Ness, Molesworth, and Hickman were soon arrested for their roles in the affair. Initially accused by Pierpoint of breaching the peace and acquitted when no witnesses appeared against him, Ness was arrested again, along with Hickman, this time for ordering his men to fire their weapons (in Ness's case) and using a halberd to fend off a member

Richard Dana, by John Singleton Copley (ca. 1770). Richard Dana, a justice of the peace in Boston during its occupation, was considered by British officers to be strongly biased against them. When a group of soldiers was brought before him, he reportedly thundered, "What brought you here? We don't want you, do you want to Murder the Inhabitants?" Descended from a French Huguenot family, Dana was a Boston patriarch with strong political views. This superb portrait, painted at about the time of the occupation, captures his forceful, imperious character.

of the crowd (in Hickman's). Molesworth was charged with inciting the soldiers to murder. In the proceedings that followed, the officers complained that their treatment by Boston's justices of the peace was anything but impartial. Various irregularities marred the proceedings, and Justice Richard Dana seemed to be especially intent on making things as hard as possible for the accused. He repeatedly refused to accept promises to stand surety for bail, and in one case even refused £100 in cash when an officer of the 14th presented it to him, though he articulated no rationale for the refusals. He allowed civilians to berate the prisoners while they stood before him; Richard Gridley, the blacksmith whose shop had taken a bullet, called the soldiers "a Parcel of Black guard Rascals." And Dana—a Boston patriarch, now seventy years old—berated them himself, at length. "What brought you here?" Dana interrupted the proceedings to ask. "We don't want you, do you want to Murder the Inhabitants[?]" He claimed that officers "Spirited up the Soldiers to Murder the Inhabitants," and that "there was no Walking in the Street by Day or Night for the Hourly abuse committed by the Soldiers." To Molesworth, Dana thundered that if one of his men had killed a townsman with his bayonet, Molesworth "wou'd have swung for it."[38] A jury eventually acquitted Ness in Superior Court. Molesworth was found guilty, though for reasons that are unclear he was apparently never sentenced.

A crowd that swarmed a detachment of soldiers; officers scrambling to impose order; a gun fired, apparently by accident; an appearance in a Boston courtroom: none of these boded well for the soldiers. In retrospect these acts would take on more significance than anyone could have known in November 1769.

CHAPTER 7

Uncertain Outcomes

FOUR MONTHS LATER, the chaos of March 5 precipitated another, more serious, crisis. As they sought to make sense of the King Street shootings, participants on all sides spun out explanations that depended upon their divergent views of the town and its occupiers. In the days and weeks that followed the shootings, the town of Boston — acting through a cohort of spokesmen who appeared over and over again in various official capacities — shaped the narrative of events to bolster long-standing complaints about the occupation. From the town's point of view, the shootings were the predictable culmination of an unjust and unconstitutional encroachment on local prerogatives. Hutchinson, acting on behalf of the crown but more deeply grounded in Boston's past than any other official involved, railed at the town's opportunism and worried that mob rule had overtaken the legitimate operations of government. For Gage and Dalrymple, the shootings dramatized the irreconcilable demands of their responsibilities. In the long months between the soldiers' arrests in March and their trials, which began in late October, everyone involved wrestled with new fears and uncertainties. Would the soldiers be convicted or acquitted, and if convicted, would they be pardoned? If pardoned, would they be lynched? Would Boston be reoccupied to prevent such an eventuality? Would the town finally break into rebellion against royal authority and military occupation? Nothing was certain, but observers freely predicted the worst outcomes they could imagine.

IMMEDIATELY AFTER THE SOLDIERS' guns had discharged in King Street on March 5, townspeople bent to the aid of the dead and wounded. Three victims died where they fell. Samuel Gray was a laborer at John Gray's ropewalk, the site of a brawl between soldiers and workers on Friday, March 2, which was widely identified as the precipitating event that led to the shootings. Eyewitness accounts disagree on the details of what happened that Friday. Some suggest that a single private of the 29th, perhaps after being insulted by a ropewalk worker, picked a fight, was beaten, and returned to his barracks for reinforcements; others describe a group of eight or ten soldiers who came to the ropewalks spoiling for a fight without provocation. The eventual result was apparently a melee in which thirty or forty soldiers of the 29th attacked a smaller group of ropewalk workers, but were beaten up in the process. Numerous eyewitnesses suggested that, having been bested, the soldiers of the 29th were eager for revenge, and this is what drove them to violence on the night of March 5. It is unclear whether Samuel Gray was involved in the brawl, but at the soldiers' trial one witness claimed that two of the accused, William Warren and Matthew Kilroy, had been present, and another thought that Kilroy intentionally targeted Gray when the firing started. Gray was "killed on the spot, the ball entering his head and beating off a large portion of his skull."[1]

Crispus Attucks also died of his wounds on the street. A sailor whose mother was a Wampanoag Indian from Natick and whose father was an African American slave, he may have been an escaped slave himself, though the evidence is inconclusive. He was waiting to ship out on a voyage, and probably working in town as a casual laborer in the meantime. The *Boston Gazette* identified him with considerable precision as a "mulatto man" who was "born in Framingham, but lately belonged to New-Providence and was here in order to go for North-Carolina." He was "killed instantly; two balls entering his breast, one of them in special goring the right lobe of the lungs, and a great part of the liver most horribly." After the shootings, he was briefly misidentified as a Michael Johnson—that is the name he was given at the coroner's inquest—but the mistake was soon corrected.[2]

James Caldwell was the third victim who died at the scene. A mate on Captain Thomas Morton's brig *Young Hawk,* Caldwell was not from Boston. He was standing in the street, facing away from the soldiers when the firing started. He was "killed by two balls entering his back." A fourth victim, Samuel Maverick, died of his wounds the next day. Maverick—"a promising youth of 17 years of age, son of the widow Maverick"—was apprenticed to Isaac Greenwood. The *Gazette* identifies Greenwood as an ivory turner (a practice that was linked to dentistry in the eighteenth century); other sources suggest that he was a carpenter. A ball pierced Maverick's "belly, & was cut out at his back: He died the next morning."[3]

Two more seventeen-year-old apprentices who were badly wounded were expected to die. Christopher Monk, a shipwright's apprentice who worked for Thomas Walker, was one of them. A "ball entered his back about 4 inches above the left kidney, near the spine, and was cut out of the breast on the same side." The other was John Clark, a native of Medford who was working in Boston as an apprentice to Captain Samuel Howard. The ball that struck him "entered just above his groin and came out at his hip, on the opposite side." It is unclear what became of Clark, but Monk survived for another decade. Unable to work, he became an object of local poor relief until his death. Patrick Carr, a thirty-year-old Irishman who made leather breeches in the shop of John Field, initially appeared to be injured less severely than Monk and Clark, but he soon became the night's fifth victim.

He was struck near the hip by a ball that passed out again "at the opposite side." He survived nine days before dying from his wound.[4]

Four others were wounded less seriously. The merchant Edward Payne was standing in front of his shop across the street when a ball struck him in the arm, shattering a bone, and then lodged in the doorpost. John Greene, a tailor who was coming up Leverett's Lane when the shots were fired, took a ball in the back of his thigh. David Parker, a wheelwright's apprentice, was also struck in the thigh, while the sailor Robert Patterson had a ball pass through his right arm, causing a "great loss of blood."[5]

The shots were fired with standard-issue Land Pattern Muskets, the firearm favored by the British army for more than a century. Nearly five feet long and weighing over ten pounds, the muskets had a .75-inch bore and fired balls that were .69 inches in diameter. This was a piece of lead large enough to tear a fearsome hole in its victim. Upon impact, these massive balls could flatten out and change shape, adding to their destructive power. The wounds inflicted on Gray and Attucks illustrate the damage they did when they found their target.[6]

The *Gazette* repeatedly stressed that the townspeople harassing the soldiers were "mostly lads," and the *Horrid Massacre* echoed that claim. They may have overstated their case, but it is worth noting that four of the eleven people struck by bullets in King Street were apprentices, and three were identified as seventeen-year-olds. This is less than a majority, but is nevertheless a substantial proportion of the victims. Perhaps equally noteworthy is the fact that three others were sailors, while a fourth was a laborer. A fifth, leather worker Patrick Carr, was a tenant in the home of his employer. The tailor John Greene and the merchant Edward Payne were the only adult men of independent means who were shot, and both were some distance from the fray. Most of the dead and wounded were laboring men and boys whose working lives would have been spent around Boston's docks or at sea on one of the vessels moored there. In both age and social status, those who were struck down disproportionately represented the lower rungs of Boston society.

THE BOSTON TOWN MEETING acted quickly to shape both the narrative and the outcome of the King Street shootings. On March 12 it appointed a committee of seven members to assemble an account of the "horrid transaction" and deliver it to key figures in London. During the second and third weeks of March, Boston's justices of the peace invited witnesses to offer affidavits relating to the events of March 5. Nearly a hundred people trooped through Faneuil Hall to give accounts of the shootings, the events leading up to them, and their immediate aftermath. At the same time the affidavits were being collected, three men — James Bowdoin, Samuel Pemberton, and Joseph Warren — began drafting the text that would eventually be printed as the *Horrid Massacre*. The town meeting approved their draft on March 19 and ordered it to be printed and sent to England. At that point, the narrative was a work in progress, since fewer than half the depositions had been collected. The printed text refers to twenty-four witnesses by name; at least nine of those twenty-four gave their depositions after the March 19 meeting. (Another name mentioned in the text, Henry Rhoads, has no corresponding affidavit in the appendix to the *Horrid Massacre*.) Unsurprisingly, given how quickly it was assembled, the narrative did not take stock of the affidavits in a comprehensive or detailed way.[7]

Once the narrative was approved, finalized, and printed, the town did its best to ensure that it was widely distributed. Initially the town meeting instructed the committee to send copies to six recipients in London whom Bostonians considered to be sympathetic to their cause. Three of the six — William Bollan, Dennys DeBerdt, and Benjamin Franklin — were current or former agents of the colony; one, Thomas Pownall, was a former governor; and two — Isaac Barré and

Barlow Trecothick—were members of Parliament well known to oppose taxing the colonies. By the time copies of the pamphlet were shipped, this short list of recipients had been expanded dramatically to include fifteen peers of the realm, including Hillsborough, the dukes of Richmond and Grafton, and the earls of Shelburne, Chatham, and Halifax; nineteen members of the House of Commons, including the current and former Speakers of the House, George Grenville, Henry Seymour Conway, Edmund Burke, and Alexander Wedderburn; and a handful of others including Thomas Hollis of the Royal Society and the prominent radical historian Catharine Macaulay. In addition to the pamphlet, each received a cover letter signed by Bowdoin, Warren, and Pemberton further justifying the town's actions.[8]

Many recipients undoubtedly—pointedly—ignored the packet of materials from Boston, but the town's committee received replies from several of them. Catharine Macaulay and William Bollan wrote short, supportive letters encouraging the town to persevere. Macaulay complimented Bostonians for their display of "patriotic resentment tempered with forbearance and the warmth of Courage with the coolness of Discretion." Longer letters from Trecothick, a London alderman and MP who was raised in Boston and had served as agent for the colony of New Hampshire, and Pownall, the former governor of Massachusetts, developed Macaulay's implicit theme of moderation. Both men expressed sympathy for the town's plight; Pownall "only wonder'd that some thing of this sort had not happen'd sooner." Both emphasized the need for Boston to proceed cautiously. Trecothick urged the town meeting to apply to Parliament "in a regular constitutional way" for relief from its grievances, while Pownall suggested that Bostonians let Parliament decide whether the practice of posting troops among the civilians in the colonies was unconstitutional. "It would be wise," he cautioned them, "to suspend all Opposition on this Point."[9]

Both Pownall and Trecothick stressed, above all, the importance of granting Preston and his men a fair trial. "One Sentiment has unanimously arisen in the Minds of all," Pownall reported: "that no Prejudice, Resentment, or party Consideration whatsoever may Operate in the unhappy Case of Capt Preston & the Soldiers, but on the Contrary it wou'd do more Honor to the Spirit & Temper of your People to shew Mercy than to exact Severe Justice." Trecothick expressed satisfaction "that the tryals of Capt Preston & the Soldiers was not precipitately brought on — any sentence of Severity would in that Case have been imputed to revenge & passion." Even the most sympathetic correspondents recognized that Boston was on thin ice in making its case to Parliament and needed to tread lightly to avoid widening the breach. The town meeting's best hope was to behave with moderation, in order to inspire moderation in Parliament. As Trecothick put it, "My most ardent Wishes are, that in both sides we may assume that temperate affectionate Conduct, which only, can become Men bound together by the united Tyes of Blood Religion & Interest."[10]

But while the town's London correspondents urged "temperate affectionate Conduct," crown officials in Boston saw little sign of it. For an observer like Thomas Hutchinson, disorder and irregularities abounded everywhere he looked. Boston was behaving like a city-state, beholden to no higher authority and sufficient unto itself. Ignoring the charter and statutes that specified the structure of the town meeting, Bostonians gave "no sort of regard . . . to any qualifications of Voters but all the inferior people meet together and at a late meeting the Inhabitants of other Towns who hap[pe]ned to be in Town mixed with them and made they say themselves near 3000 their news paper says 4000 when it is not likely that there are 1500 legal Voters in the Town." In his diary, Hutchinson added, "It could not be said to be a legal Town Meeting because the doors were open to all Men & Lads of Estate & no Estate Freemen & Servants without any inquiry or any distinction." Boston was, in Hutchinson's estimation, "under the government of the Mob."[11]

This criticism failed to acknowledge the fact that, by statute, town meetings in Massachusetts were open to everyone, "Inhabitant or Foreigner, free or not free," though voting rights were restricted to property holders. Town meeting records indicate that, even on the afternoon of March 6, attendees were "legally qualified and warned," suggesting that however many people were there, voting was likely to have been restricted to property holders. Moreover, most of the meeting's decisions and actions received unanimous support, suggesting that Hutchinson's point was a weak one.[12] At bottom, it was less the illegality of these proceedings than the populist character of the town meeting itself that troubled Hutchinson. In his view, the town stood at the bottom of the colony's hierarchy of constituted authority, but the protean power of its deliberative processes threatened to overwhelm the influence of crown officials.

The irregularities that worried Hutchinson were also spilling over into the operation of the courts. After the justices of the Superior Court had decided to delay the soldiers' trials until early June, a committee of town leaders including Samuel Adams, William Cooper, and Joseph Warren entered the court's chambers to interrupt its proceedings. With a "vast concourse of people" pressing into the chambers behind them, the committee "harangued the Justices until they alter[e]d their determination and resolved to go on with business." The town's representatives "concern themselves in the proceedings of the Superior Court all the time they are sitting," Hutchinson reported, "and several of the Judges have expressed to me their wishes that they might never hold an other Court here." Local leaders, meanwhile, "keep alive a Town meeting by short adjournments to observe how the business of the Court goes on." One judge, Edmund Trowbridge, began experiencing symptoms of a "nervous disorder." Hutchinson was determined to delay the trials as long as possible, but by the end of March he was convinced that the town's purpose was to intimidate the justices, "to act as Prosecutors and press the Court with so much earnestness that I doubt whether they will have firm-ness enough to resist it."[13]

Hutchinson was similarly concerned about the way that the town collected the affidavits that were printed along with the *Horrid Massacre*. "Nothing can be more irregular than their proceeding," he wrote. Those witnesses had been examined ex parte, as he put it: that is, only one party to the subsequent trial was involved in examin-ing them. In this way, the town could "anticipate the Evidence they are to give upon the Trial of the Prisoners and fasten the Witnesses down to Affidavits drawn by the Justices." Thus the town could ensure that "so much is contained [in the affidavits] as will serve the cause they are engaged in and no more." In effect, Hutchinson argued, the process of collecting eyewitness testimony prejudiced the witnesses in favor of the town.[14]

Boston leaders were sensitive to this charge; a passage in the *Horrid Massacre* defended their procedure and charged that the soldiers and crown officials, not the town, had collected eyewitness testimony in an indefensible way. Boston's justices of the peace had acted openly and publicly; they had also notified customs officials so that they could attend and hear the witnesses for themselves if they chose to do so. By contrast, the affidavits that were collected to vindicate the soldiers were taken secretly, "without notifying the Select Men of the Town or any other persons whatever," and then hastily carried to London by John Robinson, one of the customs commissioners who had been stationed in Boston.[15]

This instance was part of a larger narrative put forward by town leaders, who insisted that they had acted properly and justly in the wake of the shootings. Hutchinson, for example, complained that the town had decided to post a military watch every night until the last of the troops departed for Castle Island. As governor and therefore supreme commander of the provincial militia, Hutchinson refused to approve the watch. But, he wrote, the town defied him and proceeded without his authorization. "I have not the command of the Military of the Town," he concluded with exasperation. The town gave a different account. On the evening of March 6, after a long day of negotiations with Hutchinson and Dalrymple, "it was thought necessary for the safety of the Town, and for preventing a rescue of the persons committed to goal for firing upon, and killing a number of, his Majesty's subjects, that there should be a military watch." Since night had already fallen and "it was impossible a regular notification should issue from the officers of the militia," a "considerable number of respectable persons therefore offered themselves [as] voluntiers." The following day, the colonel of the Massachusetts Regiment applied to Hutchinson for permission to continue with the watch until the troops had left town. Hutchinson "declined giving any orders concerning it," but told the colonel that, as chief officer of the regiment, he could order a watch on his own authority "as he thought fit." With the governor neither ordering nor disallowing it, the military watch persisted until both regiments had moved to Castle Island. Throughout, "the Justices of the Peace in their turns attended every night: and the utmost order and regularity took place through the whole of it."[16]

WHILE THE EVENTS OF MARCH 5 allowed town leaders to reclaim the initiative in their long-running struggle to control the narrative of Boston's military occupation, it forced military officers to recalibrate the nature of their mission. Most obviously, it required Dalrymple to set in motion the complex process of removing troops to Castle Island. It also inspired a new wave of correspondence between Gage and Hutchinson over the limits of their respective authority and, more generally, over the legal implications of military-civilian conflict. This had been a running theme of their communications from the beginning of the occupation, but after the shootings they had new contingencies to consider.

Despite the decision taken on March 6 to remove both regiments to Castle Island, Dalrymple continued to explore his options. In a letter to Gage written two days later, he characterized the attack on the Custom House sentry as part of a preconcerted plan, not simply a spontaneous mob action. And it involved not only the town of Boston, but militia units from the countryside as well. "The leading men of the Militia were prepared for the matter," he wrote, "and on the concerted signal were to march into town with their men. The arms in Faniel Hall were in the hands of the people as were the town artil[l]ery." Here was the scenario about which Gage and Pomeroy had corresponded a year earlier: the town rising in armed rebellion. Dalrymple was unsure how many men were mobilized, but it was enough to cause concern: "They were short of four thousand, as they appeared to me, [but] the Governor makes mention of larger numbers being on their march." Instead of withdrawing the troops to Castle Island, Dalrymple proposed to Hutchinson that they "raise a redoubt on Fort Hill" in the South End, secure the 29th in the barracks nearby, and apply "to the Kings ship for two small guns." Hutchinson was probably appalled at Dalrymple's suggestion as he contemplated the prospect of an armed standoff between soldiers of the king and the Massachusetts militia in the streets of Boston. To dissuade Dalrymple, he argued that his men were too few, and it would be better to focus on securing the fort on Castle Island. "I offered to do that by a detachment, and at the same time adhere to the other part of the plan," Dalrymple wrote, but Hutchinson "held it improper and imprudent," and Dalrymple abandoned the idea.[17]

Still, Dalrymple dragged his feet. He was concerned that once the troops left for Castle Island, the customs officials in town would be fair game for the Boston crowd. Moreover, he had yet to receive instructions from Gage, and he was reluctant to take any decisive action before he heard from him. "I am now Sir to mention," he therefore concluded, "that I shal[l] proceed very slowly in the removal of the troops to the Castle, tho much urged, by the people." In the mean-time, he kept "the troops constantly alert" and reported that "we have never left our Barracks" since the shootings. He remained worried. "Your Excellency well knows our situation," he wrote. "With two shat[t]ered regiments"—Dalrymple estimated that he had "no more than Six hundred fit for duty"—"divided in all parts of this town, without any place of strength to make a stand on, what can be expected from us[?]" By the evening of the twelfth, he reported, the 29th Regiment would all be withdrawn to the Castle; he continued to delay the removal of the 14th.[18]

For Gage, the shootings in King Street offered the opportunity to do what he had wished for since the previous June: to remove the troops from Boston altogether. He replied to both Hutchinson and Dalrymple on March 12. "The Troops were Sent to Boston for the support of Government, and to assist the Civil Magistrates in the due Execution of the Laws," he noted, but instead "it has become the desire of Government, that the Troops should be removed out of the Town, the better to preserve Tranquility." He was only too happy to comply. He urged Dalrymple to proceed. He also informed Hutchinson that "as I do not see, that they can be of any use at Castle William," he proposed "to remove them out of the Province, and to remove one of them as Soon as Possible for, the Castle Barracks will not contain them both."[19]

At this stage in their correspondence, Gage and Hutchinson both began to backtrack. Writing to Dalrymple, Gage remarked, "It would appear extraordinary to those at a Distance" that officials in Boston would send the troops to Castle Island, where they could no longer provide prompt support. "As for myself," he wrote, "I can see no Reason to remove them out of the Town, I mean the whole of them, tho' at the Same Time am of opinion, it would be right and proper to remove the 29th Regiment, and that the People might be satisfied with that Measure." His instruction, therefore, was to remove the 29th, delay the departure of the 14th, and seek "Reconciliation" and

View of Fort William a The Neck b Light house c Saitlig out of harbour d 1770

An unknown artist painted this view of Castle Island in 1770. Thomas Pownall described the island as "a high ridge of Land running from NW to SE about Twelve hundred feet Long and Eight hundred & forty broad, with steep Cliffs, at each End and Slooping gradually on each side with a Long Low Point, a Beech running about Six hundred feet SW." Here we see the undefended side of the island that faced toward the town; this is the view a soldier might have had from the deck of a transport vessel as his regiment was relocated to the island.

"Harmony" with the town. But—Gage inserted one final reversal—if the "Officers of Government" continued to insist on it, Dalrymple should proceed to remove the 14th as well.[20]

Hutchinson, meanwhile, protested that Gage misunderstood his position. "It adds greatly to the Distress I am under," he wrote, that Gage believed he asked for the removal of the troops. "Upon first seeing Colo[nel] Dalrymple, I told him I had no authority and would give no Order for the Removal of the Troops." It was Dalrymple's decision, based on the request of the town and the advice of his council, to remove them. Now, Gage proposed removing the troops from the province altogether. "I dare by no means take such a step," Hutchinson replied, "unless it was in consequence of express orders from you upon its appearing to you that the King's service requires it."[21]

Here, once again, was the issue that plagued the occupation of Boston from beginning to end. The troops had been stationed in town by order of Gage and George III in anticipation of a rebellion, not at the express invitation of local magistrates. But in the absence of a rebellion, the troops could act only if local officials called upon them. As a crown appointee, Hutchinson—like Bernard before him—believed that his authority was insufficient for this purpose, especially when he lacked the support of his own council. Most of Boston's magistrates were adamantly opposed to the troops' presence and would not call upon them, no matter what the circumstance. The best course of action was clearly to remove the troops. But that appeared to Hutchinson and Gage to be capitulating to the mob. Unable to act, both men were reduced to vacillation and exasperated hair-splitting over questions of authority.

It fell to Dalrymple both to interpret the ambivalent orders he was receiving and to handle the complex arrangements required to house both regiments on Castle Island. To manage expenses, he hoped to get "the Barracks and houses lately occupied by the troops" put back into a reasonable order before April 7, so he could avoid paying another month's rent. With this consideration in mind, as well as the town's repeated pleas to act, Dalrymple interpreted Gage's confused instructions to mean that he could proceed with the removal of the 14th as well; by March 19 they had all been transported to the island. Dalrymple's next concern was the "vastly crowded" state of their accommodations. To ease the problem, he urged Gage to send one of the regiments elsewhere as soon as possible. On April 28, Gage sent orders to Castle Island instructing the 29th Regiment to march overland to Providence, Rhode Island, where they would board vessels for Amboy and Elizabethtown, New Jersey. Nearly a month later, Dalrymple was able to report, at last, that they were on the march. The 14th Regiment finally had the island's barracks to itself.[22]

BOTH PRESTON and the town selectmen quickly recruited lawyers to plead their cases in court. Immediately after landing in jail, Preston approached Josiah Quincy Jr. and Robert Auchmuty to ask for their aid in defending him. Quincy initially refused. He then consulted with all the principal leaders of the town meeting — Samuel Adams, John Hancock, William Molineux, Samuel Pemberton, and Joseph Warren, among others — and, on their urging, agreed: but not before telling Preston in no uncertain terms that his loyalties lay with the town. Auchmuty was apparently easier to persuade. But according to John Adams's recollection more than thirty years later, both men said they would take Preston's case only if Adams joined them. Thus, as Adams recalled, Boston merchant James Forrest visited him a day or two after the shootings "with tears streaming from his Eyes" to ask if he would assist in Preston's defense. Adams agreed.

Quincy and Adams both later reported that they faced withering criticism from townspeople for their decision to defend Preston. Quincy's father, a distinguished member of an old Massachusetts family, was outraged to learn of his son's new client. "Good God! Is it possible?" he wrote. The news "filled the bosom of your aged and infirm parent with anxiety, and distress." Quincy the son reacted impatiently to the reproaches of "ignorant slanderers." He reminded his father that the men charged with murder "are not yet legally proved guilty," and they were as deserving of counsel as anyone. And in any case, he had refused to take Preston as a client until he conferred with town leaders. Matters of principle aside, Quincy assured his father that he accepted Preston's request for aid only after he was "advised and urged to undertake it" by the leading figures in the town meeting.[23]

Those same town leaders quickly acted to ensure adequate legal support for the prosecution. The colony's attorney general—the King's Attorney—would spearhead the effort, but Boston's selectmen did not want to leave it to him alone. On March 8 they met to designate another lawyer whom they intended to hire to offer "assistance" to the attorney general. Noting that their "Enemy's" had already "avail[e]d themselves of our Neglect, & have Engag'd most or all the Lawyers in Town," they cast about for alternatives. They wrote to Robert Treat Paine—whose practice was in Taunton, not Boston—to enlist his aid. Recognizing that it was unusual (to say the least) for the town's selectmen to hire a lawyer who would assist the King's Attorney in the prosecution, they explained their reasoning to Paine. Acknowledging that it would "not be in Character for the Town to appear against the Criminals," they instead intended that Paine would "appear in behalf of the Relatives of the Deceased." Taking up those relatives' interests as its own, the Boston town meeting hired a lawyer and agreed to pay him on their behalf. (As it happened, Attorney General Jonathan Sewall left Boston for Ipswich shortly after issuing indictments for the March 5 shootings and stayed away indefinitely, perhaps to give the court grounds for delaying the soldiers' trial. In Sewall's stead, the court appointed Samuel Quincy, brother to Josiah Jr., to act on the crown's behalf.)[24]

The selectmen told Paine that he should plan to be in town on March 17, the day the court was scheduled to resume after its current adjournment, when they expected the trials of Preston and the other soldiers to come on quickly. They made extraordinary arrangements to ensure that Paine was prepared. Along with the letter of appointment, the selectmen sent him "a Printed Narrative of the Massacre, w[i]th ab[ou]t 80 affidavits by Reading of which You will Enter into the Spirit of the thing & be fully Possess'd of Substance and facts."[25]

How could the town's selectmen possibly have delivered a printed account of the massacre, complete with eighty affidavits, into the hands of their attorneys as early as March 9? At the town meeting on March 6, a committee of three men—the sheriff, William Greenleaf, along with William and Samuel Whitwell—was appointed to take depositions from eyewitnesses.[26] No formal arrangements had yet been made for preparing a narrative. Perhaps Paine was sent a draft of the version that would appear in the *Boston Gazette* on March 12. Nor had arrangements yet been made for justices of the peace to record affidavits in a public setting, as they would do for the eyewitness testimony that appeared in the *Horrid Massacre*. These earlier statements were apparently collected privately, and therefore ex parte. The town was taking an extraordinary step in prescreening witnesses in this way, as it must have realized when it later stressed the open, public character of the affidavits printed in the appendix to the *Horrid Massacre*. In their letter to Paine, the selectmen justified their actions by stressing the urgency of the moment and the justice of their cause. "I am for my own Part Convinced of Your Readiness at all Times to Espouse your Country[']s Cause," William Molineux wrote on their behalf. It was Paine's moral obligation to defend the interests of those "who have suffered by the hands of Execrable V[illain]s & Professed Murder[er]s."[27]

Above all, town leaders desired a swift outcome. The jail was crowded. It held forty-seven prisoners in mid-March, fifteen on capital charges. The town doubled the strength of its watch to prevent a jailbreak; to speed things along, it asked the governor to appoint additional judges. Instead, the court proceeded as usual. When it decided to put off the soldiers' trials until May, town leaders—as we have seen—crowded into the courtroom and forced the justices to reconsider. They expected that a quick trial, while the events of March 5 were fresh in jurors' minds, would be most likely to lead to convictions. With the same expectation in mind, Hutchinson sought to delay the trials as long as possible. "The minds of the people are so inflamed that it is much to be desired that the Trials of the Officers and Soldiers should be deferred," he wrote, "but the Town by their Committee have taken upon them to act as Prosecutors and press the Court with so much earnestness that I doubt whether they will have firmness enough to resist it." Hutchinson worried that nothing could quench the local desire for revenge. "I am doing & shall continue to do every thing in my power to prevent the unhappy persons falling a sacrifice to the Resentment of Faction," he concluded in a letter to Gage, "but greatly fear whether in the state we now are they can have a Jury without bias & strong prejudice."[28]

In the end, the trials were delayed far longer than even Hutchinson thought possible or desirable. Preston's did not come on until late October; the other soldiers' trial began almost a month after that. Not until December were all the men accused of shooting into the Boston crowd on the evening of March 5 finally brought before the bar.

DURING THE MONTHS OF WAITING, Gage, Hutchinson, and Dalrymple anticipated the worst and tried to plan for it. They had hoped that, with the passage of time, the temper of the town would cool. As it turned out, something like the reverse occurred. Within a week after the shootings, Dalrymple observed, "the malevolence of the people begins to subside relative to Captain Preston." Preston himself sent a note of thanks to the *Boston Gazette* that was printed on

March 12 — the same day the paper carried its first account of the shootings. "PERMIT me, through the Channel of your Paper," he wrote, "to return my Thanks in the most publick Manner to the Inhabitants in general of this Town. . . . I shall ever have the highest Sense of the Justice they have done me." Preston praised his legal team in particular, "who throwing aside all Party and Prejudice, have with the utmost Humanity and Freedom stept forth Advocates for Truth, in Defence of my injured Innocence." This final flourish was a bit too much for *Gazette* readers to bear; as one pointedly observed, "No Person can be satisfied of his *injured innocence,* untill he is acquitted of the high Charge laid against him, in due Course of Law."[29] Still, residents appeared to be willing to defer to the court in judging him.

But as the weeks and months in jail dragged on, the mood of the town turned against Preston. The decisive moment came in June, when Preston's chickens came home to roost. He had written a long, self-justifying account shortly after the shootings that briefly surveyed the entire period of the occupation and disparaged both townspeople and magistrates. Noting the town's "malicious Temper," Preston accused the Boston magistrates of encouraging disputes with the soldiers. Even Gage and Dalrymple — otherwise Preston's staunch defenders — recognized how inflammatory his version of events was, and hoped it would never see the light of day. Against their wishes, it was sent to England; even worse, it soon found its way into print in the London papers. Copies made their way back across the Atlantic and arrived in Boston on June 18.[30] Preston's account threw the town into an uproar; whatever patience locals had evinced toward him now appeared to evaporate altogether.

The jail seemed to Preston to offer scant protection. In a panic, he wrote to Dalrymple "expressing his great fears that the People were so enraged as to force the Gaol that night and make him a sacrifice." His concerns were not entirely misplaced, but — as Hutchinson soon learned — the "Liberty People" were not ready to take such precipitate action yet. Instead, "they have generally remarked that what ever danger there may be after the Trial it would be the heighth of madness to think of any such thing before."[31] It must have been cold comfort for Preston to learn the real danger of mob action would come only if he were acquitted or pardoned.

On July 10 the town meeting appointed a committee of nine men to "counteract the designs of those inveterate Enemies among us, who . . . are still continuing their Misrepresentations" of Boston. Chief among those was Preston, and seven of the nine members, including Samuel Adams, justice of the peace Richard Dana, John Hancock, and William Molineux, visited him in his cell later that day. How could it be, they wondered, that the same man who expressed such gratitude toward the town a week after the shootings could slander its inhabitants and officials in a private account sent off to England to explain his actions? Preston deflected their anger by telling them that his account had passed through several other people's hands before it reached England, and that the printed version had been altered along the way. The men tried to pin him down: which claims had been added later, and which statements would he recant? Pressed for details, Preston refused to say anything more. The next day he received a letter from the committee, demanding that he clarify his position. Preston never responded.[32]

By the end of July, it was commonly expected that Preston would be convicted of murder. Usually, when an army officer was convicted for actions taken in the line of duty, he could expect a royal pardon. It was under just such circumstances that John Porteous had been lynched in Edinburgh: he was tried, convicted, and sentenced to hang after his men fired into a crowd, but he remained in jail awaiting word of the king's pardon. To prevent that outcome — which would have set Porteous free — an Edinburgh mob stormed the jail and hanged him themselves. This kind of intervention in the mechanisms of royal justice was commonly understood to be a possible, even a likely, outcome. It was also widely regarded as a legitimate exercise of local prerogative. Just as magistrates worked to preserve the king's peace in the operations of their courts, a lynch mob—acting corporately as an expression of its community's will—could take matters into its own hands to ensure that justice was done. In resistance to the emerging power of a centralized, militarized state, local communities were willing to use organized vigilantism as a counterweight that asserted their right to just punishment. By defending the king's peace in the face of an impending royal pardon, a community could legitimize even such an apparently unjustifiable act as lynching, as Edinburgh had done in the case of John Porteous.[33]

Preston's supporters worried about this tradition. And for a trial taking place in the colonies, the situation was even more complicated. The king could not issue a preemptive pardon ahead of time; a pardon could be issued only in response to a verdict already rendered. Given the delays in transatlantic communication, this meant that if Preston were convicted, the colony would have to delay the execution of his sentence for two months or more to allow for even the possibility of a pardon. During that time, Preston would continue to be held in the Boston jail, susceptible every day to mob action. As an anonymous well-wisher warned him, "the popular prejudice is much against you, I have been told by many that his Majesty's pardon will avail you nothing, & by way of precedent they mention the affair of Porteous." By the end of July, this was the universal expectation: Preston would be tried, convicted, and then—if the town allowed it—pardoned. But the town would not allow it. Like Porteous before him, Preston would fall victim to the town's code of justice before word of the king's mercy could reach him. "From these circumstances," Preston's anonymous friend concluded, "I am led to believe there will be no protection for you without the aid of a military force."[34]

It remained to Hutchinson and Preston's superior officers to decide whether, when, and how to use military force in his defense. They corresponded extensively on the subject. Hutchinson noted that if the soldiers were found guilty and sentenced, it would be his responsibility "to grant a Reprieve until His Majesty's Pleasure should be known." But he worried that he might be unable to protect them. The problem was less "the rage of the People against me" than it was "our present dissolute state of Government." In an echo of the refrain they had sounded throughout the occupation, Hutchinson warned Gage that if a Boston mob decided to exact its own brand of justice against the soldiers, local officials would rather let events take their course than call upon the army to intercede. "I do not believe I have one Magistrate who would be willing to run any risque in endeavouring to prevent it," he observed dolefully.[35]

Hutchinson's pessimism was not entirely misplaced, but as it turned out there was one Boston magistrate who was willing to take a risk to help protect the soldiers. James Murray, owner of one of the warehouses that had been used as a barracks, was also a Boston justice of the peace. In July he offered the use of his facilities to the army once again. Convinced of Preston's innocence and "Zealous for the Peace and Credit of the Town," Murray informed Dalrymple, "I shall be ready, as a Civil Magistrate, to escorte two hundred men of your Regiment from the Castle to Town when the trial is come or sooner when ever there is notice of danger to him from the Mob." Once in town, the troops could remain "in Smiths Sugar house Barrack, where a Sentry from the Top of the House can hear or see a Signal from the Gaol."[36]

Murray's offer is intriguing in retrospect. Throughout the occupation, Gage, Dalrymple, and Hutchinson had repeatedly lamented that there was no magistrate in Boston who would ever call upon the soldiers to act in case of a riot; as the soldiers' trials approached, Hutchinson was trotting out the old complaint once again. But Murray's proposal seems to belie the notion that there was no Boston magistrate willing to cooperate. Unlike Richard Dana and Samuel

Pemberton—justices of the peace who were adamantly opposed to the troops' role in supporting crown officials—Murray belonged to the circle of Bostonians whom crown officers liked to call the "friends of government." One of a handful of Boston merchants who specialized in processing sugar, Murray was a Scottish-born outsider in his adopted home. He refused to sign the nonimportation agreement of 1768 and was thereafter widely resented and mistrusted by town leaders. He would eventually leave Boston for good with the British fleet that evacuated loyalists in 1776.[37] Now, with the approach of Preston's trial, he made an extraordinary offer. If he was willing to escort a detachment of soldiers through the streets of Boston in the summer of 1770, what other forms of support might he have given to the soldiers during the seventeen months of the occupation?

Nevertheless, no one took Murray's offer seriously. It was such a bad idea that Hutchinson considered it an empty gesture, intended only to curry favor with Gage. To bring soldiers back to Boston just as the court was taking up its business would produce "the very worst, & most dangerous consequences." It was not only ill advised; without a specific provocation, it would be illegal to bring soldiers back to town. As Dalrymple explained to Murray, according to the Riot Act soldiers could be called upon only "when the actual appearance of tumults vindicate the measure, and not upon every surmise of future ill intentions."[38]

In Gage's estimation, Murray was the wrong official to rely upon. "The matter in question," he wrote, "does not tally with the Duty of a Justice of the Peace." Instead, the authority to call upon troops to help protect the accused men "belongs solely to the Sheriff, whose Duty it is to secure Prisoners, bring them to their Tryal, and see Judgement executed." In the course of riots in New York, for example, Gage noted that the sheriff had requested the support of troops "to defend the jail, which he imagined the Mob intended to force." Gage offered them immediately. Now, Gage advised Dalrymple, "if you can prevail on your Sheriff to act in this Manner, I believe it will be the most regular and legal way of Acting." Once the troops were called out by the sheriff, Gage assured Dalrymple that he could respond to a request from Murray, Hutchinson, or any other "Civil Magistrate" or "Officers of Government" for assistance "as they shall require, to enable them to preserve the public Peace, and support the legal Authority of Government."[39]

These tortured calculations highlight the vagueness of the Riot Act itself, which empowered local magistrates to call upon the army for aid but offered no guidance for navigating the complex political alignments of a town like Boston. It presumed that the various authorities — in this case, a mix of local, provincial, and crown officials — would concur, and made no provision for the possibility that their opinions would be divided. In distinguishing, first, between the authority of a justice of the peace and that of the sheriff, and second, between the question of who could call out the soldiers and who could ask for help once they were deployed, Gage was employing a logic all his own. None of this was spelled out in the Riot Act. It was the product of Gage's years of experience, musing in frustration on the relationship between civil and military authority in the ill-defined netherworld of Britain's North American colonies.

FOR TOWN LEADERS, the summer of 1770 was framed by the imminent expectation of a major military crackdown on Boston. Although the 29th and 14th Regiments had been withdrawn in the spring, rumors were rife by July that Britain was about to reverse course and bring armed force to bear on the town. A large gathering at William Molineux's home — presumably a meeting of the North End Caucus — reportedly met to consider whether the town should take up arms to oppose a troop landing. If the crown did intend to reinstate a military occupation of Boston, it was essential, in Hutchinson's estimation, to present an overwhelming show of force. "If no greater numbers than were in the Town the 5[th] of March should attempt to land without a sufficient naval force to cover the landing," he warned, "I have no doubt they would be oppos[e]d."[40]

In the end, Parliament was prorogued without deciding on a new course of action in the colonies, and the rumors of an impending reoccupation abated. But in August, Gage received orders to take control of Fort William on Castle Island. For three-quarters of a century the island had been a joint outpost of provincial and royal power, a symbol of the long-standing spirit of cooperation in military matters between colony and crown. Now, based on reports they had received from March and April, the king and his ministers had concluded that Boston was verging into anarchy. Hillsborough therefore instructed Gage to put "that Island and its Fortress into such a State & Condition" that it could not only accommodate the 14th Regiment, but also serve as "a Place of Strength, and an Asylum in the last Extremity for the Officers of the Crown" in Boston, should events proceed from bad to worse. The barracks occupied by the 14th lay outside Fort William; the fort itself had remained under the control of a company of provincials throughout the occupation. Now Hillsborough instructed Hutchinson to withdraw the provincial company and cede the island to the king's soldiers, while he ordered Gage to take possession of the fort.[41]

Even as he passed along instructions to Dalrymple, Gage advised him to keep the transfer a secret as long as possible. "Till the Business is effected," he wrote, "it may be best that it should not be known." Gage, Dalrymple, and Hutchinson all recognized that given the town's sensitivity to every royal encroachment on local prerogative, the loss of the fort would trigger howls of outrage — and perhaps worse. And in fact, rumors of a major realignment of military resources were circulating once again, of which a takeover of Fort William was only a part. One report held that the navy's American squadron, which ordinarily gathered at Halifax, would be converging instead at Boston to "block up the harbour" there, and "that orders have been transmitted to General Gage, to act in concert with Commodore Gambier, in carrying into execution certain coercive measures of Government with respect to the inhabitants of the town of Boston." A second rumor suggested that the colony's provincial forts, "hitherto maintained by their own assembly, will be, in future, occupied by the King's forces; in particular, that Castle-William, situated on an island which commands the entrance into Boston harbour, will be garrisoned with a thousand regular troops."[42]

In the same issue of the *Boston Gazette* that reported these rumors, news that Castle William had been taken over by British regulars was printed as well. This gave rise to additional rumors: observers predicted that "a Citadel was to be erected on Fort Hill—and Fortifications to be built at the South Part of this Town and at Roxbury" as well. A correspondent remarked that the orders to take over Castle William "were executed with the utmost secrecy, and with so much dispatch, that the garrison in the pay of this government, were turned out in two hours." In a subsequent issue of the *Gazette,* another writer argued that there was only one way to interpret the ministry's order to commandeer Castle William: "They mean, if they have any meaning, to declare us all and in effect they have declared us all Rebels & Traitors."[43] Such rumors persisted into October, even as Preston's trial got under way. One report held that a naval squadron was about to "block up the harbour of Boston" while "a land force is to march into the town, under a pretence of supporting the Officers of the Revenue." It predicted that the assembly would be forced to meet "under the muzzle of the musket and screwed bayonet" and required "to pass such regulations as G[overnmen]t pleases, or to be dissolved, dishonoured, and deprived of their charter." And indeed, on October 10,

Commodore James Gambier arrived in Boston Harbor aboard HMS *Salisbury,* where he was saluted by guns from the Castle as well as by "the Men of War in the Harbour."[44]

But despite the fort's takeover and rumors of worse to come, the Boston town meeting registered no official complaint in the fall of 1770. When the Massachusetts General Court resumed its operations in October, it received notice in Hutchinson's opening address that the king's troops were in possession of Fort William. In response, the legislature inquired testily whether he was still in command of the fort, as the colony's charter specified. He assured them that he was, and that was the end of it. Neither body issued an official protest against the abrogation of the colony's charter rights. Hutchinson believed that the takeover of the fort initially "set [a] great part of the people into rage and fury," but that, "upon reflection," townspeople "seemed generally to be convinced they had gone too far."[45] In the fall of 1770, as the soldiers' trials approached, the town of Boston was uncharacteristically quiet.

WHEN THE SUPERIOR COURT returned to Boston at the end of August, Preston immediately petitioned to bring on his trial. Perhaps he felt another shift in local attitudes. "The alteration in men[']s minds towards him is extreamly visible," Dalrymple reported, "a degree of coolness has succeeded to the late warmth, and there are many reasons to hope an impartiality on trial of which lately there was not a ray of expectation." A few days later, on September 7, the thirteen men accused of firing into the King Street crowd — Preston, the other eight soldiers, and the four civilians accused of shooting out of the Custom House windows — were arraigned; each pled not guilty. But then, instead of proceeding to a trial, the court adjourned again until the end of October. Preston's waiting was not yet over.[46]

In all the strategizing about Preston's chances, the other eight soldiers who were jailed alongside him appear to have been all but forgotten. Adams and Quincy eventually defended them in court, but it was as Preston's counsel that they were originally engaged. Recognizing that their fate was linked to Preston's, and that they were more likely to be acquitted if they were tried together, three of the soldiers—White, Hartegan, and Kilroy—petitioned the court "to lett us have our Trial at the same time with our Captain." In articulating their rationale, they directly contradicted the claim Preston would rely upon to argue for his innocence. "For we did our Captains Orders," the petitioners insisted, "and if we don't Obay [h]is Command we should have been Confine'd and shott for not doing of it."[47]

As the soldiers well knew, Preston's acquittal would almost certainly seal their fates. If their captain had ordered them to fire into the crowd, they would have had no choice but to obey. But if Preston were tried first and a jury decided that he did not order his men to fire, then the soldiers would lose the protecting cover their commanding officer gave to their actions. "It is very hard he being a Gentelman should have more chance for to save his life then we poor men that is Oblidged to Obay his command," they wrote. If Preston were acquitted, his men could expect to bear the full responsibility for the shootings. The court denied the soldiers' petition and ordered Preston tried separately from the men serving under his command.[48]

Forgotten even more completely were the four civilians charged with firing shots at the crowd from a second-story window of the Custom House. This charge was the most incendiary of all; it was also irreconcilable with the consensus account of the shootings that would be established at trial. The case against the civilians was quickly dismissed, and just as quickly written out of popular memory and the historical record as either a plausible possibility or a meaningful misrepresentation. It was necessarily, however, one of those two things, and deserves to be subjected to its own consideration and analysis.

CHAPTER 8

Four Trials

A FTER seven and a half months of delay, the legal disposition of the March shootings unfolded over a period of five additional months, in four trials. The first two are well known. On October 24, Captain Thomas Preston was brought before the bar for ordering his men to fire into the crowd; his trial lasted six days and resulted in his acquittal. A month later, beginning on November 27, the corporal and seven privates who served under Preston were tried for murder. Their trial lasted eight days and resulted in six acquittals; two men, Matthew Kilroy and Hugh Montgomery, were convicted of the lesser charge of manslaughter. A third, rarely noted trial considered the question of whether four men — Edward Manwaring, John Monroe, Hammond Green, and Thomas Greenwood — fired shots at the crowd in King Street from a second-floor window in the Custom House. Finally, in March 1771 the principal witness in the third trial — a fourteen-year-old servant of Manwaring's named Charles Bourgatte — was convicted of perjury for changing his testimony. He was sentenced to one hour in the public stocks and twenty-five lashes; he was also required to pay his court costs.

These trials imposed a retrospective veneer of clarity on an episode that was chaotic, poorly understood, and — in important ways — inexplicable. Most people who have engaged casually with the question of what happened on March 5, 1770, come away with the impression that the answer is fairly straightforward. Historians have contributed to the impression that we know what happened that night; most scholars who have written about the shootings have pieced together a version of events that acts as a kind of best-guess narrative. To do that, however, historians — like the drafters of the *Horrid Massacre* and the *Unhappy Disturbance* — have sorted through the eyewitness testimony, amplifying some witnesses' claims while silencing others. Rather than highlighting anomalies, they have stressed areas of agreement and applied an unstated test of plausibility. To take the opposite approach — highlighting inconsistencies and confronting head on the obstacles to arriving at a plausible account of the shootings — can be powerfully illuminating. Such an approach demonstrates two things. First, testimony about the sequence of events on March 5 is sufficiently contradictory to suggest that, on several key issues, we have no way of knowing what actually happened. Second, given the contested nature of the events surrounding the shootings, the trials were as much a struggle to construct a dominant, consensus narrative as they were an attempt to attain justice for the accused. It was not only the soldiers who were on trial; the towns-people who observed, and perhaps instigated, the violence were also under scrutiny. Boston itself was on trial, and the town's character was at stake.

IN THE SMALL, tight-knit legal community of greater Boston, the five lawyers most closely involved in Preston's trial knew each other well. In his mid-forties, Robert Auchmuty Jr. was the oldest. A Boston lawyer who also served as a Vice-Admiralty Court judge, he had presided over Hancock's *Liberty* case and ordered the ship to be seized and forfeited. As Preston's lawyers prepared their defense of the captain, Colonel Dalrymple worried that Auchmuty lacked zeal;

indeed, Auchmuty told Hutchinson that he thought Preston's case a weak one. Yet, after he was acquitted, Preston singled Auchmuty out for praise. "My counsel . . . were men of parts, & exerted themselves with great spirit & cleverness, particularly Judge Auchmuty," he enthused.[1]

John Adams was a decade younger than Auchmuty, and for several years had been developing one of the busiest law practices in Boston. Later in his life, Adams described his involvement in the trials in his autobiography. As he recalled it, neither Auchmuty nor Quincy would proceed in Preston's defense unless Adams joined them in the effort. He also remembered telling James Forrest (who had come to Adams's office to ask him to represent Preston) that it was vitally important to ensure the soldiers a fair trial. Counsel, Adams recalled saying, "ought to be the very last thing that an accused Person should want [lack] in a free Country." He went on to note the magnitude of the case. "This would be as important a Cause as ever was tryed in any Court or Country of the World." Moreover, "From first to last I never said a Word about fees," Adams wrote. He claimed that he received ten guineas from Preston and another eight guineas after the soldiers' trial. "This was all the pecuniary Reward I ever had for fourteen or fifteen days labour, in the most exhausting and fatiguing Causes I ever tried." The documentary record suggests that this recollection was not entirely accurate; in Dalrymple's accounting of trial costs, lawyers' fees amount to about £125. If divided three ways, this would have come to £42 apiece, or more than double the amount Adams remembered receiving. (And it is possible that he received additional fees directly from Preston, as the phrasing in his autobiography suggests.) This is a minor point, but it highlights Adams's retrospective tendency to aggrandize his role — an understandable tendency, especially for an accomplished man reflecting on his formative experiences.[2]

The third member of the defense team, Josiah Quincy Jr., had known Adams since childhood. Adams grew up in Braintree, where

JOHN ADAMS
BENJAMIN BLYTH, 1764
Gift of JOHN ADAMS, 1956

Salem artist Benjamin Blyth completed this portrait of John Adams and another of his wife, Abigail, shortly after their marriage and about four years before the massacre trials, when Adams was a young, rising, ambitious Boston lawyer. The sober dress and oversized gray wig reflect his chosen profession. Blyth's portrait, executed in pastels, captures the volatile blend of insecurity and intelligence that were hallmarks of Adams's character in this stage of his life.

the Quincys, one of the first families of Massachusetts, owned an estate. Adams admired the Quincy family — so much so that he married into it; Abigail Smith's mother, Elizabeth Quincy Smith, was a cousin of Josiah Quincy Sr. Nine years younger than Adams, Josiah Jr. — in his mid-twenties — was at a much earlier stage of his legal career. But he was ambitious, and he had already gained a reputation for both eloquence and radical politics. He took over the practice of the promi-nent Boston lawyer Oxenbridge Thacher after Thacher's death; by 1770 Josiah Jr., like Adams, was one of the busiest and most respected young lawyers in Boston. Hutchinson wrote of Adams and Quincy that they were "both of them men of parts though the latter [was] a Tyro."[3]

Samuel Quincy, the lawyer appointed by the court to act on behalf of the crown in prosecuting the soldiers, was Josiah's older brother. Samuel was the same age as Adams, and the two became friends in Braintree and entered the legal profession at about the same time. Though he was regarded as capable, Samuel was never as ambitious as either Adams or his younger brother, and his practice was less active than theirs. (It is an ironic coincidence that Samuel led the prosecution of the soldiers, while Josiah assisted in their defense, since Josiah was well known for his radical politics, whereas his more moderate brother, the prosecutor, eventually became a loyalist exile.)[4]

The other lawyer assisting in the crown's prosecution effort was Robert Treat Paine, who had been hired by the town to join Quincy in that effort. Paine's career was more varied, and more checkered, than that of anyone else involved in the trials. Four years older than Adams and Samuel Quincy, Paine took a winding path to the practice of law. His father was a well-to-do Boston merchant, but — unlike successful military contractors Thomas Hancock and Charles Apthorp — the elder Paine lost a fortune in the midcentury wars. Though he had an estate worth more than £38,000, he was unable to cover his debts and died insolvent. Thus, Robert Treat Paine had to make his own way. Like Adams, Paine graduated from Harvard and then tried his hand as a schoolteacher. He lasted a year and a half before he decided to leave the classroom and go to sea. He worked as a sailor, master mariner, and merchant. During the Seven Years' War he applied for an officer's commission for the Crown Point expedition but failed to secure one, then became the chaplain in his uncle's regiment. In these same years he began the study of law. In 1757 he was admitted to the bar and began work in the office of the Boston lawyer Benjamin Pratt. His practice limped along, and Paine soon became known for his bad health. In 1761, unable to make a living in Boston, Paine moved to Taunton, where his reputation improved. By 1770 he was regarded as a competent lawyer, if not a brilliant one. Adams knew Paine well enough to think poorly of him. Paine was "conceited," he wrote, "and pretends to more knowledge and genius than he has."[5]

The foremost historian of the trials, Hiller B. Zobel, has argued that the outcome of Preston's trial was effectively decided in the process of jury selection. None of the jurors was from Boston; five of the twelve had a strong bias in favor of the crown's interest, while no one was seated who can be identified with the town's leaders in their ongoing controversies with the crown. Thus, Zobel concludes, "the trial, as lawyers and judges must have known, was nothing but a propaganda battle." Indeed, the principal mystery surrounding Preston's trial is why the town did not make a more concerted effort — why, in fact, it made no effort — to control the outcome of the proceedings. The town selectmen chose a roster of eighteen veniremen who were among the trial's prospective jurors, which was then vetted by the town meeting; as Zobel notes, the resulting list of prospective jurors included only two men with identifiable ties to the Sons of Liberty. Boston's veniremen joined those nominated by the other towns of Suffolk County, and Preston's counsel proceeded to challenge seventeen of the twenty-four veniremen. When the list of veniremen nominated by the towns was exhausted and only seven jurors had been seated, the remaining five places were filled with talesmen — essentially, eligible passersby who were drawn to the jury box by the sheriff. This represented another opportunity for town leaders to assert themselves by packing Queen Street and the courtroom with prospective jurors hostile to Preston and the soldiers; again, there is no evidence that they did so. Finally, as we have seen, town leaders had earlier demonstrated their willingness to disrupt the proceedings of the court when it served their purposes. But as the trial went forward, the sizable audience of five dozen or so onlookers, which included many soldiers and customs officials as well as townspeople, observed the proceedings "with the greatest order and decorum."[6]

Why, after months of wrangling, did town leaders back off so completely from any effort to influence the outcome of Preston's trial? There is good evidence to suggest that they were following the advice of their London correspondents, who had been counseling them for months to ensure a fair trial and gentle treatment for the soldiers. The letters from Barlow Trecothick and Thomas Pownall may have been especially influential. Both men advised James Bowdoin and the other town leaders that if Preston were convicted, it would be wise to intercede on his behalf, protecting him while he awaited word of a royal pardon or even applying for such a pardon on his behalf. Hutchinson reported that Trecothick's letter was "spoke of freely" when it was first received, "but afterwards there seemed to be a desire to have nothing said of it." By the time of the trials Hutchinson believed that leading Bostonians preferred an acquittal or a pardon to a conviction, which would have further provoked Parliament to act against the town.[7]

If town leaders concluded, prior to Preston's trial, that either an acquittal or a pardon would be a desirable outcome, there is no evidence that they therefore favored a weak effort to prosecute him. Nor does it appear that Paine and the elder Quincy took a halfhearted approach. On the contrary, the trial was an exhausting exercise, unprecedented in length, in which the crown's lawyers labored to demonstrate that Preston had ordered his men to fire.[8]

Nevertheless, the prosecution team performed unimpressively. In bringing twenty-three witnesses to the stand, Paine and Quincy appear to have had no clear plan for orchestrating the testimony they solicited or focusing sharply on Preston's actions. (In his closing argument, Paine acknowledged that there was "some little confusion in the evidence," then added that this should "at least destroy the supposition of a preconcerted plan to convict the Prisoner." This is an odd admission, coming from the man whose job it was to concert the prosecution.) None of the first four witnesses addressed the question of whether Preston ordered his men to fire; their role, apparently, was to set the scene. The fifth, Peter Cunningham, recalled that Preston ordered the men to "prime and load," but that he "heard no order given to fire." The seventh witness, William Wyat, was the first to positively affirm that he "heard the officer say fire." Three more — John Cole, Daniel Calfe, and Robert Goddard — said the same thing. Calfe claimed that he "look[e]d the officer in the face when he gave the word," and Goddard testified, "I was so near the officer when he gave the word fire that I could touch him." Some witnesses claimed that they heard Preston order his men to load their muskets, but did not hear him give the order to fire. Benjamin Burdick and Robert Fullerton heard someone give the command to fire, but could not say who.[9]

Perhaps the most important witness for the prosecution was Theodore Bliss. According to the depositions in the *Horrid Massacre,* Bliss was one of three men — the other two were John Hickling and Richard Palmes — standing close enough to Preston to converse with him just before the shooting started. Unfortunately for the prosecution, however, Bliss's testimony was ambivalent at best. After he spoke briefly with Preston, Bliss recalled, several soldiers were pelted with snowballs and one was struck with a three-foot stick. The soldier who was struck "sallied and then fired." "I did not hear any order given by the Capt[ain] to fire—I stood so near him I think I must have heard him if he had given an order to fire before the first firing," Bliss testified. Then, however—after the first shot was fired—Bliss thought perhaps the captain did order the rest of his men to fire. "But [I] do not certainly know," he admitted. "I heard the word fire several times but know not whether it came from the Captain, the Soldiers or the People." Coming from the prosecution's key witness, this was not nearly enough to establish Preston's guilt. In the end, only four of twenty-three witnesses testified that they had heard Preston give the order to fire, while numerous others suggested that the word "fire" was coming from the crowd. The prosecution succeeded primarily in conveying the confusion of the evening, thereby establishing abundant grounds for doubting the testimony even of those witnesses who thought they had heard Preston give the command.[10]

The defense team called twenty-three witnesses of its own. In many respects the content of their testimony was interchangeable with that of the prosecution, but there were key differences. The defense witnesses described an even more chaotic and confusing scene in King Street than the prosecution witnesses generally had. Unsurprisingly, not a single witness for the defense attributed an order to fire to Preston, though two witnesses suggested that another man, walking back and forth behind the soldiers, encouraged them to fire. Several witnesses described Preston's distress once the firing began; according to one account, Preston struck up a soldier's weapon and said, "Fire no more you have done mischief enough." Numerous defense witnesses claimed to be very close to Preston, lending credibility to their recollections.[11]

Strikingly, Preston's lawyers called three African American witnesses to the stand. One of them, a slave named Andrew who was owned by Oliver Wendell, gave the lengthiest testimony of any witness in the trial and introduced several striking details into the narrative.

He is the only witness to recall, for example, that before the conflict with the soldiers came to a head, the crowd began shouting, "Here comes Murray with the Riot Act." This would have been James Murray, the Scots merchant and justice of the peace who had rented his sugar warehouse as a barracks and, in the summer of 1770, proposed marching two hundred soldiers back into town to protect Preston and his men. Had Murray succeeded in reading the Riot Act before the crowd, it would have been obliged by law to disperse, and any subsequent violence on the part of the soldiers would have been justified. But according to Andrew, Murray never had the chance; as he approached, the crowd "turned about & pelted somebody who ran thro' Pudding lane." He implied that this was Murray, being chased off before he could perform his duty.[12]

Andrew also offered a particularly vivid account of the mayhem in King Street. As the soldiers marched from the Main Guard to the Custom House, Andrew recalled, "the men seemed to be in great rage." When they took up their positions alongside the sentry, "the People gave 3 cheers" while "the Boys at Pecks corner kept pelting snowballs over that way." Andrew wanted to get closer, so he "crowded through" the throng. As he reached Royal Exchange, which ran alongside the Custom House, he heard the grenadier nearest the corner say "Damn your blood stand off" as he struggled to keep the crowd at bay. As Andrew told it, "The People without"—that is, those who were not immediately in front of the soldiers—"were crowding in to see" while "those within [were] forcing themselves from the Grenadier who was pushing his Bayonet at 'em." Observing two men talking with Preston—probably Hickling and Palmes—Andrew also testified that people were "jumping upon their backs to hear what was said." In Andrew's telling, the crowd was surging toward the soldiers, yelling, throwing snowballs, and brandishing sticks in an especially chaotic and threatening scene. A voice cried "Fire" just before the first shot, but Andrew was certain it was not Preston's.

"I was looking at the Captain," he testified. "The officer was standing before me with his face towards the people—I am certain the voice came from beyond him."[13]

Theodore Bliss was called back to the stand by the defense; they also called Richard Palmes. (John Hickling, the third man who was supposed to have been talking to Preston just before the shooting started, did not appear at the trial; presumably he was not available.) Bliss was simply asked whether he had given an account of the evening to John Coffin; he confirmed that he had. Coffin then testified that, according to Bliss, when asked whether his men were going to fire, Preston answered, "No by no means." Richard Palmes's testimony cast further doubt on Bliss's reliability as a prosecution witness. As Palmes recalled, Bliss was already talking to Preston when he approached. "I heard him say why don't you fire or words to that effect," Palmes recalled. After Preston's response, Bliss retorted, "God damn you why don't you fire[?]" In this version of events, Bliss was acting to provoke the captain. Palmes then "step'd immediately between them and put my left hand in a familiar manner on the Captain's right shoulder to speak to him." With Hickling alongside him, Palmes asked if the guns were loaded; when Preston said they were, Palmes expressed the hope that he did not intend to fire on the inhabitants. Preston replied, "By no means." This response echoed Coffin's testimony and effectively undermined Bliss's credibility as a prosecution witness.[14]

Preston's acquittal, while certainly just, astonished many observers at a distance, who had assumed that the town would convict him. Dalrymple and Hutchinson each wrote to Gage to pass along the news. "I have the honor & pleasure to enform you that on Tuesday morn Captain Preston was acquitted & discharged on the fullest and most compleat evidence," Dalrymple wrote; "many very shamefull attempts to destroy him by perjury has been made, all which retorted on their authors." Hutchinson added, "I hope the Soldiers will meet with a fair Trial also." The most exuberant account of the acquittal to reach Gage came from Preston himself. "I take the liberty of wishing you joy, of the complete victory obtain[e]d over the knaves & foolish villains of Boston," he wrote exultantly. "The triumph is almost complete, & the Kings servants now appear with double lusture." Preston offered an astute assessment of the lawyers involved. "The Counsel for the Crown or rather the town were but poor and managd badly," he thought; "my Counsel on the contrary were men of parts, & exerted themselves with great spirit & cleverness, particularly Judge Auchmuty."[15]

Preston's trial, which focused on the question of whether he ordered his men to fire, did not entirely solve the puzzle of his actions on the night of March 5. In particular, if he did not order his men to fire, why was he so slow to intercede after the shooting began? Most accounts, both of trial witnesses and of deponents in the *Horrid Massacre,* indicated that there was a notable pause between the first shot and those that followed. Why did Preston not step in immediately and forcefully to stop the shooting before things got entirely out of hand? If he had done so, it would have gone a very long way toward limiting the damage done. The most plausible explanation is that the confrontation in front of the Custom House was so intense and chaotic that a single shot did nothing to calm the crowd or cause people to back off. Even a shot fired into their midst apparently did not discourage townspeople from further provocation.

WHEN THE SOLDIERS' trial came on a month later, this was precisely the scenario their defense team intended to prove. Having exonerated Preston, they had deprived the soldiers of their simplest line of defense: that they were merely following orders when they fired their weapons. Now it became necessary to make a more difficult case; they would have to demonstrate that the chaos in front of the Custom

House was so extreme that the men were forced to fire in self-defense. The prosecution faced difficulties of its own. It had to prove, first, that each of the eight men on trial had been present in front of the Custom House; and second, that each was involved in an act so deliberate that it could be construed as murder. For all the uncertainties that had been aired in Preston's trial, that case was straightforward by comparison.[16]

Both the prosecution and the defense responded to the complex demands of this case by bringing forward a bewildering roster of witnesses. The crown called a total of thirty-four, while the defense team called fifty-one; together, their testimony took five days. It included endless repetition and a suffocating amount of detail. Even the lawyers struggled to keep all the witnesses straight. Nothing illustrates this better than the experience of the prosecution team with the second witness of the day on Wednesday, November 28. After the court heard James Brewer's testimony, Samuel Emmons was called to the stand. When he was asked to identify which of the soldiers he had seen on the night of the shootings, Emmons replied that he could not identify any of them. "I was not in Kingstreet on the night of March 5," he added; "my Brother was."[17]

For Paine and Quincy, this must have been an embarrassing moment. For the judges, jurors, and spectators in the courtroom, it was likely a welcome moment of levity interrupting an otherwise mind-numbing exercise in recitation and interrogation. Two things are especially striking about the eyewitness testimony presented at the soldiers' trial. First, it is remarkable how many of the witnesses, particularly for the defense, did not see what happened in King Street, but testified to activities elsewhere in the town, especially in the vicinity of Dock Square. The second striking thing about the testimony at the soldiers' trial is the large percentage of witnesses who had not been heard from before. Among the thirty-three crown witnesses (not counting Samuel Emmons), eighteen had neither given

785.

THE

T R I A L

OF

William Wemms, James Hartegan, William M'Cauley, Hugh White, Matthew Killroy, William Warren, John Carrol, and Hugh Montgomery,

Soldiers in his Majefty's 29th Regiment of Foot,

FOR THE MURDER OF

Crifpus Attucks, Samuel Gray, Samuel Maverick, James Caldwell, and Patrick Carr,

On MONDAY-EVENING, the 5th of MARCH, 1770,

AT THE

Superior Court of Judicature, Court of Affize, and general Goal Delivery, held at BOSTON. The 27th Day of *November,* 1770, by Adjournment.

BEFORE

The Hon. BENJAMIN LYNDE, JOHN CUSHING, PETER O-LIVER, and EDMUND TROWBRIDGE, ESQUIRES, JUS-TICES of faid COURT.

Publifhed by Permiffion of the COURT.

Taken in SHORT-HAND by JOHN HODGSON.

B O S T O N :

Printed by J. FLEEMING, and fold at his PRINTING-OFFICE, nearly oppofite the *White-horfe* Tavern in *Newbury-ftreet.*

M,DCC,LXX.

Il vid. pa. 60.

John Hodgson took shorthand notes of the soldiers' trial, which were compiled and printed by John Fleeming shortly afterward. Though John Adams and Richard Palmes (a witness at the trial) both complained that the transcript was inaccurate, Hodgson's account provides the best trial narrative available.

a deposition for one of the pamphlets nor testified at Preston's trial. Among the fifty-one witnesses for the defense, thirty-seven offered formal accounts of their recollections for the first time.[18]

One reason for the prosecution to call new witnesses was the need to identify the soldiers on trial: Hugh White, the Custom House sentinel that night; William Wemms, the corporal who led the party from the guard house; and privates John Carrol, James Hartegan, Matthew Kilroy, William McCauley, Hugh Montgomery, and William Warren. Thirteen of the prosecution witnesses testified that they knew one or more of the soldiers and had seen them at the Custom House; eight of these thirteen had appeared neither in the pamphlets nor at Preston's trial. Most of the prosecution witnesses focused on the events that took place in King Street, though a large minority — twelve — described events elsewhere that bore, more or less directly, on the shootings.[19]

As lawyers for the soldiers' defense, Adams and Quincy (Auchmuty chose not to act as counsel in this second trial) called dozens of witnesses to the stand, many of whom had not been in King Street when the shots were fired. The first twenty-two witnesses testified primarily about events nearby in the hour or so leading up to the King Street shootings, especially in Dock Square and Boylston's Alley, where townspeople and soldiers had a menacing row. Patrick Keaton and William Davis each estimated that about two hundred people had gathered in Dock Square. William Carter then described "numbers passing in haste" toward King Street, "all with either Clubs Swords, Cutlasses or Guns." Not until the fifteenth witness did anyone describe the shootings, and not until the twenty-third did the focus of testimony shift to the events in front of the Custom House. Nathaniel Russell and William Botson testified that there were about two hundred people in King Street at the time of the shootings. Eyewitness accounts varied widely in their details. Most witnesses emphasized that the soldiers were pelted hard with snow and ice and struck with sticks before they fired, but Patrick Keaton testified that he saw nothing of the sort. As he did in Preston's trial, Andrew, the slave owned by Oliver Wendell, gave an extended, vivid account of his recollections.[20]

While the parade of witnesses must have been tiresome, the defense strategy worked. Though the testimony varied in countless details, its cumulative effect was to demonstrate beyond doubt that the streets of Boston were filled with men and boys, many of them armed with sticks and cudgels, spoiling for a fight. This was ultimately more important to the case they hoped to make than was a detailed account of what transpired immediately in front of the soldiers just before the shooting started. It enabled Quincy, in his opening remarks, and Adams, in his closing argument, to stress that the soldiers felt endangered and fired in self-defense. Quincy asked the jurors to put themselves in the soldiers' shoes. "The soldier had his feelings, his sentiments, and his characteristick passions also," he noted. Stationed in Boston, where they became symbols of imperial tyranny, the soldiers were unable to control their relations with the townspeople. "How stinging was it to be stigmatized, as the instrument of tyranny and oppression?" he asked. But, Quincy added, Boston could not be faulted for the violence either. "The inhabitants of *Boston,* by no rules of law, justice or common sense, can be supposed answerable for the unjustifiable conduct of a few individuals hastily assembled in the streets," he stressed. "Every populous city, in like circumstances, would be liable to similar commotions, if not worse." It was not Boston's judicious and reputable citizens, but "a mixt and ungovernable multitude," that had initiated the violence on March 5.[21]

Adams was even more resolute about protecting Boston's reputation, to such an extent that it threatened to compromise his effectiveness as a lawyer for the defense. His colleague Quincy had proposed to pile up evidence against the town "to prove a premeditated design to drive out the Soldiers" and detail the "frequent abuse as well as

threats" to which the soldiers were subjected. Adams objected strenu-
ously to this line of defense. If Quincy intended to "go on with such
Witnesses who only served to set the Town in a bad light," Adams
threatened to "leave the cause & not say a word more." Quincy
relented, and "many witnesses were not brought who otherwise would
have been." Adams was advocating a precarious approach to the
soldiers' defense: by insisting that he and Quincy limit any possible
damage to the town's reputation, he was also undermining the foundation of their clients' case. Having won the argument, Adams abandoned
his threat and remained on the defense team for the duration of the
trial. But, as Zobel has suggested, the price of his acquiescence was
something approaching professional malfeasance on the part of the
lawyers for the defense.[22]

In his closing argument, Adams had to face this problem squarely.
On the one hand, it was crucial for him to stress that the soldiers
faced a mortal threat prior to the shootings. Rising to a crescendo,
he vividly invoked the scene. With

> the people crying Kill them! Kill them! Knock them over! heaving
> snow-balls, oyster shells, clubs, white birch sticks three inches and
> an half diameter, consider yourselves in this situation, and then
> judge, whether a reasonable man in the soldiers situation, would
> not have concluded they were going to kill him. . . . The law does
> not oblige us to bear insults to the danger of our lives, to stand
> still with such a number of people around us, throwing such things
> at us, and threatening our lives, until we are disabled to defend
> ourselves.[23]

This dimension of the defense argument was essential to the soldiers'
cause, but it cast Boston in a distinctly unfavorable light. In his opening
argument, Quincy stressed that Boston could not be held responsible
for the "unjustifiable conduct of a few individuals hastily assembled

in the streets," but in the wake of abundant testimony suggesting that hundreds of people were involved, and that townspeople were massed in the streets through much of the evening, this dismissive approach, which sought to minimize the crowd's significance, was clearly inadequate.

Rather than minimizing the size and significance of the crowd, Adams amplified its menace. But he also made a point of distancing the participants in the mob from the town of Boston as a corporate entity. He repeatedly stressed that the people in the streets were not moderate, responsible citizens, but an indiscriminately mixed group full of outlandish characters who were prone to behave irresponsibly and violently. "Many of these people were thoughtless and inconsiderate," Adams argued, "old and young, sailors and landmen, negroes and molattos."[24] This last point was especially important. It may have been in part to emphasize to the jury the involvement of African Americans in the King Street affray that the defense team chose to rely so prominently on the recollections of Oliver Wendell's slave, Andrew.

Just as Andrew had offered the most vivid testimony in Preston's trial, so, in the trial of the soldiers, he supplied a telling detail that Adams would use to great effect. The testimony of numerous witnesses had placed Bliss, Palmes, and Hickling at the front of the crowd, talking to Preston; and several thought that someone had struck a soldier's gun before the firing started. But Andrew remembered a more intense and prolonged struggle. "I saw two or three of them hit," he testified; "one struck a Grenadier on the hat, and the people who were right before them had sticks; and as the soldiers were pushing with their guns back and forth, they struck their guns, and one hit a Grenadier on the fingers." But all this was only a prelude to the most dramatic moment of confrontation. "A stout man with a long cord wood stick" pushed his way through and "made a blow" at Captain Preston. Next he turned to a grenadier "and knocked his gun away, and struck him over the head." Then he grabbed the soldier's bayonet in his left hand "and twitched it and cried kill the dogs, knock them over." As the crowd surged in, the soldier pulled his gun out of the stout man's hand. Andrew recalled that he "heard the word fire," followed by "the report of a gun." Then the grenadier who had freed his bayonet fired, and the stout man fell. When asked if he could identify the stout man, Andrew replied, "I thought, and still think, it was the Molatto who was shot."[25]

No other eyewitness placed Crispus Attucks at the front of the crowd, and no other witness described a scene as chaotic and threatening as Andrew did. No one else recalled a man grabbing hold of a bayonet and tugging at a musket. One witness — Ebenezer Bridgham — explicitly testified that no one had grabbed a gun; when he was asked about Attucks, Bridgham did not recall seeing him in King Street. James Bailey and Patrick Keaton saw Attucks, with a cordwood stick in his hand, at the head of a crowd of twenty or thirty sailors, but they were heading up Cornhill from Dock Square; neither saw the group in King Street. Three witnesses did remember seeing Attucks in the King Street crowd. James Brewer saw Attucks standing "by the gutter" and watched him fall, but did not hear him say anything and did not observe that he held a stick. John Danbrook testified that Attucks was standing a short distance from the soldiers, leaning on a long staff; Nathaniel Russell remembered standing behind Attucks, looking over his shoulder at Preston and his men. Surveying the eyewitness testimony, Robert Treat Paine singled Andrew out for skeptical treatment. His account, Paine said, "is very curious, he tells you he saw a stout Fellow run down ye street, make his way thro' ye People & rush upon ye Soldiers; a fact which, unless all ye other Witnesses were stone-blind, or deprived of their senses, never had existence but in his own brain."[26]

Adams, however, chose to amplify Andrew's testimony to highlight the outlandish character of the crowd attacking the soldiers. Attucks's ancestry — his father was an African American slave and his mother a

Wampanoag Indian — would later enable African Americans to claim him as an honored link to the origins of the American Revolution, but in 1770 it allowed Adams to achieve something like the opposite effect. As a black man who was also a sailor, Attucks was doubly an outsider to Boston. By foregrounding his involvement, Adams could create distance between the property-holding citizens of Boston and the large, menacing, dark-skinned, club-wielding figure who led the attack.

Who, Adams asked, was responsible for the mayhem in the streets and the threats directed against the soldiers? He emphasized that it was not Boston — not the community as a corporate entity — but a mob that was to blame. Adams contended that many people hesitated to make this claim, but he was not afraid to call a violent rabble by its proper name. "We have been entertained with a great variety of phrases, to avoid calling this sort of people a mob. — Some call them shavers, some call them genius's." They could be dismissed neither as harmless children ("shavers") nor — as the term "genius" presumably implied — as thoughtful citizens acting on sound political principles: "The plain English is gentlemen, most probably a motley rabble of saucy boys, negroes and molattoes, Irish teagues and out landish jack tarrs. — And why we should scruple to call such a set of people a mob, I can't conceive, unless the name is too respectable for them."[27] This famous phrase — "a motley rabble of saucy boys, negroes and molattoes, Irish teagues and out landish jack tarrs" — is Adams's own, but it captures a widely held understanding of Boston's composition. In Adams's eyes, Boston's property holders were a respectable, solid citizenry who together constituted the town as a political body. As in any seaport, Boston also had its floating underclass: literally floating in and out of the town as they joined ships' crews and went to sea, then returned to labor on the docks or in the ropewalks while they waited for another opportunity to ship out. Although they supplied much of the port town's muscle power, they were not members of the community. But in a moment of crisis, they were especially likely to come to the fore and coalesce as a mob, giving violent form to the town's grievances. This was exactly what happened, in Adams's view, on March 5.

At the head of the mob was Attucks. James Bailey had seen "the Molatto seven or eight minutes before the firing, at the head of twenty or thirty sailors in *Cornhill,* and he had a large cordwood stick." "*Attucks* with his myrmidons," all wielding clubs, marched into King Street. "If this was not an unlawful assembly, there never was one in the world." They approached the soldiers formed up at the Custom House. When the soldiers tried to push the crowd away, "this man with his party cried, do not be afraid of them, they dare not fire, kill them! kill them! knock them over! And he tried to knock their brains out." With "this reinforcement coming down under the command of a stout Molatto fellow, whose very looks, was enough to terrify any person, what had not the soldiers then to fear? He had hardiness enough to fall in upon them, and with one hand took hold of a bayonet, and with the other knocked the man down." Seizing on Andrew's dramatic account and eliding the many complications and contradictions that had been introduced by various witnesses, Adams blamed all the night's aggression on Attucks alone, "to whose mad behaviour in all probability, the dreadful carnage of that night, is chiefly to be ascribed."[28]

Swerving momentarily from the task at hand, Adams paused in his defense of the soldiers to defend, instead, the reputation of Boston. "And it is in this manner, this town has often been treated," he noted; "a *Carr* from *Ireland,* and an *Attucks* from *Framingham,* happening to be here, shall sally out upon their thoughtless enterprizes, at the head of such a rabble of Negroes, &c. as they can collect together, and then there are not wanting, persons to ascribe all their doings to the good people of the town."[29]

By distinguishing between the town and the mob that happened to take shape within it, Adams challenged the view of crown officers like Gage and Bernard, who often explicitly equated Boston with the mob, viewing them as identical in both intent and action. They played up the roles of men like William Molineux and Samuel Adams in energizing the mob and contended that it did the town's will. Hutchinson, the native Bostonian, was slow to embrace this jaundiced view of his hometown, but in the wake of the King Street shootings he, too, endorsed it. "You used to tell me my regard for the Town made me too tender of its Interest to the damage of the publick Interest," Hutchinson wrote to Bernard in late March. "I cannot help an attachment to the place of my birth and I have some personal interest 140 or 50 pounds sterling annual rent besides the House I live in," he admitted, "but I would now give up all if the town could be separated from the rest of the province." He wished to be done with Boston. When he complained that nonvoters were overrunning the town meeting, he ended by remarking: "It is in other words being under the government of the Mob."

> This has given the lower sort of people such a sense of their Importance that a Gentleman does not meet with what used to be called common civility and we are sinking into perfect barbarism. The Province will certainly remain in this state until Parliament pass such Acts as shall when executed take away this influence of the Town.[30]

In distancing Boston's mob from Boston itself, Adams directly challenged the view held by Bernard, Gage, and — now — also Hutchinson. Adams was especially intent to discredit this view in London, where he knew his closing argument would be carefully read. Like the trial of Preston, the soldiers' trial was in large part a battle for public opinion, and Adams was mindful of the need to defend Boston in that fight. In doing so, Adams was employing a time-honored trope. After the Knowles impressment riot in 1747, for example, the town meeting claimed the fruits of the crowd action while disavowing the crowd itself. "The generality of the inhabitants" were not involved, it wrote in a subsequent message to the crown (despite the fact that several thousand people had participated); instead, "the said Riotous Tumultuous Assembly consisted of Foreign Seamen, Servants Negroes and other Persons of mean and Vile Condition."[31] It is possible that Adams was aware of the response to the Knowles riot, but it is more likely that he arrived independently at the same rhetorical device that had served the town well twenty-three years earlier. Adams's formulation exactly described the way that the respectable inhabitants of an eighteenth-century town viewed the proceedings of a mob acting in the community's interest. The mob itself could not be legitimized; it had to be disavowed. But the ministry—by taking the ill-advised step of stationing soldiers in town—could be blamed for causing the mob to form, while the deadly result of its clash with the soldiers could be viewed as a predictable outcome of that misguided policy.

Adams argued that mobs were uncommon in Boston, though they were familiar enough elsewhere. "The sun is not about to stand still or go out, nor the rivers to dry up because there was a mob in *Boston* on the 5th of *March* that attacked a party of soldiers," he noted acerbically. "Such things are not new in the world, nor in the British dominions, though they are comparatively, rarities and novelties in this town." Mob violence, he implied, was an exotic import to the normally calm town of Boston. "[Patrick] *Carr* a native of *Ireland* had often been concerned in such attacks, and indeed, from the nature of things, soldiers quartered in a populous town, will always occasion two mobs, where they prevent one.—They are wretched conservators of the peace!"[32]

Adams implied that Carr, like Attucks, was drawn by natural predisposition toward mobbish violence. The Irishman, like the mulatto, was prone to aggressive tactics; moreover, the long-standing presence of troops in peacetime had given Irishmen like Carr ample training in such affrays. Among the five victims, these two were presumed to have been provocateurs. Ropemaker Samuel Gray was doing nothing to provoke an attack when he was shot, although testimony suggested that Kilroy may have targeted him in vengeance for Gray's involvement in the ropewalk fray a few days earlier. The last two victims—Samuel Maverick, the seventeen-year-old apprentice ivory turner, son of a widow who ran a North End boardinghouse, and James Caldwell, a younger sailor who had ambitions to become a navigator—were unfortunate bystanders. As young as they were, they were exemplars of the many boys and apprentices drawn to King Street that night. Guilty only of their youthful high spirits, they did nothing to provoke the tragic fate that befell them.

The jury returned its verdict in two and a half hours. It convicted the two men whose shots most certainly felled victims—Hugh Montgomery and Matthew Kilroy—of manslaughter. The evidence suggested that one soldier did not fire, while another man shot and missed. "It is highly probable, from the places where the five persons killed fell and their wounds," as Justice Edmund Trowbridge put it in summarizing the case for the jury, "that they were killed by the discharge of five several guns only." After accounting for Montgomery's shot, which was believed to have killed Attucks, and Kilroy's, which likely killed Gray, "it will thence follow that the other three, were killed, not by the other six prisoners, but by three of them only: and therefore they cannot all be found guilty of it." On the strength of this argument, six of the eight were acquitted and discharged; they "immediately went to the Castle." Montgomery and Kilroy went back to their cell; nine days later, they returned to court for sentencing. The normal sentence for a manslaughter conviction was death, but by the eighteenth century it had become common practice to allow first-time offenders to plead the benefit of clergy and receive clemency. To ensure that Montgomery and Kilroy would not get the same consideration again, they were branded on the thumb. They were then set free and, like the other six defendants, shipped to New Jersey to rejoin their regiment.[33]

ON DECEMBER 12, a week after the conclusion of the soldiers' trial, the four civilians indicted for shooting out of a second-floor window in the Custom House — Manwaring, Monroe, Green, and Greenwood — entered the courtroom on Queen Street to be tried for murder. They were indicted based on the testimony of Charles Bourgatte, Manwaring's fourteen-year-old servant. Bourgatte's deposition in the *Horrid Massacre* describes a curious scene. He reported that, on the evening of March 5, his master left his lodgings in the North End with John Monroe to "go to the Custom-house and drink a glass of wine," leaving Bourgatte on his own. Half an hour later, bells began to ring; Bourgatte assumed they were signaling a fire and set out to investigate. He went to the Custom House and knocked on the door; Hammond Green answered it. Bourgatte saw Manwaring and Monroe go into a room on the first floor together, while another group of four or five men went upstairs, "pulling and hauling me after them." They entered a second-floor room in which there were two muskets and "a number of gentlemen."[34]

According to Bourgatte's deposition, a tall man loaded one of the guns, handed it to the servant boy, and told him to fire it out the window, threatening that if he did not do so the man would run his sword "through my guts." Bourgatte stepped up to the window and "fired [the gun] side way up the street." The gentleman reloaded the gun and again insisted that Bourgatte fire it out the window. The boy resisted, then fired "the same way up the street." By now, Manwaring had joined the group in the second-floor room. He took up a gun and pointed it out the window; Bourgatte reported that he "heard the gun go off." The tall man patted the boy on the shoulder and promised to give him some money. Then Hammond Green led Bourgatte back out the Custom House door; the latter returned to his lodgings, where he "sat up all night in my master's kitchen."[35]

Bourgatte related his story to a North End neighbor named Mrs. Waldron. Recognizing its significance, she visited justice of the peace Edmund Quincy and swore to what she had heard. On the strength of Bourgatte's claims, the four men were arrested and joined the nine soldiers in the Boston jail. But Bourgatte's reliability immediately came into question. The boy claimed that Manwaring had "licked him" for telling his story to Mrs. Waldron. This caused Bourgatte to waver. "And for fear that I should be licked again, I did deny all that I said before Justice Quincy, which I am very sorry for." Having recanted, he was jailed for "prophane swearing," and Manwaring and the others were set free.[36]

Soon, though, Bourgatte reaffirmed his original testimony. His change of heart came after William Molineux and Mrs. Waldron visited him; what transpired between them was the subject of considerable controversy. Molineux claimed that his intentions were those of a "good citizen, being anxious, if there was any truth in what the boy had related, that it might be brought to light." He said that he spoke with Bourgatte in the parlor of jailkeeper Joseph Otis's home, in the company of Otis and his wife Marcy, a young servant woman named Bathsheba Hyland, and two men named Lindsey George Wallis and Thomas Chase. In later depositions, those witnesses maintained that Molineux insisted on not being alone with the boy, and repeatedly pressed Bourgatte to "declare nothing but the truth." Molineux and the others reported that the boy reaffirmed his original version of events and swore to it again before the justice of the peace.[37]

When a grand jury convened in the week following the shootings, it repeatedly examined witnesses who had been in the Custom House. In the end, it decided to indict the four civilians who now came to trial. Once the accused were brought before the bar, however, the testimony was sufficiently contradictory and confused that the jury acquitted them, as Samuel Quincy wrote, "without going from their Seats."[38]

As a matter of law, that was certainly the most defensible outcome. But the story of the Custom House remains puzzling. If Manwaring had nothing to do with the shootings, why would his fourteen-year-old servant claim that he did? Detractors argued that Molineux had threatened the boy with the wrath of the Boston mob if he didn't testify against his master, while James Penny, a debtor who shared a cell with Bourgatte, reported that Mrs. Waldron had promised the boy gingerbread and cheese if he swore against Manwaring.[39] Perhaps Bourgatte was unhappy in his service, and saw false testimony as a way to escape it. If so, he miscalculated badly, because Manwaring went free, whereas he was tried and convicted of perjury for his efforts.

The weakness of the case against Manwaring and the others at trial has obscured some good reasons to take seriously the possibility that shots were fired from the Custom House window. The most compelling reason is the simplest: an inventory of bullets reveals a puzzling surplus. Eight soldiers were tried for the shootings. Some eyewitnesses said that they reloaded after discharging their muskets, but no one suggested that any of them fired more than once. Moreover, at their trial the most reliable testimony suggested that one of the eight never fired his musket, while another missed his target. Five people were killed by bullets, and two of them — Crispus Attucks and James Caldwell — were struck twice; six more were wounded. Three bullets were dug out of walls across the street. This makes a total of sixteen strike points. The same bullet that passed through Edward Payne's arm also lodged in the doorpost behind him, accounting for two strike points. The other two balls dug out of the wall appear to have missed any human targets, however. This leaves either four bullets (assuming that one musket was not discharged) or five to account for twelve additional strike points. While at least one or two bullets probably struck more than one victim, the likelihood that seven or eight bullets could have done all the damage is vanishingly small.

It is possible that the soldiers double-loaded their muskets; this was a street-firing technique intended to maximize firepower. The coroner's report on Crispus Attucks notes that he was killed by "a Musket or Muskets loaded with Bullets," which suggests the possibility of a single gun with more than one ball, but no one — in the pamphlets, depositions, trial testimony, or lawyers' arguments — ever explicitly contended that the muskets were double-loaded. Moreover, it was not a soldier's practice simply to jam two cartridges containing .69-caliber balls down the barrel of his musket; doing so might have caused the weapon to misfire or its breech to explode. The normal procedure was, instead, to load "buck and ball": a single .69-caliber ball with several buckshot pellets loaded behind it. These would be packed together into a paper cartridge, along with the black powder that would give them their charge. If Preston's men had loaded buck and ball, their muskets would certainly have pumped more lead into King Street than they would otherwise have done, but the effects of their firing would have been distinctive and recognizably different. In addition to the fearsome wounds inflicted by .69-caliber balls, the buckshot would have caused a larger number of smaller injuries. None of the damage in King Street that night can be attributed to smaller buckshot pellets.[40]

Though the trial of the four civilians revolved around the improbable testimony of Charles Bourgatte, he was not the only source of the claim that shots came from the Custom House. In the depositions appended to the *Horrid Massacre,* seven other witnesses said they, too, saw shots fired from a Custom House window. Jeremiah Allen recalled that he was at Colonel Ingersoll's house on King Street with William Molineux and John Simpson when he heard gunshots outside. He went out onto the balcony in time to witness four or five more shots fired in the street, and then two or three more that he saw come from a window of the Custom House—a fact upon which he remarked to Molineux and Simpson. George Costar, a Newfoundland mariner, claimed that he was standing in front of the Custom House when he heard shots fired overhead; then, "being but a small distance from the window, he heard the people from within speak and laugh, and soon after he saw the casement lowered down." Gillam Bass, Francis Read, Benjamin Frizel, Samuel Drowne, and Cato, a slave owned by Tuthil Hubbart, all reported that they saw shots fired from the Custom House window.[41]

There are two possibilities. One is that all these witnesses were wrong. If that is the case, then the further question is, were they mistaken or did they lie? It is difficult to see how they could have made the mistake honestly. Bourgatte's testimony was reported in the March 12 *Boston Gazette* account, and was likely to have been the subject of rumors in town within a day or two of the shootings, so it is possible that other witnesses heard his version of events and developed a "false-memory illusion" by vividly imagining the shots.[42] But the recollections of Jeremiah Allen and George Costar, in particular, seem too specific, too unique to their own circumstances at the time of the shooting, to be persuasively explained as a false memory. If these witnesses' claims were false, it is much more likely that they were intentionally fabricated. And if that is the case, it is worth asking what other elements of the eyewitness accounts might have been fabricated as well. If one were to argue that the depositions in the *Horrid Massacre* contained extensive, and perhaps systematic, falsification, the claim that shots were fired from the Custom House would go a long way in helping to make the case.

The other possibility is that shots were, indeed, fired from the Custom House. It seems wildly improbable that as a chaotic scene unfolded on the street, customs employees and their friends would have loaded muskets with powder and ball, flung up a second-story window, and begun to take potshots into the crowd. But it is not impossible. More than sixty years ago, the historian Oliver M. Dickerson argued that they did just that. He noted that the customs officials and soldiers in Boston were natural allies, and argued that townspeople's perception of a conspiracy against their liberties and interests was largely accurate. Customs employee Ebenezer Richardson had shot into a crowd in front of his house and killed twelve-year-old Christopher Seider less than two weeks earlier, a key source of tension in the days leading up to the King Street shootings. On the night of March 5, numerous people were coming and going from the Custom House, and arms were likely to have been present in the building. When the crowd began harassing the sentry outside, Thomas Greenwood, a servant of the customs commissioners, sent word to the Main Guard that the sentry was in trouble. Then, after the shots were fired into the crowd, Greenwood went immediately to the home of William Burch, where he reported on the event to customs commissioners Burch and Charles Paxton and board secretary Richard Reeve. Instead of lending aid to the investigation, Dickerson notes that the commissioners evaded the town's effort to collect affidavits while they gathered their own separate accounts; soon those commissioners who might be suspected of complicity had left town altogether, preferring to operate beyond the jurisdiction of Boston's courts.[43]

All of this is circumstantial, but it highlights the polarized character of the town and reinforces the point that the customs officials in Boston felt as embattled as the soldiers did. The sense that they were engaged in common cause with the soldiers could have created a bond of obligation and mutual loyalty that made the decision to fire out the windows of the Custom House less unthinkable in the heat of the moment than it now seems. Observing the beleaguered sentry trying to stand his ground and watching Preston's small detachment take up its position, it might have been tempting for customs employees inside the building to open a window and load their own muskets as they watched the violent confrontation unfold.

As an outsider to Boston, perhaps Edward Manwaring was especially inclined to take up arms in defense of the Custom House. Appointed to serve as a landwaiter and searcher in Quebec when the customs service began operating there in 1762, he was subsequently assigned the task of erecting a new Custom House in the port of Gaspé, a tiny settlement on a peninsula near the mouth of the St. Lawrence River. Then, after the creation of the American Customs Commission in 1767, Manwaring was appointed as a tide surveyor in Boston, where he was charged with "establishing such Regulations in the Port, for the Improvement of the Revenue there, as from [Manwaring's] long Experience and acknowledged Abilities might be expected." He had been in town ever since, a hated symbol — along with the customs commissioners themselves — of imperial intrusions in the local economy. As Manwaring put it, "for his Zeal and Activity in the above Service," he "became obnoxious to the People of Boston."[44]

But while Manwaring's "Zeal and Activity" might explain his motive for taking up arms in the Custom House, it is equally persuasive as an explanation for why William Molineux might have solicited a false accusation from his servant. Manwaring argued that Boston's leaders, "the more effectually to ruin his constant Efforts to serve the Revenue, had him Three times apprehended, and at last committed to Prison for supposed Murder at the Riot in Captain Preston's Affair."[45] While Green and Greenwood acknowledged they were in the Custom House on March 5, no witness except Bourgatte placed Manwaring and Monroe there. Even if it were regarded as reliable, Bourgatte's testimony describes a nonsensical scene. Who was in the room that night, and why? If their aim was to assist the troops, would they have insisted that the fourteen-year-old servant boy fire two of the three shots taken? Moreover, Bourgatte claimed that he intentionally fired away from the crowd; unless his bullets ricocheted wildly, they would not have accounted for any of the damage in front of the

Custom House. A commonsense assessment of Bourgatte's story makes it too implausible to be seriously considered.

And yet—there is the inventory of bullets. There is one other possibility worth considering. Eight soldiers were arrested, along with Preston, for their involvement in the shootings. One, Hugh White, was serving as a sentry in front of the Custom House; Preston allegedly led seven others from the Main Guard to join him. But were these the only soldiers involved? Most eyewitnesses recalled that only six or seven soldiers marched from the Main Guard to the Custom House, but Robert Goddard said there were eight or nine, William Wyat remembered eight or ten, and Ebenezer Bridgham thought there were twelve. Preston himself, in his first account of the affair, wrote that he deployed Corporal Wemms and twelve privates to go to White's aid—which would have put fourteen soldiers in front of the Custom House, with Preston alongside them. Perhaps there were that many, but when the accused were hastily rounded up on the morning of March 6, only some were identified. And perhaps, once fewer men were jailed and indicted, eyewitness recollections were influenced in turn; in giving their testimony, witnesses may have affirmed what was commonly known rather than what they actually remembered. This explanation still does nothing to unravel the puzzle of the Custom House testimony, but it could explain the surplus of bullets.[46]

One final complicating factor in assessing all the eyewitness testimony is rarely mentioned, but deserves at least passing consideration. The shootings took place at night. All the commotion in Dock Square and King Street unfolded in the dim light and deep shadows of a March evening, lit only by a quarter moon and the reflective qualities of snow-covered streets. Yet only one witness described the way that the darkness affected his perceptions. Thomas Marshall recalled that he watched a party of soldiers near the head of Quaker Lane, but "the shade of the moon light hindered me to see if they went down *Royal-exchange-lane* or went up towards the *Town-house.*" A short time later he observed Preston and his party leave the Main Guard to relieve the Custom House sentry. But "they passed out of the moon light into the dark, so that I could not see them, but I wondered to find them tarry so long."[47] Why was Marshall the only witness to note that darkness obscured his perceptions, and why does the rest of the eyewitness testimony read as if the entire episode unfolded in broad daylight?

In the end, it may not matter all that much what actually happened. But it is worth lingering on these puzzles, if only to highlight the radical uncertainty that inheres in all of our accounts of the Boston Massacre. The courtroom proceedings created a consensus view, both of what happened and who was to blame. The eyewitness accounts agree in so many ways that it is tempting to smooth out their rough edges and blend them together into a seamless narrative, ignoring contradictions and anomalies. After all, it is not surprising that memories were faulty: King Street was lit only by a quarter moon reflecting off the snow; the scene at the Custom House was chaotic; the musket fire created the kind of jarring shock that could scramble observers' recollections.

But there was more at work in these accounts than imperfect memories. Some witnesses were very probably lying. For example, the likelihood that men fired from a Custom House window is small: if so, surely more people in the street would have been aware of it. It is also exceedingly unlikely that witnesses developed a false memory of such shots after the fact; it is much more plausible that the eight witnesses who described shots being fired from the Custom House window had chosen to fabricate their testimony. And if that is the case, they almost certainly did so to support Molineux's effort to implicate Manwaring. If townspeople were willing to lie about this key detail to support Bourgatte's testimony, no matter how implausible his tale appeared to be, then what other lies were they willing to tell?

The same question can just as easily be asked of the soldiers whose depositions accompanied the *Unhappy Disturbance,* who had a much stronger incentive to cast their actions in the most favorable light than they did to tell the truth.

The shootings created a flash point around which it was necessary to generate a narrative web. No party to that process was disinterested: everyone had a motive to suppress details, to bend the facts, or simply to lie in order to impart a desired shape to that narrative. What happened, and what people subsequently said had happened, were two quite different things.

WHATEVER LIES were told about the events of March 5, only one witness was tried, sentenced, and punished for doing so under oath. After the acquittal of the four civilians, Edward Manwaring pressed a perjury charge against Charles Bourgatte, the fourteen-year-old servant boy who had apparently betrayed him. The boy was bound over for trial in March 1771 and found guilty; on March 20 he was sentenced to spend an hour in the pillory, receive twenty-five lashes, and pay court costs. The first time he was led to the whipping post — which stood in King Street, near the building that had served as the Main Guard for the troops while they were in town — Bourgatte's lashes were postponed because a "riotous Multitude" intervened on his behalf to protest his punishment. The delay was temporary, however; the sentence was carried out on March 29, and then the young Bourgatte was transported out of the colony.[48]

By that time the first anniversary of the King Street shootings had passed. Though the trials had unspooled over an extraordinarily long period of time, the legacies of the Boston Massacre were still only beginning to take their shape.

CHAPTER 9

Contested Meanings

B EGINNING ON FRIDAY NIGHT, October 19, 1770, and continuing through Saturday — four days before the beginning of Captain Preston's trial — a massive nor'easter rolled across the New
England coast and lashed Boston Harbor. A "violent Storm of Wind
and Rain," it was the most severe Boston had experienced in many
years. High tide, which came around noon, was "the highest . . . that
has been known at this Place for near 50 Years past." Warehouses,
cellars, and stores were inundated "in all Parts of the Town," resulting
in the "Loss of Sugars, Salt, and other Articles." The wind and
waves also swept away several thousand cords of wood, along with
"Boards, Staves, and Shingles, &c from different Parts of the Town."
Wharves were carried off. The town of Boston "became one Island,
the waters having made a junction across the Neck, which is entirely
embarrassed with Timber, Fences Boats &c." Water flowed in King
Street as high as the British Coffee House; "in many other streets
the Communication was by Boats." Several houses and barns lost
their roofs, "and sundry Stores in Town were carried off and removed
by the Current." A fisherman in South Boston fell overboard and
drowned while he was attempting to secure his boat. In the harbor,
forty merchant ships were damaged and sixteen more men drowned.
Sixteen or seventeen vessels were "cast ashore" on the flats in

Braintree Bay and on various islands, and several captains were obliged to cut away their masts. A schooner washed ashore on Deer Island "without any Person on board, supposed to have drifted from Lynn or Marblehead." In nearby Plymouth, nearly sixty vessels were driven ashore "and 40 or 50 Lives lost." In Boston alone, the damages were estimated at £50,000.[1]

On Castle Island, Captain John Montresor surveyed the destruction. Gage's most accomplished engineer had recently returned to the island on the general's orders. In 1768 Montresor had been present to facilitate a possible invasion of Boston; now, his assignment was to ensure that the barracks were sufficient to house the 14th Regiment. Montresor had undertaken a survey of the island's defenses and accommodations. The engineer's ambitions were, as usual, at war with the general's desire for economy, and the two had been wrangling for some weeks about the appropriate extent of modifications and new construction on the island. The storm rendered their earlier correspondence largely moot. "The height of Water," Montresor reported, "was four feet higher than any Spring tide known these last 50 years." The island's wharf was broken up, the barracks took on sixteen inches of water and had to be evacuated, and several sentry boxes were carried off. The barrack-master lost more than sixty cords of firewood. All kinds of construction materials were lost. "Most of our squared timber & frame work[,] four thousand Pallisades ready squared and pointed, three thousand Boards of pine besides a thousand Plank, . . . Pickets & Brush, and the store near the water side with 50 H[ogs]h[ea]ds of Lime fill'd with the sea, and several lighters of sand washed away." The storm brought a special misfortune to Montresor himself. "The Stack of Chimneys belonging to my Room in the Castle [was] blown down directly into the body of the Room," he wrote, "demolishing most of my Books & Papers together with my Bedstead, Bedding, Instruments, and part of my Cloaths and a Fusil."[2]

In the wake of the storm, Montresor had his work cut out for him. He remained on Castle Island for two more months, rebuilding the crown's foothold in Boston Harbor; in the years to come, he returned to the island repeatedly, shoring up its decaying defenses. Soldiers no longer occupied barracks or rented rooms in the streets and alleyways of Boston, but they were close at hand: on Castle Island, first the 14th Regiment and then the 64th continued to keep watch over the city. Boston merchants continued to supply the troops, and Boston carpenters, masons, watermen, and laborers assisted Montresor in his work. After years of service to the province, the fort was now firmly under the control of the crown. It was doubly useful as a base of operations, since its gaze turned both inward, toward Britain's most troublesome North American port town, and outward, toward the hostile spaces of the Atlantic world. In the fall of 1770, the soldiers on Castle Island and the townspeople of Boston had little idea where the future would take them. For the moment, they were two islands caught in a single storm: its dimensions unclear, its duration indefinite, its costs as yet unknown.

IN THE FIRST YEAR AFTER THE shootings in King Street, their meaning and legacy were contested and uncertain. The courtroom resolution appeared paramount, both to townspeople and to crown officials: acquittal of the soldiers would imply condemnation of Boston as a mobbish town; convictions and death sentences would vindicate Boston as a community victimized by unnecessary aggression. Although town leaders had resisted the temptation to pack the jury, and many of them apparently agreed with Barlow Trecothick and Thomas Pownall that a pardon carried off without a lynching — or even the peaceful acceptance of an acquittal — would help Boston's reputation in London, feelings continued to run high through the trial. Samuel Adams, for one, remained passionate in his view that the soldiers had violated English law and custom by firing on the King Street crowd, and that they must be held accountable for it. Among Robert Treat Paine's papers from the trial is a sheet of "suggestions and remarks" passed by Adams to Paine in the midst of the soldiers' trial. Adams identified weaknesses and contradictions in witness testimony, suggested lines of argument, and raised points of law. Clearly, he was an interested observer hoping to see the soldiers' conviction.[3]

The soldiers' acquittals prompted cries of outrage. Immediately after the trials, an impassioned indictment of the verdicts was tacked to the Town House door. "To see the Court *cheat* the injured people with a *Shew* of Justice which yet we near can taste of," it read, "drive us like *Wrecks* down the rough Tide of Power while no hold is left to save us from Destruction, all that bear this are slaves, & we as such not to rise up at the great Call of Nature & free the world from such domestic Tyrants." Technically, this was a call to arms against royal justice that amounted to an act of treason. As lieutenant governor and commander in chief of the province, Hutchinson condemned the sentiment and offered a reward to anyone who could help bring the author to justice.[4]

In the aftermath of the trials, Bostonians continued to debate the merits of the case and defend themselves in print. Samuel Adams, writing as "Vindex," took to the pages of the *Boston Gazette* to rehash the events of March 5 and insist that the soldiers had been the aggressors. Jonathan Sewall, the attorney general who had absented himself to avoid prosecuting the soldiers, responded under the pseudonym "Philanthrop." He contended that "Vindex" must have been one "of those who did not hear the trials, and whose former prejudices therefore still remain." As the trial of Charles Bourgatte approached, William Molineux published a lengthy defense of his role in eliciting the servant's testimony, including depositions from five witnesses who claimed that Molineux never spoke privately with the boy and only urged him to tell the truth. In similar fashion, Richard Palmes published a statement a week later, defending his trial testimony and criticizing the account that had appeared in the narrative of the trial based on John Hodgson's shorthand notes that was published in December. All of these arguments and defensive parries suggest that the topic of the trials' outcomes remained very much alive in the early months of 1771, and that participants were especially sensitive to the criticisms that were circulating in town.[5]

When the town meeting convened in March 1771, its members evinced a similar inclination to argue about who was to blame for the shootings. Many residents were deeply unhappy with Hodgson's published account of the second trial, which appeared to vindicate the soldiers and place responsibility for the massacre on Boston's unruly mob. At the year's first town meeting, residents considered the question of whether "some steps may be taken to vindicate the Character of the Town Inhabitants," who had been "grosly injured by some partial and false Publications relative to the Tryals of Capt. Preston &c." A committee concluded that Hodgson had offered only a "mutilated and partial Account" of the soldiers' trial, and recommended that the town should consider appointing another committee "who shall be directed to prepare and draw up a true and full account of those Tryals and what preceded them."[6]

Tellingly, however, no further action was taken. The time for such arguments was passing. In the spring of 1771, Bostonians turned from contestation to commemoration: from arguing about who was to blame for the massacre to cementing the event in public memory and ensuring that its larger significance would not be forgotten.

FROM THE BEGINNING, the symbolic power of the Boston Massacre transcended its details; in the first year after the shootings, a series of commemorative undertakings ensured that its iconic power would not be lost in the muddle of a legal resolution. However complicit Bostonians may have been in triggering the catastrophe on King Street, a large majority of the town's residents were unequivocal in asserting their aggrieved innocence. More than anything that had yet transpired between Britain and its colonies — far more than the Stamp Act, the Townshend Duties, or the creation of the American Board of Customs Commissioners — the Boston Massacre drove a deep wedge between those like Thomas Hutchinson who continued to temporize on behalf of an ill-defined imperial constitution, and others, including Samuel Adams, Paul Revere, and William Molineux, for whom the shootings represented an irreparable breaking point in that relationship.

Beginning on the day after the shootings, town leaders orchestrated public events and demonstrations of solidarity to dramatize the town's outrage and its unequivocal rejection of the occupation's legitimacy. By organizing local militiamen into a town watch — whose principal purpose was to keep soldiers from storming the jail and freeing the prisoners — town leaders asserted the primacy of their locally controlled military apparatus over that of the empire. On March 8 a mass funeral was organized for the first four victims. "Such a Concourse of People I never saw before," John Rowe remarked. "I believe Ten or Twelve thousand." The procession wound through the streets of Boston: the victims' coffins, followed by family members, then the town selectmen, and finally the enormous throng of inhabitants. The procession ended at the Granary burying ground, where the four were interred in a single grave. "It is supposed," according to the *Boston Gazette,* "that there must have been a greater Number of People from Town and Country at the Funeral of those who were massacred by the Soldiers, than were ever together on this Continent on any Occasion." Patrick Carr died on March 14; three days later, another procession accompanied his coffin to the Granary burying ground, where it joined the others.[7]

Soon, local printers were advertising two nearly identical engravings that purported to represent the massacre. Based on a painting by Henry Pelham, one was engraved by Pelham, and the other by Paul Revere. Both prints show seven soldiers, arrayed in a line, firing simultaneously; Preston stands behind them, sword raised, apparently giving the command to fire. Puffs of smoke are also visible in a second-story window of the Custom House. The dead and dying are arrayed before the soldiers while a respectable assemblage of townspeople looks on in horror. Pelham's print is headed with the line "THE FRUITS OF ARBITRARY POWER, OR THE BLOODY MASSACRE"; beneath the image, the text of the Ninety-Fourth Psalm is flanked by a skull and crossbones on one side and a sword shattered by a lightning bolt on the other.

Revere's print differs in a few key details—most notably, Revere included a sign on the Custom House that reads "Butcher's Hall"—and bears different text above and below the image. It is headed "THE BLOODY MASSACRE perpetrated in King-Street BOSTON on March 5th 1770 by a party of the 29th REGT." Below, an eighteen-line poem laments the shootings and implies that if the soldiers are not convicted in an earthly court, they will eventually face "a JUDGE who never can be brib'd." Jonathan Mulliken, a Newburyport clockmaker, engraved a third version of the scene soon thereafter.

The image depicted in these engravings served as a powerful visual icon for Bostonians. At the trials, jurors were swayed by Adams's argument that Bostonians had violently assaulted the soldiers, leaving them no alternative but to defend themselves. The Revere, Pelham, and Mulliken engravings told a different story. By reorienting the scene to place the soldiers in the foreground and make them the unquestioned aggressors, the prints must have stoked outrage at the shootings; they lent credence to the belief that a standing army was an instrument of tyranny. It is unclear how many copies of these images were printed or how widely they circulated. Almost certainly,

Henry Pelham's engraving of the massacre scene, based on his own painting. It is very similar to Paul Revere's more familiar print, but the central image varies in a few details, and the surrounding text is entirely different.

Paul Revere's engraving of the "Bloody Massacre," based on Henry Pelham's painting. This copy, owned by the William L. Clements Library, is still in its original frame, which is believed to have been made in Revere's own workshop.

their significance outside of Boston has been exaggerated. The initial run of the Revere print was two hundred copies. It was definitely reprinted, but it is not clear how many additional runs were made. Henry Pelham was angry with Revere for hijacking the scene he had painted and beating him to the printer's office. Advertising his version for sale a week after Revere's had come on the market, Pelham complained that he had been "deprived" of the "Advantage" he had expected to gain. Indeed, Pelham's print fell into relative obscurity; only two known copies of his version survive. Even the Mulliken version, printed in a small North Shore town, has more surviving copies, seven. The Revere print has come down to us in larger numbers. Clarence S. Brigham, who published the most comprehensive account of these images in the mid-twentieth century, personally viewed thirty-six of them. Brigham noted that about half the surviving copies of the Revere print still have their original frames, suggesting that they were printed, colored, and framed for sale in the local market. Christian Remick, a Massachusetts sailor and painter, apparently added the watercolor to at least some of the original images.[8]

Three English reprints of the Boston Massacre scene were published in London within a few months of the shootings.[9] It is not surprising that English radicals would be interested in broadcasting the image, which cast such strong aspersions on Britain's American policy. Strikingly, however, no American imprints survive from any printer outside of Massachusetts Bay. Historians have sometimes suggested that Revere's Boston Massacre print became an important image throughout British North America, helping to fuel the patriotic fervor that allowed the thirteen colonies to unite in rebellion. There is no evidence for this proposition. The fact that half the surviving copies of the Revere print were framed in the printer's workshop suggests that they traveled only very short distances from the place they were produced. Most of the prints were almost certainly purchased and displayed by residents of Boston or nearby towns.

But if the Revere print had little impact elsewhere, there is no doubt that in Boston itself it was an important image that shaped local perceptions of the shootings. Like the *Horrid Massacre,* the Revere print put the onus squarely on the backs of the soldiers. The *Horrid Massacre,* however, was not intended for local circulation. Copies were shipped to England immediately, while the remaining stock in Edes and Gill's print shop was held back, by order of the town meeting. Though the *Horrid Massacre* did eventually come onto the Boston market, so that it was widely available by the time of the trials, for the first several months after the shootings it was the Revere print that gave townspeople their most vivid image of the massacre. Framed and colored prints of Revere's engraving must have hung in many Boston homes, coffeehouses, and taverns. In his defense of the soldiers, Josiah Quincy Jr. invoked the power the prints exercised over local imaginations. "The prints exhibited in our houses have added wings to fancy," he argued, "and in the fervor of our zeal, reason is in hazard of being lost."[10]

The image was also reproduced in other contexts in the months and years to come. Almost immediately after Edes and Gill struck off the first run, they used Revere's plate to illustrate a large broadside that also included the text of the original *Boston Gazette* account. In 1771 a small woodcut based on Revere's image (and, in all likelihood, engraved by Revere himself) appeared in an almanac published in Boston by Isaiah Thomas. In the following year, the same woodcut was used again, this time to illustrate a Boston broadside. And in 1775 Revere reused the image when he was employed by Massachusetts Bay to engrave two paper money issues.[11] These derivative engravings kept the images in circulation for several years beyond the shootings. Yet, it bears emphasizing that these were the only examples of derivative engravings produced from the famous massacre print in the eighteenth century. And, as with the original prints, they were intended for local consumption. Whether any version of the Revere

In the years following the original publication of Paul Revere's "Bloody Massacre" print, the image was occasionally reused, as it was on this 1772 broadside *(above)* and this 1771 almanac page *(opposite)*.

the BOSTON MASSACRE, perpetrated on
March the 5th, 1770.

WHILE BRITONS view this scene with conscious dread,
   And pay the last sad tribute to the dead ;
What though the shafts of justice faintly gleam,
And ermin'd miscreants ridicule the scene ;
Ne'er let one breast the generous sigh disclaim,
Or cease to bow at FREEDOM's hallow'd fane ;
Till with the thought let Fame's loud Clarion swell,
And Fate to distant time the MURDER tell.

print would have been widely recognized or known outside of Massachusetts is doubtful.

Popular awareness of March 5 as a date worthy of commemoration was similarly limited to Boston and its immediate environs. A search of almanacs published in British North America from 1770 until 1786 finds that only one — the *Massachusetts Calendar,* published by Isaiah Thomas in 1772 — used an image to depict the Boston Massacre, while twenty-four more placed the date on their calendars. Of those twenty-five almanacs, published from 1771 to 1785, fourteen were printed in Boston and twenty-one in eastern Massachusetts. Prior to 1775, only Boston publishers had taken note of the massacre. Thereafter, it appeared in almanacs published in Boston, Newburyport, Worcester, Salem, and Danvers, as well as Providence, Rhode Island; Portsmouth, New Hampshire; and Bennington, Vermont. No almanac published outside of New England ever noted March 5 before 1786, and beyond Boston there is little evidence to suggest that it was remembered in more than a passing way.[12]

In Boston, however, March 5 became a date of prime importance. As the first anniversary of the shootings approached, a series of public events allowed townspeople to preserve the memory of the shootings and to reflect on their meaning. On March 5, 1771, the bells of several churches in Boston began tolling at noon and continued for an hour. In the evening, a crowd gathered at the Manufactory House — where residents had resisted Bernard's efforts to house troops in the fall of 1768 — to hear an oration by Thomas Young. Afterward, the bells tolled for another hour while townspeople streamed past Paul Revere's home. He had illuminated three windows with scenes recalling the events of the previous year. In the first, the ghost of Christopher Seider shared the space with a "monumental Obelisk" containing the names of the five men who died in the massacre. The second window showed the same scene that was depicted in Revere's famous print: "the Soldiers drawn up, firing at the People assembled before them." The third window displayed a woman representing America, wearing a liberty cap and holding a staff, with one foot "on the head of a Grenadier lying prostrate grasping a serpent"—an image very similar to the one in the cartouche of Revere's engraving depicting the arrival of the troops on Long Wharf in 1768. "The whole was so well executed," the *Boston Gazette* reported, "that the Spectators, which amounted to many Thousands, were struck with solemn Silence, and their Countenances covered with a melancholy Gloom."[13]

A week later, the town meeting convened for the first time since the previous fall. Despite the success of the anniversary commemoration that had already taken place, the meeting appointed a committee to "determine upon some suitable Method to perpetuate the memory of the horred Massacre." The committee, in turn, suggested that the town should choose someone "to deliver an Oration at such Time as may be Judged most convenient." It nominated Samuel Hunt, the master of Boston's North Grammar School, and James Lovell, usher of the South Grammar School, as candidates. The town voted for Lovell, and he delivered his oration on April 2. The town meeting convened that morning in Faneuil Hall as usual; when the time for the oration arrived, it adjourned to the more spacious Old South Meeting House. Lovell spoke to "a crow[d]ed assembly." The town thanked him for his efforts and requested a copy to send to the printers. It also appointed a committee to make arrangements for the following year's commemoration.[14]

Beginning in 1772, the opening date for the town meeting was moved to March 5. This change ensured that each year's round of public business began with a day devoted to the memory of the Boston Massacre. The meeting would convene in the morning, approve the work of the commemoration committee, and then adjourn to a larger venue for the afternoon's oration. Joseph Warren was the speaker in 1772;

the records of the town meeting report that he spoke to "a crowded assembly," as had Lovell the year before. His address, like Lovell's, was printed by order of the town. In 1773 Dr. Benjamin Church reportedly delivered his oration "to a large and crowded Audience, and [was] received by them with great applause"; thereafter, this precise phrase was inserted into the town records each year to describe the oration and its reception. John Hancock delivered an "elegant and spirited oration" at the Old South Meeting House in 1774; again, "a large crowded Audience" responded with "great Applause"; again, the town printed the text of the oration afterward.[15]

In this way, the date of the massacre was established as Boston's most important and consistently remembered public holiday. By 1774, March 5 had become the centerpiece of Boston's corporate identity. It was a day to remember the fallen, to recall the horrors of military occupation, and to reinforce resistance to the tyrannical rule of an imperial state that paid no regard to local prerogatives.

The tone—and with it, the purpose—of these orations evolved quickly. Lovell's inaugural oration in 1771 tentatively probed the significance of the shootings. Lovell briefly mentioned "the horrid bloody scene we here commemorate" before asking his listeners to put aside the "shocking . . . course of rancor and dispute" that Boston's occupation had engendered. He moved first to offer historical reflections on the threat standing armies posed to a free people. Then, rehearsing arguments that would have been familiar to anyone who had read John Dickinson's "Letters from a Pennsylvania Farmer" or Samuel Adams's "Vindex" essays in the *Boston Gazette,* he steered farther away from the massacre to talk about illegal taxation. Though it was impassioned in its own way, Lovell's oration did little to capitalize on the strong emotions aroused by the shootings. His reflections ranged widely across the constitutional arguments circulating in the colonies at the time, but mostly failed to draw the attention of his fellow Bostonians to their special plight.[16]

In the following year, Joseph Warren took a markedly different approach — one that set the tone for all the orations that followed. Warren abandoned Lovell's sober tones in favor of an emotionally charged harangue designed to arouse and incite his listeners. "THE FATAL FIFTH OF MARCH, 1770, CAN NEVER BE FORGOTTEN," he thundered. "The horrors of THAT DREADFUL NIGHT are but too deeply impressed on our hearts — Language is too feeble to paint the emotions of our souls, when our streets were stained with the BLOOD OF OUR BRETHREN, — when our ears were wounded by the groans of the *dying,* and our eyes were tormented with the sight of the mangled bodies of the *dead.*" As if this opening salvo were not sufficient to arouse his audience, Warren built to an even more dramatic crescendo:

> When our alarmed imagination presented to our view our houses wrapt in flames, — our children subjected to the barbarous caprice of the raging soldiery — our beauteous virgins exposed to all the insolence of unbridled passion, — our virtuous wives endeared to us by every tender tie, falling a sacrifice to their worse than brutal violence, and perhaps like the famed LUCRETIA, distracted with anguish and despair, ending their wretched lives by their own fair hands.[17]

By invoking not only what residents heard and saw, but also what they imagined and feared, Warren found a way to catalogue the full scope of afflictions that might be visited on the town by a "raging soldiery." He used the massacre both to recall the horrors of the event itself and to expound upon the much worse things that might have come from Boston's military occupation. This was not an oration calculated to instruct Bostonians in constitutional principles. It aimed to arouse them — even infuriate them. From that point forward, the massacre oration served to galvanize local sentiments and orchestrate unanimity of feeling.

Nine months later, John Adams was asked to deliver the 1773 oration. He begged off, arguing that his ill health and advanced age (he was thirty-seven years old) left him unfit to "make Declamations." When he was pressed, he admitted to misgivings. He feared that, having defended the soldiers at their trial, delivering a massacre oration would expose him "to the Lash of ignorant and malicious Tongues on both sides of the question."[18] Adams was probably right to refuse the invitation — though the subsequent course of his life would amply demonstrate that he was not yet too old to speak in public. It was not public speaking in general but the particular demands of this occasion that gave Adams pause. He understood that Joseph Warren's 1772 oration set a pattern he did not want to emulate. Though he was eminently capable of passionate speech, his thoughts on the subject of the shootings were, in all likelihood, considerably more complex and even-handed than the ones Warren had expressed. But the massacre oration was no place to air them: Adams recognized that a measured or lukewarm reflection on the Boston Massacre would not be well received. Rather than present himself as an ambivalent patriot, Adams chose to refuse the invitation and leave such public declamations to other men.

WHEN THE 29TH and 14TH REGIMENTS moved to Castle Island in the weeks after the massacre, and the 29th was subsequently reassigned to New Jersey, it appeared that a new day was dawning in Boston's relations with Great Britain. And indeed, the repeal of the Townshend Duties and a more conciliatory attitude on the part of the North administration meant that the three years following the Boston Massacre were relatively free of conflicts between colonies and empire. In Boston, though, the annual commemoration of the massacre helped keep alive a deep mistrust of British intentions. When Parliament approved a plan to ship British East India Company tea directly to the colonies, Bostonians interpreted the policy as a renewal of the conspiracy against American liberties and tried to block the tea. Then, on December 16, 1773, a group boarded three ships in the harbor and threw 342 chests of tea overboard. In retaliation, Parliament closed the port of Boston and revised the colony's charter, fulfilling at last the hope that Bernard, Gage, and other friends of government had vainly entertained five years earlier. Massachusetts government was reorganized to make the Governor's Council appointive rather than elective, give the governor more control over town meetings, and limit the power of Massachusetts courts. The apparent calm of the previous three years was shattered, and Boston was in Parliament's crosshairs once again.

Castle Island became the staging ground for Britain's effort to assert control over the troublesome port town. It had been continuously occupied since the troops left Boston proper. The 14th Regiment remained on the island until July 1772, when it was sent to St. Vincent to serve in the Carib War and was relieved at Fort William by the 64th. (In 1771, when war with Spain over possession of the Falkland Islands appeared imminent, the 64th and 65th boarded transports to Castle Island in preparation for a campaign against Louisiana, but they soon returned to Halifax when Britain and Spain reached a diplomatic settlement.) During the years of relative calm, the army continued to pour money into local pockets. John Robertson, Gage's barrack-master general, was spending between £1,100 and £1,500 per year to supply the island's regiment, but this amount was dwarfed by the expenses Montresor incurred, first in fitting up the barracks and then rebuilding the island's defenses after the epic October 1770 storm. The work progressed in stages. During the course of 1770, Montresor spent nearly £3,000 on improvements to the barracks and stopgap repairs to the fort's defenses. Beginning in mid-1771 and continuing through 1772, he directed a much more ambitious and comprehensive rebuilding process. Carpenters, masons, and laborers in his employ replaced wharves, platforms, and gun carriages; dug wells; built ovens; repaired shingles, doors, windows, and frames; and undertook a variety of other tasks. In this second phase, Montresor paid out another £11,000, most of it to Boston suppliers, craftsmen, and laborers. By the end of 1772, Montresor had spent £14,000 on Castle Island.[19]

Following the passage of the Coercive Acts in 1774, troops returned once again to Boston: this time, nine regiments and parts of two others, or some three thousand soldiers in all. Montresor was hastily dispatched to secure accommodations. Between August and December, he spent nearly £20,000 "Fitting, & Repairing Houses Hired for Barracks, Hospitalls, Guard Houses, Centry Boxes, Together with all the Materials for Carrying on Said Work, for Ten Regiments & Detachment of the Royal Artillery, & for Building a Magazine for Stores at Castle William, Repairing the Wall, &ca &ca &ca." In the first half of 1775, he spent an additional £11,700 for "Fortifying, & making Batterys" on Copps Hill, Beacon Hill, Bunker Hill, and Tileston's Wharf, along with expenditures for a hospital and an ironworks. At the same time, Captain William Spry fortified Boston Neck. He spent £4,056 digging entrenchments, setting platforms, building two large guardhouses, and "Picqueting the Works."[20] Throughout the summer of 1774, British troops — most of them new to North America — disembarked in Boston to help enforce the Port Act, which closed the town to all maritime trade. As in the fall and winter of 1768–1769, they sought accommodations in town, but on an even larger scale. Once again, privates were housed in warehouses

John Montresor completed this detailed plan of Castle Island in 1771 *(opposite)*. It shows the fort and its bastions facing the harbor channel, the barracks placed behind them, and the wharf on the island's lee side.

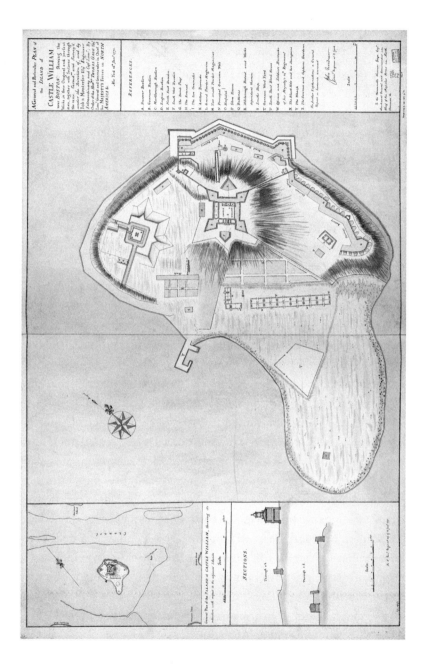

A General and Particular PLAN of
the ISLAND of
CASTLE WILLIAM
near BOSTON: Shewing the
Works in their Original and present
state, together with Sections through
the same: General and Survey'd
under the Direction of, and by
John Montresor Eng. Engineer
Extraordinary and Captain: By
Order of the Honble THOMAS GAGE Esq.
Lieut. General and Commander in Chief of
his MAJESTYS Forces in NORTH
AMERICA.

New York 4th June 1775.

REFERENCES.

A.   Hanover Bastion.
B.   Governors Bastion.
C.   Marlborough Bastion.
D.   Kingston Bastion.
E.   North East Bastion.
F.   South West Bastion.
G.   The Ravelin Proof.
H.   The Arsenal.
I.   The Gun Granadier.
K.   Artillery Barracks.
L.   General Powder Magazineine.
M.   Two small Powder Magazines.
N.   Principal Garrison Well.
O.   Hospital.
P.   Store House.
Q.   Bakehouse.
R.   Hillsborough Redout and Works
        appendant thereon.
S.   Smiths Shop.
T.   Garrison Wharf Yard.
U.   South West Point Platform.
W. Officers and Soldiers Barracks
        of his Majesty's 64th Regiment.
X.   The Mount Hill and her Dependents.
Y.   The Wreck.
Z.   The Governor and Captains Gardens
        Perfective Perpendicular, or General
        Report, as herewith annexed.

John Montresor
Chief Engineer at Large

Scale

SECTIONS.

General Plan of the ISLAND of CASTLE WILLIAM, shewing its
extendent with respect to the adjacent Islands.

Scale

General Plan of the ISLAND of CASTLE WILLIAM, shewing its
extendent with respect to the adjacent Islands.

Scale

Through a b

Through c d

Scale

and camped on the Common, while officers filled boardinghouses and looked for rooms to rent.

In 1768 troops had occupied Boston to offer aid to local magistrates. By the fall of 1774, with the First Continental Congress meeting in Philadelphia and Samuel Adams proposing that Massachusetts raise twenty thousand militiamen to resist the troops in Boston, something more like a military operation was under way. British troops had besieged Boston from within.

ON JANUARY 18, 1775, the officers occupying Boston celebrated the birthday of Charlotte of Mecklenburg-Strelitz, wife of George III and queen of Great Britain and Ireland. The celebration was organized by "The Loyal and Friendly Society of the Blue and Orange," a group founded by the King's Own (4th) Regiment to honor the memory of the Glorious Revolution and the accession of the House of Hanover; they invited Generals Thomas Gage and Frederick Haldimand and Admiral Samuel Graves, along with other distinguished guests. (After the passage of the Massachusetts Government Act, Gage was appointed governor of Massachusetts Bay, an office he held at the same time he continued to serve as commander in chief of British armed forces in North America.) Beginning at noon and continuing until 9:00 P.M., the queen's birthday celebration consisted of a dinner and a program of music, punctuated throughout the day by marching, volleys, and public toasts. A royal salute fired by the artillery company announced the commencement of festivities. Next, an army color guard marched into King Street and discharged three more volleys. Warships in the harbor fired a salute in response. A group of sixty-eight officers and supporters then gathered for dinner at the British Coffee House in King Street, where they banqueted to the accompaniment of an army band that was stationed on the Coffee House balcony overlooking the street.[21]

When the toasts began, they were shouted into King Street. An officer joined the band on the balcony; as each toast was proposed and then cheered in the banquet hall, he repeated it for the benefit of the crowd below. Across the street, twenty-three grenadiers of the King's Own Regiment fired a volley in response to each toast. Each volley was followed by more drums and music. For residents of Boston who took pride in their effort, five years earlier, to drive the soldiers from their city, the martial character of this display must have made it a galling spectacle. Many toasts were intended to disparage the town. A toast to the "Sixteenth of April, '46, A Similar Chastisement to All Rebels" recalled the decisive and bloody defeat of the Jacobite rebellion at the battle of Culloden and linked that uprising to the current state of affairs in the colonies. The Bostonians who were looking on said nothing. But when a toast was offered to Lord North, architect of the Boston Port Bill and the rest of the Coercive Acts, their silence was broken. As the soldiers in the street cheered the toast, the townspeople began to hiss. Someone called out, "Damn him!" In response, the toastmaster shouted, "Bless him!" The shouting continued and intensified, until the commander of the grenadiers gave the order to disperse the crowd and clear King Street. The King's Own grenadiers complied, with fixed bayonets.[22]

The events of January 18 dramatized the circumstances in which Bostonians found themselves in early 1775. The sights and sounds of the day carried an unmistakable message. Soldiers dressed in bright uniforms and marching in measured ranks presented a metaphor of the proper relationship between sovereign authority and loyal obedience, in dramatic contrast to the chaotic, antiauthoritarian qualities that Gage and his officer corps had come to associate with Boston. From the salute of the color guard that was answered by volleys from warships in the harbor, to the band playing on the Coffee House balcony and the toasts called out into King Street, to the long series of volleys accompanying them, it was impossible for anyone within earshot to ignore the celebration. As soldiers paraded into King Street, they dramatically reenacted the occupation of the town and staked the army's claim to define and control the tenor of public life. With the army band on the balcony and an officer alongside, calling out toasts that affirmed the orthodox doctrines of loyalty and submission to authority, the challenge to the rebellious sentiments of Boston's radical faction was clear. Nothing drove the point home more clearly than the array of grenadiers standing across the street, firing volleys in response. The last time British regulars had discharged weapons in King Street was, of course, on a moonlit night in March 1770, when shots were fired into a civilian crowd. No one in King Street on the queen's birthday could have failed to make the connection.

The reoccupation of Boston set the massacre oration of 1775 in an entirely new context. In previous years, the occasion had affirmed local sentiments that seemed to be held almost unanimously by the town's inhabitants, and which only grew stronger with the passage of time. Now, in March 1775 — as the queen's birthday celebration had unmistakably demonstrated — the town had lost control over its own affairs. For the second time in four years, the massacre oration committee selected Joseph Warren to deliver the address. Warren, a Harvard graduate and a respected physician, was active in the town's radical political leadership. Handsome and graceful, with a high forehead, clear brown eyes, and a pleasing smile, Warren was a commanding presence. He combined a cultivated ease with fiery eloquence, and he had emerged in the years of rising tension between Britain and its colonies as one of Boston's most capable and persuasive advocates for local prerogative and resistance to tyranny. It was presumably because of the success of his oration in 1772 that he was asked to deliver the address again only three years later, in circumstances that had changed dramatically for the worse.[23]

As with the queen's birthday celebration, the organizers of the massacre oration intended the event to reflect their view of the proper relationship between government and the governed, and to dramatize Boston's place in a larger history of liberty and oppression. In contrast to the spectacle of authority staged two months earlier in King Street, the oration was delivered, once again, in the Old South Meeting House, a site more appropriate to didactic instruction. The Old South stood near enough to the governor's house that the mere act of staging the oration offered an implicit challenge to the legitimacy of Gage's tenure in that office. Four years' tradition had established a clear tone and purpose for the event, but this oration would be different: none of its antecedents had been delivered in the presence of British troops. This time, in the midst of "an immense concourse of people," a "great number" of army and navy officers were in attendance. Many crowded into the front of the meetinghouse. The feeling in the room was electric.[24]

Warren, ascending the pulpit before the packed house, began his oration in the spirit of republican self-deprecation. He addressed his "ever honoured fellow-citizens" and avowed a "most humiliating conviction of my want of ability." He hoped that his sincerity might compensate for his lack of eloquence. But then — in an elegantly constructed address that belied his initial protestations — he began to unfold a series of reflections on natural rights, anarchy, and arbitrary government. "Even *anarchy itself*," he suggested, "that bugbear held up by the tools of power (though truly to be deprecated) is infinitely less dangerous to mankind than *arbitrary government. Anarchy,*" after all, "can be but of short duration," while "*tyranny,* when once established, entails its curse on a nation to the latest period of time." It could only be thrown off by "some daring genius, inspired by Heaven," who might "bravely form and execute the arduous design of restoring liberty and life to his enslaved, murdered country." If the toasts and volleys of the January birthday celebration had implied that Bostonians were rebels, Warren suggested that, when it was directed against a tyrant, rebellion was an act of divine genius.[25]

Soon, Warren's general observations gave way to direct criticisms of British policies. He began by arguing that Parliament had violated the principle of taxation by consent. Warren then condemned the presence of the army. "Martial law and the government of a well regulated city are so entirely different," Warren contended, "that it has always been considered as improper to quarter troops in populous cities. . . . Standing armies always endanger the liberty of the subject. But when the people on the one part, considered the army as sent to enslave them, and the army on the other were taught to look on the people as in a state of rebellion, it was but just to fear the most disagreeable consequences. Our fears, we have seen, were but too well grounded."[26]

Having set the contexts that gave the Boston Massacre its meaning, he proceeded to the event itself. "Approach we then," he intoned, "the melancholy walk of death." A victim's "gay companion," a "tender mother," a "widowed mourner," her "infant children": Warren called upon all of them to view the scene in King Street. "Take heed, ye orphan babes, lest, whilst your streaming eyes are fixed upon the ghastly corpse, *your feet slide on the stones bespattered with your father's brains.* Enough! . . . Nature reluctant shrinks already from the view."[27]

What explains the city's sudden ruin?

We wildly stare about, and with amazement, ask, who spread this ruin round us? What wretch has dared deface the image of his God? Has haughty France or cruel Spain sent forth her myrmidons? Has the grim savage rushed again from the far distant wilderness? Or does some fiend, fierce from the depth of Hell, with all the rancorous malice which the apostate damned can feel, twang her destructive bow and hurl her deadly arrows at our breast? No. None of these—but, how astonishing! It is the hand of Britain that inflicts the wound. The arms of George our rightful king have been employed to shed that blood which freely would have flown at his command when justice or the honour of his crown had called his subjects to the field.

Bostonians, outraged by the shootings, initially felt the urge to revenge their townsmen, but resisted. "The storm subsides—a solemn pause ensues—You spare upon condition they depart. They go—they quit your city—they no more shall give offence.—Thus closes the important drama."[28]

But recent events demonstrated that the larger crisis had not passed. "Our streets are again filled with armed men," Warren noted: "Our harbour is crouded with ships of war." How should Bostonians respond? "These cannot intimidate us," he admonished his audience; "our liberty must be preserved; it is far dearer than *life,* we hold it even dear as our *allegiance;* we must defend it against the attacks of *friends* as well as *enemies;* we cannot suffer even BRITONS to ravish it from us." In a sustained crescendo that built through the final fifteen minutes of his address, Warren reminded his listeners what was at stake. Act now to secure the blessings of liberty "to future generations," he proclaimed, and they, "fired by your example, shall emulate your virtues, and learn from *you* the heavenly art of making millions happy."[29]

It was a spellbinding performance. A compact, powerful oration of fewer than forty-four hundred words, it would have taken no more than forty-five or fifty minutes to deliver. The *Boston Gazette* described it simply as "elegant and spirited"; the minutes of the town meeting reported, in their formulaic construction, that it was delivered "to a large and crouded Audience, & received by them with great Applause." But those brief descriptions fail to capture the real tone of the event. All the eyewitness accounts agree that the atmosphere in the Old South was explosive. More than a hundred officers were present, "determined to take notice of, and resent" any insult to the honor of the military. The townspeople "certainly expected a Riot, as almost every man had a short stick, or bludgeon, in his hand." Decades later, an "old Bostonian" recalled that the smallest disturbance that day might have "deluged that Church in blood," and remarked, "It has always been a wonder to me, that the war did not commence on that day."[30]

It is worth pausing to note that only four eyewitness accounts of the oration offer sustained descriptions of the event, and they were all written by British officers. Two appear in soldiers' diaries: one (the most detailed and straightforward account) by Lieutenant Frederick Mackenzie of the Royal Welch Fusiliers, the other by Lieutenant John Barker of the King's Own Regiment. The other two are anonymous letters printed in James Rivington's conservative New York newspaper within a few weeks of the event. The anonymous letters are pointedly sardonic in tone, in keeping with the editorial bias of Rivington's paper. (The publication was reviled in Boston, where it was commonly referred to as *"Rivington's New-York (lying) Gazeteer."*) Nevertheless, the essential consistency of the four accounts suggests that they are broadly accurate.[31]

All agree that a violent confrontation was a very real possibility, and that violence was forestalled because Warren avoided any direct affront to the honor of army or crown. One report claimed that an officer stood nearby with an egg in his pocket; if Warren had insulted the king or the army directly, he would have thrown it in Warren's face, "and that was to have been a signal to draw swords, and they would have massacred Hancock, Adams, and hundreds more." But the oration, though it was "severe on the conduct of the Military, and evidently calculated to excite the resentment of the populace against them, contained nothing so violent as was expected." The egg was never thrown; swords were never drawn. One of the anonymous accounts claims that "the officers frequently interrupted Warren, by laughing loudly at the most ludicrous parts, and *coughing* and *hemming* at the most seditious, to the great discontent of the *devoted citizens,*" but that was probably an embellishment. Mackenzie wrote that the oration "was delivered without any other interruption than a few hisses from some of the Officers." Samuel Adams wrote that the officers "behaved tollerably well till the Oration was ended."[32]

Even without them drawing their swords, the presence of so many officers profoundly unsettled the townspeople who crowded the meetinghouse. The event ended in a chaotic scene. When Warren finished, Samuel Adams rose to announce that a speaker would be chosen to deliver the next year's oration. In doing so, he made reference to " '*the bloody and horrid massacre perpetrated by a party of soldiers under the command of Captain T. Preston.*' " Throughout his oration, Warren had refrained from any direct assertion that Preston and his men had perpetrated a massacre. Now, Adams had given the officers an opening; they "could no longer contain themselves." One of them "exclaimed, *Fie, shame!* and, fie, shame! was echoed by all the navy and military in the place; this caused a violent confusion, and in an instant the windows were thrown open, and the affrighted Yankies jumped out by fifties, so that in a few minutes, we should have had an empty house."[33]

It may seem surprising that the officers' response would have provoked such a strong reaction in the assembled townspeople, but all four eyewitness accounts agree in saying that when the officers began voicing their displeasure, the crowd rose from their seats and, as Barker put it, got "out as fast as they cou'd by the doors and windows." (Or, in the words of the most satirical anonymous account, "The gallerians . . . bounced out of the windows, and swarmed down the gutters, like rats into the street.") Mackenzie, Barker, and one of the anonymous writers assumed that the audience misunderstood and believed the officers were crying "fire." Perhaps this is true—but even if it were, the word "fire" would have had an ambiguous meaning. Was the meetinghouse about to burn, or were the officers about to discharge their arms? According to one account, the confusion was intensified by the "Drums & fifes of the 43rd Regiment which happened to be passing by from Exercise." The noise might have caused townspeople to fear that a concerted attack on the meetinghouse was under way.[34]

Two accounts note that there were many women present. Mackenzie wrote that the misunderstanding "created a Scene of the greatest confusion imaginable. As there were numbers of Women in the Meeting, their cries encreased the confusion." The merchant John Andrews attributed the chaos to a captain of the Royal Irish regiment, who had "exposed himself by behaving in a very scandalous manner at the South meeting, while Doctor Warren was delivering the oration." Andrews proceeded to remark that the captain "got pretty decently frighted for it. A woman, among the rest, attack'd him and threatened to wring his nose."[35] It is unclear whether the confrontation occurred in the meetinghouse at the end of the oration or sometime later, perhaps in the street — or whether it was a detail invented by Andrews. If the attack occurred, such a direct affront to the honor of a British officer must have occasioned talk among both townspeople and the officers themselves.

Order was soon restored, and the town meeting proceeded to its conclusion. "As soon as the mistake was discovered, and things grew quiet," Mackenzie wrote, ". . . the Select men proceeded to the Choice of some public Officers, which being finished, the people dispersed." Samuel Adams wrote more briefly that some of the officers "began a Disturbance, which was soon suppressed & the remaining Business of the Meeting went on as usual."[36] Nevertheless, the uproar must have brought the massacre oration to an unsettling end for the many Bostonians who hurried from the Old South in a panic.

One of the anonymous eyewitness accounts has an especially satirical tone. The meetinghouse, according to this version, was "crowded with mobility and some Gentlemen," who "sat gaping at one another above an hour" awaiting Warren's arrival. Finally, Warren arrived and changed into a "Ciceronian Toga" in an apothecary's shop across the street. Then, "having robed himself," he crossed the street, entered the Old South, and took his place in the pulpit. "He then put himself into a Demosthenian posture, with a white handkerchief in his right hand." This account claims that Warren's oration received a mixed response: "He was applauded by the mob, but groaned at by the people of understanding."[37] The image of Warren appearing in a Ciceronian toga is absurd; clearly, the writer intended to mock Warren's self-conscious identification with the republican traditions of ancient Rome. It was an unmistakable jab at his inflated pretensions to both oratorical skill and moral virtue.

In later years, as subsequent generations of Bostonians came to recognize the drama and significance of the occasion, Warren's massacre oration passed into folklore. Writers who wanted to imbue the scene with a more dignified and patriotic tone recast the eyewitness accounts, altering details and adding embellishments that effectively inverted the character and significance of the event. Failing to recognize the absurdity in the image of Warren appearing in a toga, it became common to repeat this detail as a fact. Rather than satirizing his pretensions to republican virtue, in the eyes of later writers his choice of attire confirmed it. Instead of frantic Bostonians rushing in disorder out the windows at the oration's end, writers instead depicted Warren climbing a ladder outside the building and *entering* through a window: an invented detail that helped to suggest how crowded the Old South was, and also allowed Warren to appear before his audience, demigod-like, from on high.[38]

In a similar vein, later versions of the oration story suppressed any mention of a panicked response on the part of Warren's audience. In its place, they substituted a single disruptive soldier who was silenced by patriotic eloquence and virtue. As one such alternative account described the scene, the officer who cried "fie!" held up a handful of bullets as he did so. Though the audience was initially alarmed, the house was quieted when Warren dropped a handkerchief over the officer's hand—a detail suggested, perhaps, by the handkerchief the anonymous writer in Rivington's *Gazette* had placed in his hand to complement the toga. Then William Cooper, the town clerk who was at the front of the meetinghouse, "rose and said . . . 'there is no fire, but the fire of envy, burning in the hearts of our enemies, which I hope soon to see extinguished.'"[39] Thus retold, Warren's gesture and Cooper's spirited remark silenced the soldier's attempt to disrupt the proceedings.

All of these modifications to the original eyewitness accounts of the oration began to appear in print for the first time nearly half a century after the fact, as writers sought to ennoble the characters of Warren and the other heroes of the era and wrap the second occupation of Boston in a shroud of patriotic glory. But in the pews of the Old South Meeting House in 1775, the glory of Boston's radical cause remained far from assured. Warren's massacre oration, like the queen's birthday celebration preceding it, was a single dramatic episode in a larger contest over cultural politics in an occupied town. In little more than a month, on the road leading from Boston to Lexington and Concord, the contest between British soldiers and Massachusetts militiamen would move from the realm of word and symbol to the field of battle. And in three months' time Warren would lie dead on the battlefield at Bunker Hill, a loss that devastated many of his townsmen, who regarded him as one of the most brilliant and talented men of his generation.

As war descended on the colonies, the massacre oration continued to serve an important didactic purpose. In the spring of 1775, Boston's radical leaders (and many others) fled the occupied town and took up residence in nearby communities. Thus, in 1776 Peter Thacher delivered the massacre oration in the Watertown Meeting House. But—to the amazement of many observers—the British army abandoned Boston for New York a few short weeks later, and residents who had fled the town now reoccupied it. In subsequent years, the oration continued without interruption, and the minutes of the town meeting reported on the event each year in a formulaic litany that never varied. The town meeting convened for its first session of the year on the morning of March 5; the organizing committee identified a speaker; the town approved the choice; the time was set—sometimes noon, sometimes 12:30—and the town meeting adjourned to reassemble in the chosen location. The Old South was a wreck: during the occupation, soldiers had torn out the pews and hauled in dirt and gravel to create a stable and riding ring. In its place, in 1777 the oration moved to the Old Brick, where it remained throughout the war. The oration was delivered to "a large and crowded Audience, and receieved by them with great Applause."[40]

A few changes were introduced over the years. Beginning in 1774, a collection was taken each year for Christopher Monk, "a young Man, now languishing under a Wound he received in his Lungs, by a Shot from Preston's Butchering Party of Soldiers on the 5th of march 1770." In the first year, it raised nearly £320. In 1781, after Monk had finally died, Robert Patterson petitioned the town for a collection since he was wounded in his right arm by one of Preston's men. "Since the Death of Mr. Monk," the petition noted, Patterson was "the only one of the unhappy number then badly wounded, that survives." The town concurred, and Patterson's collection replaced Monk's. Beginning in 1779, "the several Bells" in town tolled to mark the occasion. With the exception of Warren, no orator performed more than once. Benjamin Hitchburne was chosen in 1777, followed by Jonathan William Austin, Colonel William Tudor, Jonathan Mason Jr., Thomas Dawes Jr., George Rogers Minot, and, in 1783,

Dr. Thomas Welsh. Every year, as it had done from the beginning, the town requested a copy of the oration and had it published.[41] The pattern was so deeply rooted that it seemed it would go on indefinitely. But instead, at war's end the tradition of the massacre oration came suddenly to its end.

Customarily, on the occasion of each year's oration the town meeting appointed a committee to organize the event for the following year. But in 1783, after Thomas Welsh delivered his address, town clerk William Cooper made a motion to reconsider the practice. His motion acknowledged that the massacre oration had served "excellent purposes." But it had now run its course. Cooper suggested that it was time to replace the massacre oration with another public occasion that would have some other theme and purpose — perhaps the Fourth of July. Orators could expound upon a variety of topics, any of which would be more appropriate to postwar civic culture now that Britain had ceded control of its former colonies. The town quickly endorsed the suggestion. "It is therefore Resolved that the Celebration of the fifth of March from henceforwards shall cease; and that instead thereof the Anniversary of the 4th Day of July A.D. 1776 (a Day ever memorable in the Annals of this Country for the declaration of our Independence) shall be constantly celebrated by the Delivery of a Publick Oration." A committee was chosen to select the first July 4 orator and organize the event, and the tradition of the massacre oration passed into oblivion. To mark its final passing, in January 1785 Peter Edes collected all the orations into a single volume, which he offered for sale in Boston.[42]

From its earliest years, when orators helped to solidify a local consensus about the massacre's larger meaning, to the dark days of Boston's reoccupation, through the difficult trials of war, the annual commemoration of the Boston Massacre served as a vital touchstone that articulated grievances and principles and stoked popular emotions. The imperial crisis — with its prolonged twists and turns of policy, its repeated calls to coercion against neighbors, and the tangled complexities of constitutional principles — could all too easily inspire ambivalence and divided loyalties. But the Boston Massacre was vivid and clear. Its memory united Bostonians in outrage and schooled them in the dangers of equivocation. It became a vital wellspring of shared experience.

But by war's end it had served its purpose. No longer useful to a local audience that had won its independence from Great Britain, it fell into relative obscurity. Only gradually would a widely shared memory of the Boston Massacre be revived. Its revival was driven by new contexts, new questions, and new concerns; it became important to various people for various reasons. As they rediscovered the Boston Massacre, they adapted the story to new purposes and shared it with new audiences. Yet, even as its meanings shifted and multiplied, the essential tensions at its core remained.

CHAPTER 10

A Usable Past

A MONG THOSE WHO LIVED through the events of the American
Revolution and had personal memories of the Boston Massacre,
many wrote accounts for posterity: by 1820 perhaps a dozen histories
of the Revolution had been published. They vary widely in quality,
and many passages in later texts derive directly from accounts in
earlier ones. Two stand out: the narratives of David Ramsay and
Mercy Otis Warren illustrate with great clarity the tension at the
heart of the massacre story. Both writers agreed that it would have
been better if the soldiers had never fired their guns. But who was
at fault? Who was the aggressor in the confrontation between soldiers
and townspeople? Could Boston be portrayed as the aggrieved innocent, or did the story make sense only if Boston was a mobbish town?
In the version of events familiar from the *Boston Gazette* and the
Horrid Massacre, the soldiers were on the rampage on the night of
March 5; initially, only boys were involved with the Custom House
sentry; nothing untoward occurred to provoke the shootings. But the
published account of the trial suggested something close to the opposite: a surging mob created a scene so chaotic that gunfire was all but
inevitable. As these two early histories of the American Revolution
suggest, at war's end this essential inconsistency had not been
resolved.

David Ramsay was born in Pennsylvania in 1749, where he trained as a physician before relocating to Charleston, South Carolina. He built an active medical practice, but was also drawn into politics at the onset of the American Revolution. He served in the South Carolina legislature from 1776 to 1783 and in the Continental Congress for four years in the 1780s. In the following decade he was elected to three terms in the South Carolina Senate. Alongside his work as a physician and his long period of public service, Ramsay also became one of the first and most eminent historians of the Revolutionary era. He published a two-volume history of the war in South Carolina in 1785; four years later his two-volume *History of the American Revolution* appeared in print.[1] It was the first such history published in the United States.

Mercy Otis Warren had an impeccable pedigree as a Massachusetts Whig. Born in 1728 and raised in West Barnstable, Massachusetts, she was the oldest daughter of James Otis Sr. and Mary Allyne Otis. Though she was not formally schooled, she received tutoring comparable to that of her brothers. In 1754 she married James Warren (not closely related to Joseph) of Plymouth, Massachusetts. They became active in the radical politics of the 1760s and 1770s. Mercy Otis Warren gave birth to five sons between 1757 and 1766; then, beginning in the 1770s, she began to publish plays and poems. She also undertook a history of the American Revolution. Though the writing was slowed by ill health and personal misfortunes, in 1805 her *History of the Rise, Progress, and Termination of the American Revolution* was published in three volumes.[2]

Both Ramsay and Warren offer accounts of the Boston Massacre, but the differences between them are instructive. Throughout his history, Ramsay's tone is measured and moderate, with due attention to the aims and interests of both Great Britain and the colonies. As Parliament softened its line on colonial policy in 1769 and 1770, he notes, "many hoped that the contention between the two countries was finally closed. In all the provinces, excepting Massachusetts, appearances seemed to favour that opinion." Massachusetts was the exception—the one colony that remained unreconciled to the new direction in colonial policy—because "the stationing a military force among them, was a fruitful source of uneasiness." Ramsay then sketched an account of the "dreadful scene" that unfolded on March 5, 1770. "The soldiers, when under arms, were pressed upon, insulted and pelted by a mob armed with clubs, sticks, and snowballs covering stones," he began. "They were also dared to fire. In this situation, one of the soldiers who had received a blow, in resentment fired at the supposed aggressor. This was followed by a single discharge from six others." The victims "were buried in one vault . . . to express the indignation of the inhabitants at the slaughter of their brethren, by soldiers quartered among them, in violation of their civil liberties." Preston and his soldiers were jailed and tried, with seven acquittals and two convictions of manslaughter. "It appeared on the trial, that the soldiers were abused, insulted, threatened, and pelted, before they fired," Ramsay continued. "These circumstances induced the jury to make a favourable verdict. The result of the trial reflected great honour on John Adams, and Josiah Quincy, the council [*sic*] for the prisoners, and also on the integrity of the jury, who ventured to give an upright verdict, in defiance of popular opinions."[3]

Ramsay proceeded to take note of the ongoing importance of massacre commemorations in the life of the community. "The events of this tragical night, sunk deep in the minds of the people, and were made subservient to important purposes," he remarked. "The anniversary of it was observed with great solemnity. Eloquent orators, were successively employed to deliver an annual oration, to preserve the remembrance of it fresh in their minds."[4] By giving as much significance—and almost as much space—to the commemorations as to the event itself, Ramsay acknowledged the symbolic power of the massacre; yet he placed the responsibility for the events of March 5 squarely on the backs of the townspeople and lauded the trials' outcomes.

Mercy Otis Warren, like Ramsay, noted that the occupation of Boston set Massachusetts apart from the other colonies. Since "no military force had been expressly called in aid of civil authority in any of them, except the Massachusetts," she wrote, observers in other colonies "began to flatter themselves that more lenient dispositions were operating in the mind of the king of Great Britain, as well as in the parliament and the people towards America in general." But Bostonians held a different view. They "had suffered almost every species of insult from the British soldiery. . . . All authority rested on the point of the sword, and the partizans of the crown triumphed for a time in the plenitude of military power." The result was "continual bickerings . . . between the soldiers and the citizens." In contrast to Ramsay, who expended only a few sentences on the shootings, Warren devoted eight paragraphs to the events of March 5 and 6 alone. Warren's version of the shootings began, not with an aggressive mob, but with the Custom House sentinel, who "seized and abused a boy" who had insulted an officer. Some "other lads" gathered, and they "took the childish revenge of pelting the soldier with snow-balls." The Main Guard was alerted to the "rising tumult," and Captain Preston led a detachment to the scene. Soldiers and "the lower class of inhabitants" had previously gotten into scrapes, so "probably both were in a temper to avenge their own private wrongs." When "the cry of fire was raised" throughout town, "the mob collected, and the soldiery from all quarters ran through the streets sword in hand, threatening and wounding the people, and with every appearance of hostility, they rushed furiously to the centre of town."[5]

The "unusual alarm . . . naturally drew out persons of higher condition, and more peaceably disposed, to inquire the cause." They were appalled by what they discovered. "Their consternation can scarcely be described, when they found orders were given to fire promiscuously among the unarmed multitude. Five or six persons fell at the first fire, and several more were dangerously wounded at their own doors."[6]

Ramsay and Warren agree on the essential significance of the Boston Massacre story. For both writers, it highlighted the dangerous consequences of granting police powers to soldiers in peacetime. Yet, this agreement on principle notwithstanding, it is striking how differently they describe the events of the massacre. Ramsay was certainly drawing on the text of *The Trial of William Wemms* in preparing his account; in the spirit of the trial narrative, he frankly characterizes Boston as a mobbish town. The soldiers were assaulted with clubs and sticks; even the snowballs were snow-covered rocks. No order was given to fire. Instead, the first shot came from a soldier who had just been struck by a townsman. Six other shots followed in ragged succession. The trial established that the soldiers "were abused, insulted, threatened, and pelted, before they fired." In seeking their acquittal, Adams and Quincy acted bravely against the sentiments of their fellow Bostonians.

By contrast, Warren gives us a kind of executive summary of the *Horrid Massacre* account, unleavened even by a mention of the trial outcomes. The conflict started innocently, in the roughhousing play of boys. Echoing the accounts of the *Boston Gazette* and the *Horrid Massacre,* Warren's version of the conflict begins with lads who were abused by soldiers; as tempers rose, the boys were joined by a mob composed of people of "the lower sort." Disregarding the courtroom proceedings, Warren blithely claims that Preston had given the order to fire "promiscuously among the unarmed multitude." Boston's "persons of higher condition, and more peaceably disposed," were drawn into the street only in time to observe the aftermath of the shootings.

These two contrasting narratives illustrate the double-edged character of the Boston Massacre. In Ramsay's version of events, which appears to a modern eye to be the more measured and defensible one, Bostonians had provoked the shootings by acting aggressively against the soldiers. But Warren captures the sensibilities of local residents, who had to make sense of the massacre in deeply personal terms. Her account also reflects a Bostonian's understanding of the relationship between the town, as a collection of responsible, property-owning citizens, and the mob, whose behavior, though understandable, was not endorsed by "persons of higher condition." Warren's account depicts rampaging soldiers acting against an aggrieved and victimized town. She does not need to invoke the trial outcomes, because the moral lesson of the massacre is contained in the event itself. For Ramsay, the massacre is more problematic; in its eagerness to provoke the soldiers, the town is as much to blame as they are. The story reaches its proper conclusion only with the trials, when Adams, Quincy, and the jurors acted honorably in the face of popular disapproval. The town's actions on the night of March 5 had been indefensible; only the soldiers' acquittals vindicated Boston's character and gave the episode a conclusion worthy of the emerging republican values of the new American nation.

While this may seem like a minor point of disagreement, in fact the mobbish character of the events of March 5 dogged Bostonians for generations, preying on the minds and imaginations of that city's respectable citizens and inspiring a deep ambivalence about the massacre. In fact, Boston's distinctive role in the American Revolution came to appear, upon reflection, to be inseparable from mob activities. The demolition of Andrew Oliver's warehouse and Thomas Hutchinson's house in 1765; the provocation of the soldiers in 1770; the destruction of East India Company tea in 1773: in each case, iconic events of critical importance to the patriot cause were triggered by acts of mob violence. The destruction of the tea — so critical to the creation of continent-wide political organization and to the coming of war — was recast in the 1830s, as Alfred Young has shown, as a "tea party," an appellation that helped to impose retrospective order and a certain kind of respectability on this carefully staged act of violent political theater.[7]

The "bloody massacre" of 1770 received no comparable recasting. As Boston's political and cultural leaders sought to reshape the events of the Revolution into a form that appeared useful and respectable, they regarded the March 5 rioters as a lawless rabble, unworthy of celebration or commemoration.

IT WAS INSTEAD BOSTON'S African American community that first gave sustained attention to the massacre. Beginning around 1840, black activists laid claim to Crispus Attucks as an African American patriot who was the first man to die for the cause of American independence. William Cooper Nell was Attucks's foremost champion. An African American who grew up in Boston, Nell was an abolitionist, a printer who trained under William Lloyd Garrison, and a historian. In a series of newspaper essays and books that appeared in the 1840s and 1850s, Nell introduced Attucks to his readers, which included the community of Boston abolitionists and black activists.[8]

Ironically, Nell learned most of what he knew about Attucks from an Italian historian. Carlo (or, as his American publishers would have it, Charles) Botta's three-volume history of the American war for independence was first translated into English in 1820; it quickly achieved great popularity, passing through seven editions in fifteen years. Botta, like Ramsay, relied heavily upon *The Trial of William Wemms* for his account of the Boston Massacre. But Botta focused on a feature of the trial that Ramsay had passed over: he made Crispus Attucks the central figure in the night's events. Botta described rioters furiously attacking the Custom House sentinel. When Preston's men marched to his relief, "they encountered a band of the populace, led by a mulatto named Attucks." As the violence and confusion escalated, "the mulatto and twelve of his companions, pressing forward," surrounded the soldiers and urged the townspeople not to be afraid. "The mulatto lifted his arm against captain Preston, and having turned one of the muskets, he seized the bayonet with his left hand." The musket was discharged, and Attucks was the first man killed.[9] Among the dozens of eyewitnesses who offered a version of these events, only Oliver Wendell's slave, Andrew, had remembered them this way. But John Adams chose to amplify Andrew's account in his closing arguments to protect the reputation of Boston, and now Botta, in search of dramatic interest, made Attucks the central figure in his narrative.

William Cooper Nell saw in Crispus Attucks something other than the outlandish figure that Adams had intended to make of him. For Nell and other black activists of the 1840s, Attucks became a patriot forebear. In 1851 Nell and six other African Americans from Boston petitioned the state legislature to appropriate funds for a monument to Crispus Attucks, "the first martyr of the American Revolution."[10] From that point forward, the question of whether the Boston Massacre would be publicly remembered was bound up with the status of Crispus Attucks as a symbol of African American citizenship.

Crispus Attucks became a familiar name in Boston at the same time that the moral depravity of slavery was becoming an urgent public issue. In 1852 New England native Harriet Beecher Stowe published *Uncle Tom's Cabin,* a novel that pricked the consciences of many northerners. Two years later, the case of Anthony Burns dramatized for Bostonians the worsening plight of American slaves. The Fugitive Slave Law of 1850 had given federal agents intrusive new powers to recapture escaped slaves and required local officials to aid their efforts. For decades, escaped slaves like Frederick Douglass had secured their freedom in the North; the new law was intended to change that. Burns, a Virginia slave who had escaped to Boston, was arrested by federal agents, tried in a local court, and led down State

Boston Massacre, March 5th 1770, drawn by William Champney, lithography by
J. H. Bufford, published by Henry O. Smith (1856). This chromolithograph
reflects the growing awareness of Crispus Attucks as a central figure in the shootings. Printed two years after Anthony Burns was led through a huge crowd lining
State Street on his return to slavery in Virginia, Champney's image echoes the
Pelham and Revere prints but portrays a more chaotic scene. The soldiers appear
to be under assault; at the center of the image is Crispus Attucks, grasping a
bayonet just before he is shot. Townspeople armed with clubs surge through
the scene, while half a dozen guns are being discharged from the windows and
balcony of the Custom House.

Street (formerly King Street) through a crowd of thousands of astonished and dismayed onlookers to the cutter that would carry him back
to Virginia.[11]

But even in Boston — the center of abolitionist and antislavery activ-
ism in the mid-nineteenth century — the idea of a monument to Crispus

Attucks was explosive. African Americans, denied full citizenship in every state in the Union, clustered in Boston's poorest neighborhood and were regarded with ambivalence by most residents. For many, the idea that Crispus Attucks was a worthy symbol of American independence was laughable. Referring to the monument petition, one local writer expressed astonishment. Attucks was no patriot hero. He "was a very fireb[r]and of disorder and sedition: the most conspicuous, defying inflammatory and uproarious of the misguided populace on that unhappy night. If Crispus had not been lucky enough to fall as a martyr, he would richly have deserved to be hanged as an incendiary."[12]

Nell confronted this characterization directly. "If the leader, ATTUCKS," deserved to hang, he wrote, "is it not a legitimate inference, that the citizens who followed on are included, and hence should swing in his company on the gallows? If the leader and his patriot band were misguided, the distinguished orators who, in after days, commemorated the 5th of March, must, indeed, have been misguided" as well. John Hancock, James Lovell, Thomas Dawes Jr., and Joseph Warren; even George Washington was supposed to have invoked the memory of the massacre when he exhorted his troops during the siege of Boston on March 5, 1776. If Attucks was a firebrand and an incendiary, Nell contended, then so too were all of these revered patriots who came after him.[13]

The 1851 petition to erect a monument in Attucks's honor failed, as did several others that followed. But his reputation spread. In Boston, a writer mentioned Attucks in a letter criticizing school segregation; in New York, James McCune Smith, the prominent physician and abolitionist, invoked Attucks in condemning the African colonization movement; in Philadelphia, activists noted Attucks's example in making their case for African American voting rights. In response to the Supreme Court's 1857 *Dred Scott* decision, in 1858 Nell and his associates in Boston began commemorating March 5 as

Crispus Attucks Day. And in the year of Abraham Lincoln's election to the presidency, as the crisis of union approached in 1860, Boston's African American community formed a quasi-military organization called the Attucks Guards. In 1863 the Fifty-Fourth Massachusetts Volunteer Infantry Regiment — the famous all-black regiment led by Robert Gould Shaw — marched through State Street. As Nell pointed out to his readers, this was the site where Attucks had fallen ninety-three years earlier. During the course of the 1850s and 1860s, the name of Crispus Attucks and his status as the first martyr of the American Revolution had been indelibly stamped in the minds of civil rights activists and abolitionists, both black and white, throughout the Northeast.[14]

Nell and his colleagues continued to petition the Massachusetts legislature for a monument to honor Attucks, but their progress was slow. After Nell's death, it was Lewis Hayden who finally broke through. A former slave born in Kentucky, Hayden escaped to Boston and became a leader of its African American community. He was elected to the Massachusetts Senate in 1873. His last political act was to organize one more petition requesting that the state erect a "suitable memorial" to the victims. He gained the support of dozens of prominent white men, including every living former governor of Massachusetts.[15] Their political clout ensured that the resolution passed both the senate and the house unopposed.

Before Governor Oliver Ames signed the bill into law, it was presented to the members of the Massachusetts Historical Society for consideration. Society president George E. Ellis introduced the discussion. Ellis, a Boston native who was a Unitarian minister as well as an amateur historian, thought the General Court's decision to erect a massacre monument was ill conceived. He argued that oppressive British policies of the 1760s and 1770s had inspired two kinds of resistance: "the one of peaceful, earnest, patriotic protest and resistance by our wise and resolute popular leaders; the other of riots and mobs, resulting in the destruction of private property and in personal insults to officials." It was only because of the rioters that troops had been sent to Boston in the first place. Once in Boston, the soldiers "were exasperated by the threats, gibes, insults, and missiles of a mob of these rioters, and discharged their guns into it in self-defence. Those who fell in this hap-hazard conflict came to be described as the victims of a 'massacre,'" but he believed the term was an unfortunate misnomer that gave the victims too much credit. It seemed incredible that the Commonwealth of Massachusetts, which had "never as yet raised any monumental memorial of a person or of an event in its history," would now "pay its highest monumental honors to commemorate those victims."[16]

Other Historical Society members concurred. "These men were not acting in the character of patriots, but of rioters," John D. Washburn noted indignantly. Charles Deane attributed the attack on the soldiers to "a mere mob, inspired by no elevated sentiments, and fatally bent on mischief." By chance, a few "were killed, and for that reason they became martyrs. . . . Thus the martyr's crown is placed upon the brow of the vulgar ruffian."[17]

Only one member dissented from this majority opinion. Lucius Robinson Paige, an elderly Universalist minister, reminded the society that, at the time of the shootings, Bostonians believed the massacre victims "had lost their lives in the cause of liberty; and the whole town rendered such funeral honors as had seldom been witnessed." In the years that followed, the tradition of the massacre oration arose "to keep the memory of that event green." In all the texts of all the orations, "he could not recall a single disparaging remark concerning the victims." Moreover, before the Declaration of Independence, it was not only the massacre victims who could be called lawless rioters: all acts of opposition to British authority were "technically rebellious and treasonable." There was no clear way to distinguish the attack on soldiers in King Street from the "unorganized skirmish" in Lexington and Concord a few years later, or even from the "more orderly but illegally organized struggle on Bunker Hill." Having made his point, however, Paige retreated. He could not support a statement that condemned the massacre monument; "yet, as there seemed to be a desire that the action should be unanimous, he would not vote against it, notwithstanding he so strongly doubted its propriety and expediency."[18]

Once the members achieved consensus, it remained to decide on a strategy. Washburn argued that if the Historical Society merely issued a statement of disapproval, it would have little effect. But if it created a committee, led by the president of the society, to "wait on the Governor," then they might "prevail on the Executive to interpose his veto." They would only succeed, he quickly added, if the governor were "not more likely to be influenced by the negroes and the cheaper politicians than by the educated men." But that was precisely the rub. When Washburn's suggestion was formally proposed, President Ellis declined to serve. He "had been informed of some of the influences under which the legislative measure had been carried," and he was persuaded that nothing could be done to block the passage of the resolution: Washburn's "negroes and cheaper politicians" were bound to carry the day. Instead, the society adopted a brief statement "applauding the sentiment which erects memorials to the heroes and martyrs of our annals," but concluding that only a "misapprehension" of the King Street shootings could have led to the decision to grant the victims "recognition at the public expense."[19]

The efforts of the Massachusetts Historical Society notwithstanding, Governor Ames signed the resolve into law. A German sculptor named Robert Kraus won the design competition, the governor selected a site on the Boston Common, and a committee of nineteen gentlemen, including Lewis Hayden and many of the other petitioners, made arrangements for the unveiling and dedication ceremony. It took place on November 14, 1888. In "most delightful" weather, a huge public procession marched from the corner of Beacon and Charles Streets past the State House and City Hall and then circled back to the site of the monument on a triangular lot facing Tremont Street. State and city officials took their places on a temporary platform in front of the monument, while an enormous throng gathered around them and spilled into Tremont Street. After an invocation and remarks by the chairman of the Citizens' Committee and by Governor Ames, a "canopy of American tricolor" fell away from the monument, producing "a concerted shout of delight by the assembled thousands." The procession then made its way to Faneuil Hall for a more extended ceremony.[20]

Though the monument honored all five victims of the massacre, Attucks was the focus of attention. From the beginning, it was called the Crispus Attucks Monument. At Faneuil Hall, the governor began by welcoming the African Americans in attendance. "Those men who are our special guests to-day are representatives of a race whose brother, Attucks, was the first one to fall in the great massacre," he noted. The mayor followed with brief remarks that enlarged on the theme. "I am aware that the monument to Crispus Attucks and his martyr associates has been the subject of more or less adverse criticism," he began, "and that by some they are looked upon as rioters, who deserved their fate." But, he insisted, the "Boston Massacre was one of the most important and exciting events that preceded our Revolution," and with it the Declaration of Independence, "that immortal document which pronounced all men free and equal without regard to color, creed, or nationality." Erecting "the Attucks Monument on Boston Common," he concluded, "ratifies the words of that declaration" and ensures that "the memory of the martyrs whose blood was shed in the cause of liberty in 1770 will thus be preserved and honored for all time." The exercises also included a long poem written by John Boyle O'Reilly, entitled simply "Crispus Attucks," which enlarged at length on Attucks's heroism and the unity of mankind.[21]

John Fiske, the well-known philosopher and historian, delivered the dedication address. He was not the organizing committee's first choice: they invited Frederick Douglass, America's most famous former slave, to speak, and settled on Fiske only when Douglass declined. Fiske departed from the day's script in a way that Douglass surely would not have. For Fiske, the Boston Massacre could only be explained and justified in context, and he provided an abundance of it. Beginning with the writs of assistance issued to revenue officers in 1761, he traced the effects of the Stamp Act, explained the Townshend Duties, discussed the nonimportation movement and the *Liberty* riot, and focused on Bernard's decision to call for troops in Boston. He explained the quartering controversy that accompanied the arrival of the troops; he described the debate between Bernard and Gage, a few months later, over the question of whether the troops should be removed; he enumerated the ways in which the troops annoyed local residents.

Finally Fiske came to the night of March 5, when a crowd gathered in the street. "Conspicuous among the throng," he noted, "was a very tall colored man, who seemed to be acting as a leader." This was Attucks, who received only passing attention in the afternoon's oration. Relying on the narrative that was presented at the soldiers' trial, Fiske laid out the events of the evening in detail. But he quietly amended the version of events, drawn from Andrew's testimony, which Adams had presented in his closing argument. Instead of portraying Attucks leading the assault on the soldiers, Fiske relied on the testimony of John Danbrook to offer a more peaceful, contemplative Attucks. He was shot, Fiske told his listeners, while he "was standing quietly at a little distance leaning upon a stick." It is unclear how many members of his audience were surprised by this innovation. And in any case, the details of the shootings meant little to Fiske. For him, the great significance of the massacre came in its aftermath, when townspeople calmly but firmly insisted on the removal of the troops from Boston. "Nature is apt to demand some forfeit in accomplishing great results, and for achieving this particular result the lives of those five men were forfeit," he remarked. "It is, therefore, historically correct to regard them as the first martyrs of American independence."[22]

At the same time that Fiske sought to validate the monument, his primary theme was to emphasize that Boston was a respectable town, not a mobbish one. Setting aside the destruction of Hutchinson's house in the Stamp Act riot, which Fiske called a "disgraceful affair" that was "at once disowned and condemned by the people of Boston," he repeatedly stressed the civil character of the town's public actions. Though he narrated the events of March 5 at length, Fiske was less impressed by that outburst of violence than he was by the fact that it was an isolated incident. In that light, the Boston Massacre story "furnishes an instructive illustration of the high state of civilization that had been attained by the people among whom it happened." That only five people were killed during a seventeen-month occupation "is a fact highly creditable to both the discipline of the soldiers and to the moderation of the people." And that Bostonians were so deeply affected by the shootings, yet allowed the soldiers "to be dealt with in the ordinary course of law, is a striking commentary upon the general peacefulness and decorum of American life; and it shows how high and severe was the standard by which our forefathers judged all lawless proceedings." Attucks was largely an afterthought to Fiske, and he sidestepped the question of whether the victims were rioters or patriots.[23]

For most of those involved with the monument dedication, however, Attucks was central to its meaning. The monument itself illustrates the symbolic power of the first African American martyr to American independence. Made of Concord granite, its central feature is a twenty-five-foot pillar with the victims' names inscribed near the top, beginning with Crispus Attucks. Embedded in the base is a bronze bas-relief showing a modified version of the street scene made famous by Henry

Pelham and Paul Revere. The setting is the same, but the crowd is more turbulent and chaotic, with townspeople appearing more active and less like innocent victims. At the front of the scene, already prostrate, with sticks and clubs strewn around him, lies the figure of Crispus Attucks. Quotations from Daniel Webster ("From that Moment we may date the Severance of the British Empire") and John Adams ("On that night the Foundation of American Independence was laid") are inscribed in the upper corners of the scene. Above the bas-relief is a seven-foot bronze statue called *Free America*. In the tradition of images depicting America and liberty, it is a loosely draped female figure. A huge eagle is lighting near her feet, at the edge of the plinth. The royal crown is crushed under her right foot. In one hand she holds a flag—not yet unfurled—and in the other a length of broken chain.[24] The chain creates a powerful visual link between the chains of empire and the chains of slavery, and Attucks is the historical figure who makes the connection meaningful.

The prolonged controversy over the Crispus Attucks Monument recast the old debate about whether Boston was a mobbish town. Opponents held—as John Adams had argued more than a century earlier—that the March 5 mob was a disorderly rabble, acting not on principle but on violent impulse. In the post–Civil War era, opponents of the monument feared that public acclaim would only encourage present-day radicals to destroy property and threaten disorder. And as Crispus Attucks came to the fore as the central figure in that night's events, the racial dimension of this argument only grew more prominent. The disorder of the Boston Massacre mob was embodied and symbolized by the huge mulatto man who led the charge against the troops. But supporters of the monument argued that the victims constituted a patriot vanguard. The first martyrs for American liberty, they were guilty of nothing more than anticipating the frustrations of their countrymen, who would soon die in much larger numbers in the face of British arms.

The Boston Massacre Monument, by Robert Kraus, in a photograph taken ca. 1904. Crispus Attucks is listed first among the victims, and the broken chain in the hand of the *Free America* statue symbolically links the end of colonial status with the end of slavery.

In the decades following the monument controversy, Crispus Attucks became an increasingly important figure. His name began to appear on public institutions, including a Norfolk, Virginia, theater, a high school in Indianapolis, a Chicago academy, a Brooklyn grade school, and a community center in York, Pennsylvania. He was also a powerful symbol for African American activists during the civil rights struggles of the 1950s and 1960s. In 1967 the National Committee of Negro Churchmen met at the base of the Crispus Attucks Monument on the Boston Common to announce a "national campaign to complete 'the unfinished American revolution' through a multimillion dollar fund for economic development of the Negro community." And in 1968 the public schools of Newark, New Jersey, closed on March 5 to honor Attucks. Mayor Hugh J. Addonizio proudly declared that Newark "was the first school system in the nation to declare a holiday for a Negro." Two and a half weeks later, some twenty-five thousand Newark citizens turned out for a parade in Attucks's honor.[25] A divisive figure through much of the nineteenth century, Attucks became an accepted addition to the pantheon of Revolutionary heroes in the era of the civil rights movement.

ON THE FIRST WEEKEND in May 1970, the Ohio National Guard was mobilized to the campus of Kent State University to restore order after a series of violent incidents. On Thursday, President Richard Nixon had announced his decision to send U.S. troops into Cambodia. That Friday night, unrest over Nixon's decision spilled into the streets of downtown Kent, Ohio; a growing crowd of students stopped cars, broke storefront windows, and threw rocks at policemen who tried to intervene. The next day, campus demonstrations culminated in an attack on the ROTC building, which was burned to the ground. On Sunday, the university declared a state of emergency and banned outdoor gatherings; twice on Sunday evening, officials read the Ohio

Riot Act to large groups of students and insisted that they disband. The next day—Monday, May 4—students began to gather on the campus commons in the late morning, many of them in anticipation of a protest rally scheduled for noon. In response, the guardsmen's commanding officer, General Robert Canterbury, issued orders to disperse the crowd. Ninety-six soldiers and seven officers formed up and marched through the center of campus. Students shouted at the guardsmen and threw rocks, while the guardsmen fired tear gas canisters into the crowd. Near the top of Blanket Hill, the guardsmen later claimed they heard a sharp noise, like gunfire. In an apparent panic, they fired in response. In thirteen seconds, twenty-eight guardsmen fired a total of sixty-one rounds. Four students were killed and nine were wounded.[26]

The military force of a great world power shooting into an unarmed crowd of its own civilians: the analogy to the Boston Massacre immediately suggested itself. Eight days later, a company called SBS Creative Designs published a poster featuring Paul Revere's famous engraving, with large red banners across the top and the bottom. The top banner said "Boston Mar. 5, 1770," while the bottom read "Kent State May 4, 1970." Four coffins—very similar to the ones printed in the *Boston Gazette* two hundred years earlier—punctuated the lower banner. The soldiers' coats and the victims' blood were colored red, while the rest of the print was in black and white.[27]

The firepower at Kent State was much greater than it had been two hundred years earlier: the guardsmen discharged more than sixty rounds in about thirteen seconds, and none of the four victims who were killed was within a football field's length of the soldiers. But in other ways the event was sufficiently similar to the shootings in Boston that some observers who reflected on Kent State made the comparison explicit. Student protests brought hundreds of college campuses to a standstill in the weeks following the shootings. At Brooklyn Polytechnic, a hundred students staged a lie-in, wearing the names of people who had been killed in wars and "other civil disturbances dating back to the pre–Revolutionary War Boston Massacre." When an interviewer asked about the larger significance of an event that left four students dead, Kent State student Michael Stein remarked, "Only five people were killed in the Boston Massacre." In a letter to the editor in *Time,* John J. Guiniven drew out the implications of the comparison. "In March 1770 a military unit took offense at being called names and being pelted with rocks," he wrote, "and fired into a crowd of unarmed civilians. They called that the Boston Massacre. Then they started a revolution."[28]

Peter Stone, an award-winning writer for film and stage whose *1776* had recently won the Tony Award for Best Musical, had a similar point in mind when he published an editorial in the *New York Times* entitled "Afraid of Revolution?" It began, "A group of protesters gathers in the streets to decry government policies — they are angry, they are loud and abusive, they are demanding disobedience. Facing them is a unit of militia. . . . Suddenly, somehow, a guardsman fires into the crowd. . . . Kent State, 1970? No. Boston, 1770." Americans, Stone went on to argue, had lost touch with their radical origins and, in the era of the Vietnam War, clung instead to an unreflective patriotism.[29]

The parallels between Kent State and the Boston Massacre extend beyond the obvious fact of soldiers firing into a civilian crowd. The victims included both active participants in a crowd action and innocent bystanders. From the beginning, eyewitness accounts differed dramatically; soldiers and their defenders claimed that the crowd was increasingly aggressive and menacing, while critics argued (and, in the case of Kent State, photographic evidence demonstrates) that people mostly kept their distance. In the aftermath of both shootings, many people expressed surprise that the soldiers' weapons had live ammunition, and in both cases it was unclear whether the soldiers were ordered to fire. Conspiracy theories took shape immediately. In

Boston, townspeople believed that soldiers and customs officers were acting together and developed the claim that shots were fired from the Custom House window. In Kent, multiple conspiracy theories emerged: that ten of the soldiers agreed to fire on the students upon a prearranged signal; that an armed undercover FBI informant fired a pistol, triggering the soldiers' response; that the federal government had decided that it was time to act decisively against campus demonstrations, and officials in Kent proceeded accordingly.[30]

Nor do the similarities stop there. In the wake of Kent State, a spate of publications aimed to tell the story from the victims' point of view. Photographs of the shootings began to circulate almost immediately afterward, just as the Pelham and Revere prints had done two hundred years earlier. Annual commemorations on the Kent State campus recalled the victims and decried the violent act that killed them, while Neil Young's song "Ohio"—recorded and released only a few weeks after the shootings—broadcast a sense of anguish more widely. Kent State, like the Boston Massacre, quickly became a cultural icon for everyone engaged in a movement challenging government policy and decrying its coercive and violent tactics. In Kent, as in Boston, the legal resolution of the shootings—delayed in both cases—exonerated the soldiers. Both events appear, in retrospect, to have been decisive turning points in an ongoing political conflict. The Boston Massacre radicalized that community and ensured its role as the crucible of the American Revolution. The Kent State shootings enflamed antiwar activists and undermined the credibility and legitimacy of the Nixon administration, both in its decision to go to war in Cambodia and in its attempts to crack down on dissidents at home.[31]

Kent State, like the Boston Massacre, gave rise to controversies over monuments. In Boston, the erection of a monument was delayed by more than a century. In Kent, campus officials rejected a bronze statue by George Segal representing Abraham and Isaac at the moment when the biblical patriarch was about to slay his son. Segal inscribed the work "In Memory of May 4, 1970," and intended it to represent the moral dilemma faced by soldiers and agents of the state as they confronted student protesters. University president Brage Golding considered the image too violent and refused to accept the work. Instead, campus officials created a May 4 Memorial Committee, which sponsored a national competition to design an appropriate memorial. Bruno Ast, the winning designer, conceived an ambitious, fourteen-hundred-square-foot plaza that would cost an estimated $1.2 million. But the campus imposed a budget of $100,000 and installed a dramatically scaled-down version.[32]

One final similarity between the Boston Massacre and the Kent State shootings is perhaps more important than all the others. Both events had a double-edged character: while soldiers could be criticized for firing into a crowd, members of the crowd were equally subject to criticism for their behavior. Thus, while students like Michael Stein and writers like Peter Stone used an analogy with the Boston Massacre to validate the actions of Kent State students and condemn the national guardsmen who fired upon them, most Americans took a different view. In response to Stone's *New York Times* editorial, for example, the Reverend William S. Reisman of Garrison, New York, wrote a scathing letter to the editor. Stone's "thesis is typical of current revisionist efforts to give cachet to today's radical anarchists and mindless 'trashers,'" he wrote. If Stone understood the Boston Massacre more clearly, he would recognize that his comparison was unflattering to the Kent State students. The "Boston rabble of 1770" were lawless rioters; in King Street on the night of March 5, the soldiers "were in danger of being stoned to death by a mob that was determined to force a volley." Defended in their trial by "none other than John Adams," the British soldiers were "acquitted in a fair trial by a jury." The national guardsmen in Kent, Reisman implied, were no more guilty than their redcoat counterparts had been.[33]

Nor was Reisman alone in that opinion. In a letter to the editor of Kent's newspaper, the *Record-Courier,* Diane Foster remarked, "The National Guard made only one mistake — they should have fired sooner and longer." A national Gallup poll conducted in the weeks after the shootings found that 58 percent of Americans considered the protesters to have been primarily responsible for the tragedy, while only 11 percent placed the blame on the national guardsmen. On the basis of that finding, William A. Gordon has noted, "one could argue that these were the most popular murders ever committed in the United States."[34]

Less than two weeks after the Kent State shootings, dozens of police and highway patrol officers responded to reports of a riot on the campus of Jackson State College in Jackson, Mississippi. Jackson is the capital of Mississippi, and Jackson State is a historically black campus bisected by Lynch Street, a major thoroughfare for the town's white population and the site of frequent hostile interactions between students and townspeople. On the night of May 14, 1970, a crowd gathered on campus near Lynch Street, throwing rocks at cars and setting fire to a dump truck. In response, about seventy lawmen armed with shotguns, carbines, rifles, and submachine guns approached Alexander Hall, a women's dormitory, where the crowd of students and black townspeople was gathered. A chain-link fence separated them. Someone threw a bottle into the street; law officers later claimed that they thought they were caught in the crossfire of snipers on campus rooftops. In response, they unleashed a twenty-eight-second barrage in which more than 150 rounds were fired, leaving 400 bullet or buckshot holes in the façade of Alexander Hall. One college student, Phillip Gibbs, and one local high school student, James Earl Green, were killed; twenty-two others, mostly women who had been inside the dormitory, were wounded.[35]

The Jackson State and Kent State shootings were immediately linked in the national press, but in subsequent weeks and months Jackson State received considerably less attention from the national news media. Jackson State faculty member Gene Young has argued that it may have been only the Kent State tragedy ten days earlier that brought any national attention at all to the Jackson State campus. And strikingly, the Boston Massacre analogy was much less in evidence in the case of Jackson State than it had been with Kent State. A different context supplied the most meaningful narrative for understanding the Jackson shootings: the violence against blacks that ran through the era of the civil rights movement. The legacy of southern violence against African Americans supplied the interpretive frame for everyone involved in the shootings. "The black survivors of Jackson State appear to view themselves as part of a larger group," notes one commentator, "a group which includes all black survivors of white violence. The tradition of struggle against white injustice and willing or unwilling martyrdom to the cause of black freedom is part of the fabric of black southern community life." Seven years earlier, civil rights activist Medgar Evers had been assassinated in his driveway in Jackson, Mississippi. On the night of the Lynch Street riot, Jackson State students heard a rumor that Evers's brother, Charles—the mayor of Fayette, Mississippi, whose daughter attended Jackson State—had been shot. In Orangeburg, South Carolina, in 1968, highway patrolmen had fired into a crowd of black protesters at South Carolina State College, killing three and injuring twenty-eight. The context of southern violence against blacks was much more immediate and salient to students at Jackson State than their kinship to the mostly white students in Kent, Ohio.[36]

Yet the connection between Lynch Street in Jackson and King Street in Boston was not neglected entirely. In July 1970, two months after the shootings, the *Chicago Tribune* featured a long essay by the Reverend Jesse Jackson that sought to explain "what blacks of

Chicago want." Jackson argued that black Chicagoans wanted to "share responsibility in the reshaping" of their city. In return, they wanted inclusion: "Blacks seek the freedom to be judges, jurors, and policemen in proportionate numbers to their population ratio," he contended. White Americans needed to recognize, according to Jackson, that "there is no more red-blooded an American group than the nation's black citizenry." To drive the point home, he asked, "Did you know this? The first blood shed for this land's liberty was that of a black man, Crispus Attucks." And blacks continued to shed blood for their nation. "Now," he wrote, "black boys are being wounded and killed in Viet Nam at two to three times the rate of white boys." But despite their contributions to American interests, blacks were still violently oppressed at home. "We have shed mortal blood, too, for freedom even in domestic combat against poverty and racism," Jackson noted, "such as did Fred Hampton of Chicago's West Side, James Chaney and Emmet Till in neo-primitive Mississippi, the South Carolina State College martyrs in Orangeburg, and the Jackson State College martyrs." In Jackson's account, the Boston Massacre belonged not only to a narrative of American nationhood; through Crispus Attucks, it also represented—as it had done more than a century earlier for William C. Nell—the starting point for a narrative of African American citizenship.[37]

After 1970 the Boston Massacre receded into the shadows again. That began to change in the 1990s, when critics became increasingly concerned about the militarization of law enforcement. In expressing their concerns, they used the Boston Massacre as a meaningful point of reference. More recently, the fear of militarized police forces has intersected with the issue of race in many urban settings. For leaders of the Black Lives Matter movement, it is useful to trace a genealogy from Crispus Attucks to Michael Brown, the eighteen-year-old African American who was shot and killed by a Ferguson, Missouri, police officer in August 2014.[38] As concern about police brutality against African Americans grows into a nationwide movement, the legacy of Crispus Attucks is relevant once again.

ALL OF THESE CONTROVERSIES illustrate the usefulness of the Boston Massacre as a touchstone of American identity, and also the limits of its power to generate a consensus response. Because it occurred at the dawn of a successful revolution against British authority, the double-edged character of the Boston Massacre is easy to overlook, at least initially. In the case of the Kent State shootings, it cropped up many times in the first few weeks after May 5, but then became less common. After 1989 the repression of student protests in Tiananmen Square appeared to protesters to be a more useful comparison. Though there are many dissimilarities, both are cases in which the armed forces of a powerful government suppressed student protest. And in both cases, the government that suppressed the protest remained in power.

If the Boston Massacre seems superficially unproblematic, it is because the government that sponsored the repression of crowd activity was subsequently overthrown. It became an important symbol of imperial injustice in the narrative of events that ran from the Stamp Act riots to the Declaration of Independence. Even the exoneration of the soldiers could be folded into a patriotic narrative. The outcome of the trials illustrated the civil, rules-bound character of Boston — and, by extension, of the thirteen united colonies — even in the midst of a rebellion. Boston was a wronged community that nevertheless abided by laws intended to protect life and property. The American Revolution was a campaign for order in the midst of imperial disorder.

But the potential to see something else entirely in the Boston Massacre always lay just beneath the surface. John Adams's closing argument in the soldiers' trial gave subsequent critics all the ammunition they needed to elevate criticism of the Boston mob above criticism of the soldiers' behavior. It also introduced a volatile element of race into the narrative: by vividly invoking the image of a club-wielding mulatto, Adams summoned the specter of black disorder and violence at the same time that he — unwittingly — helped to create an African American patriot hero. In the monument controversy and the aftermath of Kent State, the effort to invoke the Boston Massacre as an unproblematic symbol of American identity — a symbol that legitimated protest and condemned its violent repression — met with opposition from critics who drew upon Adams's arguments and turned the analogy against the behavior of the crowd. For leaders of the Black Lives Matter movement, the example of Crispus Attucks helps to legitimize the aggressive assertion of rights in opposition to armed agents of an oppressive government.

As a symbol, the Boston Massacre refuses to resolve itself. Instead it asks us to define, over and over again, the limits of legitimate authority, and to place them in the balance against the limits of legitimate popular protest. In this respect, the symbolic import of the Boston Massacre is of a piece with the contested meanings of the American Revolution itself.

APPENDIX

ABBREVIATIONS

NOTES

ACKNOWLEDGMENTS

ILLUSTRATION CREDITS

INDEX

Eyewitness Accounts

Boston Massacre
Witnesses and Deponents

Last name	First name	Inquest[1]	SNHM[2]	FALUD[3]	Other depositions[4]	Preston MS[5]	Wemms MS[6]	TWW[7]
Anonymous					Y			
Adams	Matthew		18					
Allen	Jeremiah		64					
Allen	Joseph		84					
Alline	Benjamin		60					
Allman	John		87					
Andrews	Benjamin		93					
Appleton	John						Crown	Crown
Appleton	Nathaniel		31				Crown	Crown
Archbald	Francis		50			Crown	Crown	Crown
Atwood	Samuel		35					
Austin	Jonathan W.					Crown	Crown	Crown
Bailey	James						Crown	Crown

(*continued*)

Last name	First name	Inquest[1]	SNHM[2]	FALUD[3]	Other depositions[4]	Preston MS[5]	Wemms MS[6]	TWW[7]
Bass	Gillam		59					
Bass	Henry		25				Prisoners	Prisoners
Bass	Jedediah						Crown	Crown
Basset	James			113				
Belknap	Jeremiah		32					
Belknap	Joseph					Crown		
Bliss	Samuel			114				
Bliss	Theodore					Crown & Prisoner	Prisoners	Prisoners
Bostwick	Samuel		23					
Botson	William						Prisoners	Prisoners
Bourgatte	Charles	Y	58					
Bowman	Archibald						Prisoners	Prisoners
Brailsford	John		14					
Brailsford	Mary		12					
Brewer	James						Crown	Crown
Bridgham	Ebenezer						Crown	Crown
Broaders	Bartholomew		38					
Broughton	Hugh				Y			
Brown	John		22					
Brown	William Jr.			115				
Buckley	John						Prisoners	Prisoners
Buckley	Thomas			106a				
Burdick	Benjamin Jr.		43			Crown	Crown	Crown
Cain	Thomas		46					

APPENDIX

Last name	First name	Inquest[1]	SNHM[2]	FALUD[3]	Other depositions[4]	Preston MS[5]	Wemms MS[6]	TWW[7]
Calfe	Daniel		40			Crown		
Carter	James						Crown	Crown
Carter	William						Prisoners	Prisoners
Cary	Jonathan						Crown	Crown
Church	Benjamin Jr.		88					
Clark	Samuel						Crown	Crown
Coburn	John		33					
Cockran	David		3					
Coffin	John					Prisoner		
Cole	John					Crown		
Condon	Samuel		48					
Conner	Charles	Y						
Cookson	John						Prisoners	Prisoners
Copeland	Asa		13					
Cornwall	Daniel					Prisoner	Prisoners	Prisoners
Costar	George		67					
Cox	John						Crown	Crown
Crafts	Edward		83					
Crawford	James						Prisoners	Prisoners
Croswell	Joseph						Crown	Crown
Cruickshanks	Alexander					Crown	Prisoners	Prisoners
Cullen	Henry				Y			
Cunningham	Peter		47			Crown		
Danbrook	John						Crown	Crown
Davies	William			99			Prisoners	Prisoners

(*continued*)

{ 289 }

Last name	First name	Inquest[1]	SNHM[2]	FALUD[3]	Other depositions[4]	Preston MS[5]	Wemms MS[6]	TWW[7]
Davis	Benjamin					Prisoner	Prisoners	Prisoners
Davis	Benjamin Jr.						Prisoners	Prisoners
Dickson	Hugh			110a				
Dixon	William						Prisoners	Prisoners
Dodge	James						Crown	Crown
Dorr	Ebenezer			82				
Dougan	Henry			121	Y			
Drowne	Samuel			68				
Edwards	Joseph					Prisoner		
Emmons	Samuel						Crown	
Fallass	William			85				
Fenno	Ephraim			91				
Ferreter	Nicholas			5			Crown	Crown
Field	Catherine						Prisoners	Prisoners
Fisher	John			7				
Fosdick	Nathaniel			51		Crown	Crown	Crown
French	Jeremiah				Y			
Frizel	Benjamin			63				
Frost	John					Prisoner	Prisoners	Prisoners
Fullerton	Robert					Crown		
Gammell	John			57				
Gardner	Mary			86				
Gerrish	Edward					Crown		
Gifford	James					Prisoner		

Last name	First name	Inquest[1]	SNHM[2]	FALUD[3]	Other depositions[4]	Preston MS[5]	Wemms MS[6]	TWW[7]
Gillespie	John			104		Prisoner	Prisoners	Prisoners
Goddard	John		39					
Goddard	Robert	Y	72			Crown		
Goldfinch	John			108			Prisoners	Prisoners
Gould	Archibald						Prisoners	Prisoners
Gray	Harrison Jr.					Prisoner	Prisoners	Prisoners
Gray	John		9					
Green	Hammond		95					
Green	John		94					
Greenwood	Thomas		96	111				
Gridley	John						Prisoners	Prisoners
Hall	Thomas						Crown	Crown
Hallwood	Henry			116				
Helyer	Joseph					Prisoner	Crown	Crown
Hemmingway	Samuel						Crown	Crown
Hewes	George		75					
Hickling	John		73					
Hill	Edward			105		Prisoner		
Hill	John		8				Crown	Crown
Hinckley	Ebenezer		49			Crown		
Hinckley	Joseph						Prisoners	Prisoners
Hirons	Richard						Prisoners	Prisoners
Hobby	Charles		44					
Hooton	Joseph Jr.		52					

(*continued*)

Last name	First name	Inquest[1]	SNHM[2]	FALUD[3]	Other depositions[4]	Preston MS[5]	Wemms MS[6]	TWW[7]
Hubbard	Thomas					Crown		
Hughes	Shubael						Prisoners	Prisoners
Hunter	William						Prisoners	Prisoners
Hutchinson	Thomas					Prisoner		
Inman	John			98				
Jackson	Thomas Jr.		76					
Jackson	William					Prisoner		
Jeffries	John						Prisoners	Prisoners
Keaton	Patrick						Prisoners	Prisoners
King	Matthias		37					
Kirkwood	James		36					
Kneeland	Bartholomew		30				Crown	Crown
Knight	Thomas						Prisoners	Prisoners
Knox	Henry		55			Crown	Prisoners	Prisoners
Langsford	Edward G.					Crown	Crown	Crown
Lawrie	Andrew			120				
Leach	John	Y	42					
LeBaron	William		26					
Lee	Benjamin					Prisoner	Prisoners	Prisoners
Leslie	Samuel			102				
Lewis	William		27					
Lockhead	Thomas			100				
Loring	David		92					
Mall	Alexander			101	Y			
Mansfield	John						Prisoners	Prisoners

Last name	First name	Inquest[1]	SNHM[2]	FALUD[3]	Other depositions[4]	Preston MS[5]	Wemms MS[6]	TWW[7]
Marshall	Thomas		41			Crown	Crown	Crown
Mason	Edmund			103			Prisoners	Prisoners
Mason	Jonathan		80			Crown		
Mattear	Daniel			119				
McCann	Hugh				Y			
McNeil	Archibald Jr.		10					
Michelson	David						Prisoners	Prisoners
Minchin	Paul			107				
Morton	Dimond		62			Crown		
Murray	Matthew					Prisoner	Prisoners	Prisoners
Napier	William			117				
Newhall	William		4					
Noyes	Nathaniel		15					
O'Hara	Barbason						Prisoners	Prisoners
Paine	Edward						Crown	Crown
Palmes	Richard	Y	53	112		Prisoner	Crown	Crown
Parker	Isaac		29					
Parker	William						Prisoners	Prisoners
Patterson	Robert		69					
Payne	Edward		56				Crown	Crown
Peck	Thomas H.					Prisoner		
Petty	Joseph	Y						
Pierce	Isaac		81			Crown		
Pierpont	Robert		21					
Polley	Robert		34					

(*continued*)

Last name	First name	Inquest[1]	SNHM[2]	FALUD[3]	Other depositions[4]	Preston MS[5]	Wemms MS[6]	TWW[7]
Prince	Newton					Prisoner	Prisoners	Prisoners
Pryce	Thomas			97				
Read	Francis		61					
Rhodes	William		89					
Richardson	Jeffrey		6					
Riordan	John		77					
Ross	Alexander			118	Y			
Ruddock	John						Prisoners	Prisoners
Russell	Mary		90					
Russell	Nathaniel						Prisoners	Prisoners
Sawyer	William					Prisoner		
Selkrig	James						Prisoners	Prisoners
Short	John						Prisoners	Prisoners
Simmons	Thomas						Prisoners	Prisoners
Simpson	Josiah		65				Crown	Crown
St. Clair	David			110b				
Steele	Thomas			106b				
Stewart	John						Prisoners	Prisoners
Strong	William						Prisoners	Prisoners
svt to Hubbart[8]	Cato		70					
svt to Lloyd	Jack					Prisoner		
svt to Wendall	Andrew					Prisoner	Prisoners	Prisoners
Swan	Caleb		19					
Swansborough	Margaret		20					

Last name	First name	Inquest[1]	SNHM[2]	FALUD[3]	Other depositions[4]	Preston MS[5]	Wemms MS[6]	TWW[7]
Tant	William		45					
Thayer	Mary		11					
Thayer	Nathaniel		28				Crown	Crown
Thompson	James						Prisoners	Prisoners
Townsend	Gregory						Prisoners	Prisoners
Tuckerman	Abraham		78					
Tyler	William		24					
Usher	Daniel		71					
Usher	Jane		17					
Vibart	James			122				
Walker	Spencer		79					
Ward	Richard	Y	16					
Warwell	Michael Angelo			123				
Weir	John			109				
Whiston	Obadiah		74			Crown		
Whitehouse	Jane					Prisoner		
Whittington	William						Prisoners	Prisoners
Wilkinson	Thomas						Crown	Crown
Williams	John						Prisoners	
Williams	Robert						Crown	Crown
Willis	Charles						Prisoners	Prisoners
Wilme	John		1					
Wilme	Sarah		2					
Wilson	Archibald						Prisoners	Prisoners

(*continued*)

Last name	First name	Inquest[1]	SNHM[2]	FALUD[3]	Other depositions[4]	Preston MS[5]	Wemms MS[6]	TWW[7]
Wilson	John		66					
Woodall	James					Prisoner	Prisoners	Prisoners
Wyat	William		54			Crown		

[1] Inquest: Depositions in the Revolutionary War Manuscript Collection, Boston Public Library, online at https://archive.org.

[2] [James Bowdoin, Joseph Warren, and Samuel Pemberton], *A Short Narrative of the horrid Massacre in Boston; Perpetrated In the Evening of the Fifth Day of March, 1770, by Soldiers of the XXIXth Regiment; Which With The XIVth Regiment Were then Quartered there: With Some Observations on the State of Things Prior to that Catastrophe* (Boston: Edes and Gill, 1770). The numbers refer to the order in which the depositions are printed.

[3] [Anon.], *A Fair Account of the Late Unhappy Disturbance at Boston in New England . . .* (London, 1770). The numbers refer to the order in which the depositions are printed.

[4] Other depositions: Anonymous, reported by captain of the *Senegal,* 11 Mar. 1770, CO5/759, NAUK; Broughton, Cullen, Dougan, French, Mall, McCann, and Ross, July–Aug. 1770, CO5/88, NAUK.

[5] Manuscript testimony from Preston trial: CO5/759, NAUK. "Crown" denotes that the witness testified for the prosecution; "Prisoner" indicates that the witness testified for the defense.

[6] Manuscript testimony from the trial of the soldiers: CO5/759, NAUK. "Crown" denotes that the witness testified for the prosecution; "Prisoners" indicates that the witness testified for the defense.

[7] *The Trial of William Wemms, James Hartegan, William McCauley, Hugh White, Matthew Killroy, William Warren, John Carrol, and Hugh Montgomery . . . ,* taken in shorthand by John Hodgson (Boston: J. Fleeming, 1770). "Crown" denotes that the witness testified for the prosecution; "Prisoners" indicates that the witness testified for the defense.

[8] Three slaves gave depositions or testimony, each identified by a first name only and as "servant" to an owner. They are listed together here as "svt to" their respective owners.

Abbreviations

AHR	*The American Historical Review.*
ANB	*American National Biography,* ed. John A. Garraty and Mark C. Carnes, 24 vols. (New York: Oxford University Press, 1999).
BEP	*Boston Evening-Post.*
BG	*Boston-Gazette, and Country Journal.*
BR	*Boston Records Commissioners' Reports (1674–1822),* 39 vols. (Boston, 1876–1909).
CGTG	Clarence Edwin Carter, ed., *The Correspondence of General Thomas Gage with the Secretaries of State, and with the War Office and Treasury, 1763–1775,* 2 vols. (New Haven, CT: Yale University Press, 1931–1933).
CTH	John W. Tyler and Elizabeth Dubrulle, eds., *The Correspondence of Thomas Hutchinson* (Boston: Colonial Society of Massachusetts, 2014–).
DAB	*Dictionary of American Biography,* 30 vols. (New York: Charles Scribner's Sons, 1928–1995).
DAR	K. G. Davies, ed., *Documents of the American Revolution, 1770–1783,* 19 vols. (Shannon, Ireland, 1972–1981).
DLTH	Thomas Hutchinson and Peter Orlando Hutchinson, *The Diary and Letters of His Excellency Thomas Hutchinson, Esq.: Captain-General and Governor-in-Chief of his late majesty's province of Massachusetts Bay, in North America,* 2 vols. (London: S. Low, Marston, Searle and Rivington, 1883–1886).

ABBREVIATIONS

DNB	*Dictionary of National Biography,* 66 vols. (Oxford: Oxford University Press, 1885–1901).
FALUD	[Anon.], *A Fair Account of the Late Unhappy Disturbance at Boston in New England* . . . (London, 1770).
GPAS	Gage Papers, American Series, William J. Clements Library, University of Michigan.
GPW	Gage Papers Warrants, William J. Clements Library, University of Michigan.
HPMB	Thomas Hutchinson, *The History of the Province of Massachusetts-Bay,* 3 vols.
	Volume 1: *From the First Settlement Thereof in 1628 until its Incorporation with the Colony of Plimouth, etc.* (Boston: Thomas & John Fleet, 1764).
	Volume 2: *From the Charter of King William and Queen Mary; in 1691, Until the Year 1750* (Boston: Thomas & John Fleet, 1767).
	Volume 3: *From 1749 to 1774, Comprising a Detailed Narrative of the Origin and Early Stages of the American Revolution* (London: John Murray, 1778); ed. John Hutchinson (London: W. Clowes, 1828).
JAH	*The Journal of American History.*
LPJA	L. Kinvin Wroth and Hiller B. Zobel, eds., *Legal Papers of John Adams,* 3 vols. (Cambridge, MA: Belknap Press of Harvard University Press, 1965).
MA	Massachusetts Archives, Boston.
MHR	*Massachusetts Historical Review.*
MHS	Massachusetts Historical Society, Boston.
NAUK	National Archives of the United Kingdom, Kew, England.
NEQ	*New England Quarterly.*
NYT	*New York Times.*
PFB	Colin Nicholson, ed., *The Papers of Francis Bernard: Governor of Colonial Massachusetts, 1760–1769,* 6 vols. (Boston: Colonial Society of Massachusetts, 2007–).

ABBREVIATIONS

PJQJ Daniel R. Coquillette and Neil Longley York, eds., *Portrait of a Patriot: The Major Political and Legal Papers of Josiah Quincy Junior,* 6 vols. (Boston: Colonial Society of Massachusetts, 2005–2014).

RTPP Robert Treat Paine Papers, Notes and Letters on the Boston Massacre Trial, 1770–1771, microfilm, reel 14, MHS.

RWMC-BPL Revolutionary War Manuscript Collection, Boston Public Library, online at https://archive.org.

SNHM [James Bowdoin, Joseph Warren, and Samuel Pemberton], *A Short Narrative of the horrid Massacre in Boston; Perpetrated In the Evening of the Fifth Day of March, 1770, by Soldiers of the XXIXth Regiment; Which With The XIVth Regiment Were then Quartered there: With Some Observations on the State of Things Prior to That Catastrophe* (Boston: Edes and Gill, 1770).

TWW *The Trial of William Wemms, James Hartegan, William McCauley, Hugh White, Matthew Killroy, William Warren, John Carrol, and Hugh Montgomery . . . ,* taken in shorthand by John Hodgson (Boston: J. Fleeming, 1770).

WMQ *The William and Mary Quarterly,* 3rd series.

WSA Harry Alonzo Cushing, ed., *The Writings of Samuel Adams,* 4 vols. (New York: Octagon Books, 1968 [orig. pub. G. P. Putnam's Sons, 1904).

Notes

{INTRODUCTION}

1. Walter Benjamin articulated a similar view when he wrote: "The true picture of the past flits by. The past can be seized only as an image which flashes up at the instant when it can be recognized and is never seen again. . . . To articulate the past historically does not mean to recognize it 'the way it really was' (Ranke). It means to seize hold of a memory as it flashes up in a moment of danger." Benjamin, *Illuminations,* ed. Hannah Arendt, trans. Harry Zohn (New York: Schocken Books, 1969 [orig. pub. Frankfurt, 1955]), 255. I am grateful to Stanley Thayne for suggesting the connection. On the relationship between memory and narrative, see especially William J. Cronon, "A Place for Stories: Nature, History, and Narrative," *JAH* 78 (1992): 1347–1376.

2. For especially useful introductions to the literature on memory and the construction of identity, see, e.g., Yael Zerubavel, *Recovered Roots: Collective Memory and the Making of Israeli National Tradition* (Chicago: University of Chicago Press, 1995); David G. Roskies, *The Jewish Search for a Usable Past* (Bloomington: Indiana University Press, 1999); W. James Booth, *Communities of Memory: On Witness, Identity, and Justice* (Ithaca, NY: Cornell University Press, 2006); W. Fitzhugh Brundage, "Introduction: No Deed but Memory," in *Where These Memories Grow: History, Memory, and Southern Identity,* ed. W. Fitzhugh Brundage (Chapel Hill: University of North Carolina Press, 2000), 1–28; Jim Cullen, *The Civil War in Popular Culture: A Reusable Past* (Washington, DC: Smithsonian Institution Press, 1995); and, in a different vein, Marita Sturken, *Tangled Memories: The Vietnam War, the AIDS Epidemic, and the Politics of Remembering* (Berkeley: University of California Press, 1997). I am especially indebted to Maeera Shreiber and David Kieran for conversations and suggestions on this subject.

3. Two complementary strands of scholarship shed useful light on the kind of analytical problem presented by the Boston Massacre. Robert Darnton uses the term "incident analysis" to refer to scholarly works that offer detailed explications of a single occurrence: Darnton, "It Happened One Night," *New York Review of Books* 51, no. 11 (June 24, 2004). For an especially good example of this kind of analysis, see John Brewer, *A Sentimental Murder: Love and Madness in the Eighteenth Century* (New York: Farrar, Straus and Giroux, 2004). William H. Sewell Jr. coined the phrase "event history" to denote the study of events that triggered structural social transformations: Sewell, *Logics of History: Social Theory and Social Transformation* (Chicago: University of Chicago Press, 2005), esp. chap. 8, "Historical Events as Transformations of Structures: Inventing Revolution at the Bastille," 225–270. The Boston Massacre occupies a middle position between these two cases: it possessed deeper and more immediate political and social significance than the murder described by Brewer, but it did not result in the kind of structural change ascribed by Sewell to the storming of the Bastille.

4. *Oxford English Dictionary Online,* accessed 18 Mar. 2016. The term was borrowed from the French in the mid-sixteenth century; the examples there suggest that it was in the twentieth century that the word took on the additional expectation that a massacre results in a large number of deaths. The phrase "unhappy disturbance" comes from the title of a pamphlet that aimed to exonerate the soldiers' actions: [Anon.], *A Fair Account of the Late Unhappy Disturbance at Boston in New England* . . . (London, 1770).

5. Fred Anderson, *A People's Army: Massachusetts Soldiers and Society in the Seven Years' War* (Chapel Hill: University of North Carolina Press, 1984).

6. Lois G. Schwoerer, *"No Standing Armies!": The Antiarmy Ideology in Seventeenth-Century England* (Baltimore: Johns Hopkins University Press, 1974); John Brewer, *The Sinews of Power: War, Money, and the English State, 1688–1783* (Cambridge, MA: Harvard University Press, 1990); Lawrence Stone, ed., *An Imperial State at War: Britain from 1689 to 1815* (New York: Routledge, 1993); Stephen Conway, *War, State, and Society in Mid-Eighteenth-Century Britain and Ireland* (Oxford: Oxford University Press, 2006).

7. For the constitutional dimension of this conflict, see John Phillip Reid, *In Defiance of the Law: The Standing-Army Controversy, the Two Constitutions, and the Coming of the American Revolution* (Chapel Hill: University of North Carolina Press, 1981).

8. To write a book on Revolutionary-era Boston is to follow a well-trodden path, and I have drawn gratefully on the work of many scholars. I have been especially influenced by John Shy, *Toward Lexington: The Role of the British Army in the Coming of the American Revolution* (Princeton, NJ: Princeton

University Press, 1965); G. B. Warden, *Boston, 1689–1776* (Boston: Little, Brown, 1970); Pauline Maier, *From Resistance to Revolution: Colonial Radicals and the Development of American Opposition to Britain, 1765–1776* (New York: Random House, 1972); Bernard Bailyn, *The Ordeal of Thomas Hutchinson* (Cambridge, MA: Belknap Press of Harvard University Press, 1974); Dirk Hoerder, *Crowd Action in Revolutionary Massachusetts, 1765–1780* (New York: Academic Press, 1977); Gary B. Nash, *The Urban Crucible: Social Change, Political Consciousness, and the Origins of the American Revolution* (Cambridge, MA: Harvard University Press, 1979); John Tyler, *Smugglers and Patriots: Boston Merchants and the Advent of the American Revolution* (Boston: Northeastern University Press, 1986); Alfred F. Young, *The Shoemaker and the Tea Party* (Boston: Beacon Press, 1999), and *Liberty Tree: Ordinary People and the American Revolution* (New York: New York University Press, 2006); Benjamin L. Carp, *Rebels Rising: Cities and the American Revolution* (New York: Oxford University Press, 2007); Richard Archer, *As If an Enemy's Country: The British Occupation of Boston and the Origins of Revolution* (New York: Oxford University Press, 2010); and Mark A. Peterson, *The City-State of Boston* (New Haven, CT: Yale University Press, forthcoming). On the Boston Massacre itself, I have profited immensely from the work of Hiller B. Zobel, whose masterful book on the subject did so much to excavate the period of Boston's occupation. In its treatment of the soldiers' trials and other legal matters attendant upon the occupation, Zobel's book is unsurpassed, and likely to remain so: Hiller B. Zobel, *The Boston Massacre* (New York: W. W. Norton, 1970). I have also learned a great deal from Neil L. York, "Rival Truths, Political Accommodation, and the Boston 'Massacre,'" *Massachusetts Historical Review* 11 (2009): 57–95, and *The Boston Massacre: A History with Documents* (New York: Routledge, 2010); Serena R. Zabin, *An Intimate History of the Boston Massacre* (New York: Houghton Mifflin Harcourt, forthcoming); and Robert J. Allison, *The Boston Massacre* (Beverly, MA: Commonwealth Editions, 2006).

{CHAPTER 1 · A WAR OF WORDS}

1. The third paper that gave an account on March 12 was the *Massachusetts Gazette, and Boston Post-Boy and Advertiser,* published by John Green and Joseph Russell. It was similar in tone to the *Evening-Post* (Thomas and John Fleet, publishers) and the *Boston-Gazette* (Benjamin Edes and John Gill), but briefer. The first Boston newspaper to mention the shootings was the twice-weekly *Boston Chronicle,* in its March 8 issue. Published by John Mein and John Fleeming, the *Chronicle* was generally hostile to Boston's radical leadership, and its account of the shootings — "a most

unfortunate affair"— was brief and restrained in tone. It concluded, *"We decline at present, giving a more particular account of this unhappy affair, as we hear the trial of the unfortunate prisoners is to come on next week."* In this expectation the editors were mistaken; nevertheless, the *Chronicle* offered no further account of March 5. For Boston's press in this era generally, see Mary Ann Yodelis, "Boston's Second Major Paper War: Economics, Politics, and the Theory and Practice of Political Expression in the Press, 1763–1775" (PhD diss., University of Wisconsin, 1971).

2. *BG,* 12 Mar. 1770; *BEP,* 12 Mar. 1770.

3. *SNHM.*

4. Ibid., 16–26; quotes: 17, 20–21.

5. Ibid., 26–28.

6. Ibid., 12–16; quote: 15.

7. *FALUD.*

8. *FALUD,* deposition nos. 104, 100, 99, 106; appendix, pp. 7, 3–4, 9; narrative, p. 15. N.B.: *FALUD* includes twenty-eight depositions, but they are numbered beginning with no. 97, so that they follow sequentially from the ninety-six depositions of the *SNHM.*

9. *FALUD,* 17–20.

10. Ibid., 20–21.

11. A crowd of thirty to forty: depositions of Samuel Condon (no. 48) and Benjamin Alline (no. 60), *SNHM,* 33–34, 46–47; a crowd of fifty to sixty: depositions of Ebenezer Hinckley (no. 49) and Francis Archbald Jr. (no. 50), ibid., 34–36; a crowd of about seventy: deposition of Richard Palmes (no. 53), ibid., 38–40; a crowd of seventy to eighty: deposition of Henry Knox (no. 55), ibid., 42; quote: deposition of Samuel Drowne (no. 68), ibid., 54–55. (Page numbers here refer to the appendix containing depositions, which is paginated separately from the text of the pamphlet.)

12. Deposition of Nathaniel Fosdick (no. 51), *SNHM,* 36–37; deposition of Capt. Samuel Leslie (no. 102), *FALUD,* appendix, p. 5; Capt. Edmund Mason (no. 103), ibid., appendix, pp. 5–6.

13. Deposition of Richard Palmes (no. 53), *SNHM,* 38–40; deposition of Henry Knox (no. 55), ibid., 42.

14. Deposition of John Hickling (no. 73), *SNHM,* 59–60; deposition of Thomas Greenwood (no. 111), *FALUD,* appendix, pp. 12–13.

15. Deposition of William Wyat (no. 54), *SNHM,* 40–42.

16. "The Case of Captain Preston," encl. in Preston to the Earl of Chatham, 17 Mar. 1770, 30/8/97 (Pt. 1), NAUK. There are multiple versions of this document; they vary slightly, primarily in capitalization and punctuation. Printed versions can be found in Albert Matthews, "Captain Thomas Preston and the Boston Massacre," in *Publications of the Colonial Society of*

Massachusetts, vol. 7, *Transactions, 1900–1902* (Boston, 1905), 2–22; and as an enclosure in Lieut.-Col. William Dalrymple to Earl of Hillsborough, 13 Mar. 1770, *DAR* 2:60–66.

17. "Case of Captain Preston."
18. Ibid.; James Bowdoin to William Bollan, 27 Mar. 1770, Winthrop Papers microfilm, reel 47, Bowdoin-Temple Papers, MHS.
19. Thomas Hutchinson to Major-General Thomas Gage, 6 Mar. 1770, *DAR* 2:51–53; deposition of Joseph Belknap, Jeremy Belknap Collection 161.A.69 [microfilm], MHS.
20. Deposition of Joseph Belknap, MHS.
21. Deposition of Isaac Pierce (no. 81), *SNHM,* 65.
22. Robert Treat Paine's minutes of Hutchinson's testimony at the trial of Thomas Preston, 27 Oct. 1770, and Hutchinson's testimony, anonymous summary of defense evidence, 27 Oct. 1770, *LPJA* 3:87, 80–81. For England's Riot Act, see Danby Pickering, ed., *The Statutes at Large,* 46 vols. (Cambridge, UK: Joseph Bentham et al., 1762–1807), 13:142–146, at 1 George I Stat. 2 c 5; and for Massachusetts, *The Acts and Resolves, Public and Private, of the Province of Massachusetts Bay,* 21 vols. (Boston: Wright and Potter, 1869–1922), 3:544–546. For a fuller discussion of the Riot Act and its implications for the soldiers in Boston, see Chapter 5.
23. Deposition of Isaac Pierce (no. 81), *SNHM,* 65; Hutchinson, anonymous summary, *LPJA* 3:81; deposition of Joseph Belknap, MHS.
24. Deposition of Joseph Belknap, MHS; Hutchinson, anonymous summary, *LPJA* 3:81; "Case of Captain Preston."
25. Deposition of Joseph Belknap, MHS; Hutchinson, anonymous summary, *LPJA* 3:81.

{CHAPTER 2 · TOWN AND CROWN}

1. *DAB* 9:439–443.
2. As the building's name implies, the Town House originally housed the Boston town meeting as well as the assembly and council. But in the early 1740s the Huguenot merchant Peter Faneuil erected a new building to serve as a public market and town hall, and beginning in September 1742 the town meeting convened in Faneuil Hall. See [Anon.], *Re-dedication of the Old State House, Boston, July 11, 1882,* 4th ed. (Boston: Rockwell and Churchill, 1887), 65.
3. *HPMB* 3:272; Hutchinson's testimony, anonymous summary of defense evidence, 27 Oct. 1770, *LPJA* 3:87, 80–81; deposition of Joseph Belknap, Jeremy Belknap Collection 161.A.69 [microfilm], MHS; John Rowe, *Letters and Diary of John Rowe,* ed. Anne Rowe Cunningham (New York: Arno Press, 1969 [orig. pub. Boston, 1903]), 286; Peter Oliver, *Peter Oliver's*

Origin and Progress of the American Rebellion: A Tory View, ed. Douglass Adair and John A. Schutz (Stanford: Stanford University Press, 1961), 117; Thomas Hutchinson, memoranda and diary for 1770, Egerton MS, 2666, British Library. For Molineux's background, see J. L. Bell, "William Molineux, Forgotten Revolutionary," and "William Molineux: A Wolverhampton Wanderer?," at *Boston 1775,* http://boston1775.blogspot.com/2007 /06/william-molineux-forgotten.html and http://boston1775.blogspot .com/2007/06/william-molineux-wolverhampton-wanderer.html.

4. Captain Thomas Preston's account, in Lieut.-Col. William Dalrymple to Earl of Hillsborough, 13 Mar. 1770, *DAR* 2:60–66; Andrew Oliver Jr. to Benjamin Lynde, 6 Mar. 1770, in *The Diaries of Benjamin Lynde and of Benjamin Lynde, Jr., with an Appendix* (Boston: n.p., 1880), 226–228; John Tudor, *Deacon Tudor's Diary,* ed. William Tudor (Boston: Wallace Spooner, 1896), 31; quote: deposition of Joseph Belknap, MHS.

5. Oliver to Lynde, 6 Mar. 1770, in *Diaries of Benjamin Lynde,* 226–228; Hutchinson to Hillsborough, 12 Mar. 1770, *DAR* 2:58–60; Tudor, *Diary,* 31–32; Preston's account, *DAR* 2:60–66. Preston says that three justices were present, but Hutchinson and Tudor concur in saying there were two. No surviving source explains how the eight arrested soldiers were identified.

6. Hutchinson to Hillsborough, 12 Mar. 1770, *DAR* 2:58–60; quote: 59.

7. Town meeting minutes, 6 Mar. 1770, *BR* 18:1–4; quote: 3. The Boston selectmen were John Hancock, Joshua Henshaw, Henderson Inches, Joseph Jackson, Jonathan Mason, Samuel Pemberton, and John Ruddock. The committee chosen by the town meeting included Hancock, Henshaw, and Pemberton, and added to their number Samuel Adams, William Molineux, William Phillips, and Joseph Warren—the latter four perhaps the most outspoken and articulate advocates for the town's interests in the face of parliamentary power and royal prerogative.

8. *HPMB* 2:7–10.

9. Ibid., 3:166. For James Otis Jr., see *DAB* 14:101–105.

10. Hutchinson, *HPMB* 3:234–235; Bernard to Shelburne, 5 Mar. 1768, *PFB* 4:112–118. See Francis G. Walett, "The Massachusetts Council, 1766–1774: The Transformation of a Conservative Institution," *WMQ* 6 (1949): 605–627.

11. On town meeting government generally, see especially Robert E. Brown, *Middle-Class Democracy and the Revolution in Massachusetts, 1691–1780* (Ithaca, NY: Cornell University Press, 1955), 78–99; and for the Boston town meeting in particular, G. B. Warden, *Boston, 1689–1776* (Boston: Little, Brown, 1970), 28–33, 40–44; quote: 28. In 1770 Hutchinson estimated that Boston had about fifteen hundred eligible voters. The Massachusetts

Township Act required voters to have a £20 ratable estate—a modest requirement, but one that limited voting to property-owning townspeople. A 1765 census found 1,676 houses in Boston, 2,069 families, and 2,941 white males above the age of sixteen. If the number of Bostonians with a £20 ratable estate was roughly the same as the number of houses in town, then about half the town's males over sixteen years of age would have been eligible to vote, and Hutchinson's guess would be reasonably accurate. See Hutchinson to John Pownall, 21 Mar. 1770 (private), MA 26:464, from the MHS typescript, 1007–1009; "An Act for Regulating of Townships . . . ," in *The Acts and Resolves, Public and Private, of the Province of Massachusetts Bay*, ed. Ellis Ames et al., 21 vols. (Boston: Wright and Potter, 1869–1922), 1:64–68; Warden, *Boston*, 40–43; J. H. Benton Jr., *Early Census Making in Massachusetts, 1643–1765* (Boston: Charles E. Goodspeed, 1905), 74–75. The provision that all men could attend Massachusetts town meetings dates to the Charter of Liberties of 1641 and was first codified in 1649; see *The General Laws and Liberties of the Massachusetts Colony, Revised and Reprinted* (Boston, 1672), 90, printed in *The Colonial Laws of Massachusetts: Reprinted from the Edition of 1672* (Boston: Rockwell and Churchill, 1890).

12. Records of the town meeting from 1634 to 1822 are contained in *BR* vols. 2, 7, 8, 12, 14, 16, 18, 26, 31, 35, and 37.

13. For the complexities attendant upon property qualifications in town meetings, see Warden, *Boston*, 40–44; for the estimate of fifteen hundred voters, see note 11 above. The Boston town meeting convened on twelve days in 1743 and 1744, and on eleven days in 1745; *BR* 14:1–76. For meetings in 1770, see *BR* 18:1–38; for voting 1763–1774, see Alan Day and Katherine Day, "Another Look at the Boston 'Caucus,'" *Journal of American Studies* 5 (1971): 37–38.

14. Warden, *Boston*, 67–79, 92–97, 124–126, 130; Day and Day, "Another Look at the Boston 'Caucus,'" 19–42.

15. *DAB* 9:439; Bernard Bailyn, *The Ordeal of Thomas Hutchinson* (Cambridge, MA: Harvard University Press, 1974), 1–34; quote: 12.

16. See especially Margaret Newell, *From Dependency to Independence: Economic Revolution in Colonial New England* (Ithaca, NY: Cornell University Press, 1998), 107–213.

17. William Douglass, *Summary, Historical and Political, of the first Planting, progressive Improvements, and present State of the British Settlements in North America*, 2 vols. (Boston, 1749–1751 [repr., New York: Arno Press, 1972]), 1:310.

18. Newell, *From Dependency to Independence*, 214–222.

19. Ibid., 222–235; Warden, *Boston*, 132–139.

20. William V. Wells, *The Life and Public Services of Samuel Adams,* 3 vols. (Boston: Little, Brown, 1865), 1:6–13, 23–28.

21. Jacob M. Price, "Economic Function and the Growth of American Port Towns in the Eighteenth Century," *Perspectives in American History* 8 (1974): 138–160, 176; Committee report, 16 Mar. 1742/43, *BR* 14:12–14. Three years later, conditions had only worsened; see *BR* 14:98–100. The immediate local effects of the War of Jenkins' Ear were more complex than the town's petition suggests. At the beginning of the war, Boston experienced a shipbuilding boom before the bottom dropped out; in 1741, 164 ships were reportedly under construction in Boston shipyards. Certain local merchants made fortunes in war contracting. Local sailors found their services to be in high demand, and their wages shot up. And Boston, like the rest of Massachusetts, contributed many soldiers, especially to the Cartagena and Louisbourg campaigns; as a result, much of the growth in poor relief in Boston was due to an increase in the number of widows. For an introduction to all these issues, see Gary B. Nash, *The Urban Crucible: Social Change, Political Consciousness, and the Origins of the American Revolution* (Cambridge, MA: Harvard University Press, 1979), 165–173.

22. Bernard Bailyn, *The New England Merchants in the Seventeenth Century* (Cambridge, MA: Harvard University Press, 1955); Bernard Bailyn and Lotte Bailyn, *Massachusetts Shipping, 1697–1714* (Cambridge, MA: Harvard University Press, 1959), 105, 20, 56; Stephen Innes, *Creating the Commonwealth: The Economic Culture of Puritan New England* (New York: W. W. Norton, 1995), 272; Warden, *Boston,* 81, 102; Price, "Economic Function and the Growth of American Port Towns," appendix B, p. 176.

23. Price, "Economic Function and the Growth of American Port Towns," 138–160, 176.

24. Nash, *Urban Crucible,* 165–173; W. T. Baxter, *The House of Hancock: Business in Boston, 1724–1775* (Cambridge, MA: Harvard University Press, 1945), 103–107 and following.

25. Warden, *Boston,* 28–132.

26. Belcher to Hutchinson, 11 May 1741, *CTH* 1:93.

27. See especially Warden, *Boston,* 127–173.

28. Wells, *Samuel Adams,* 1:5–6, 11–12, 24; *DAB* 1:95–96; Adams, Petitions to the Freeholders of the Town of Boston, 14 Mar. 1768 and 13 Mar. 1769, *WSA* 1:199–200, 319–322; *BR* 16:92, 143, 201, 218–219, 241–243, 271–272; John Adams diary, 30 Dec. 1770 [electronic edition], *Adams Family Papers: An Electronic Archive,* MHS, http://www.masshist.org/digitaladams/. For an especially insightful sketch of Adams, see Pauline Maier, *The Old Revolutionaries: Political Lives in the Age of Samuel Adams* (New York: Knopf, 1980), 3–50.

29. For Otis, see especially James M. Farrell, "The Writs of Assistance and Public Memory: John Adams and the Legacy of James Otis," *NEQ* 79 (2006): 533–556; Adams "flame of fire" quote (in caption to Otis's portrait), 542.

30. Warden, *Boston,* 140–144; Benjamin Carp, *Rebels Rising: Cities and the American Revolution* (New York: Oxford University Press, 2007), 32; John W. Tyler, *Smugglers and Patriots: Boston Merchants and the Advent of the American Revolution* (Boston: Northeastern University Press, 1986), 285n17.

31. Warden, *Boston,* 163–164, 214–218; Pauline Maier, *From Resistance to Revolution: Colonial Radicals and the Development of American Opposition to Britain, 1765–1776* (New York: Random House, 1972), 85–86 and following.

32. *DNB* 2:380–381; Colin Nicholson, "Introduction," *PFB* 3:3–8 and following.

33. For the Stamp Act generally, see Edmund S. Morgan and Helen S. Morgan, *The Stamp Act Crisis: Prologue to Revolution* (Chapel Hill: University of North Carolina Press, 1953); for Oliver, see Troy O. Bickham, "Oliver, Andrew (1706–1774)," *Oxford Dictionary of National Biography* (Oxford University Press, 2004), http://www.oxforddnb.com/view/article/20718; quotations: Thomas Hutchinson to [Richard Jackson], 16 Aug. 1765, *CTH* 1:279–282. In the month following this episode a copper plate engraved with gold letters was affixed to the elm designating it "The Tree of Liberty"; see *BG,* 16 Sept. 1765, Supplement.

34. Hutchinson to [Richard Jackson], 16 Aug. 1765, *CTH* 1:279–282; Bernard to Board of Trade, 15–16 Aug. 1765, *PFB* 2:301–307.

35. Hutchinson to [Richard Jackson], 16 Aug. 1765, *CTH* 1:279–282.

36. Thomas Hutchinson to Richard Jackson, 30 Aug. 1765, and Thomas Hutchinson to William Bollan, 1 Sept. 1765, *CTH* 1:291–294, 296–298.

37. [Francis Bernard], "Observations on the Massachusetts Indemnity Act" [ca. 7–19 July 1766], appendix 1.2, *PFB* 3:441–448.

38. For this paragraph and the next, see generally Nicholson, "Introduction," *PFB* 3:6–24. Francis Bernard to Conway, 21 Jan. 1766 and 23 Jan. 1766, *PFB* 3:70–77.

39. Francis Bernard to Conway, 23 Jan. 1766, *PFB* 3:73; Earl of Shelburne to Francis Bernard, 13 Sept. 1766, *PFB* 3:224–225; and see their subsequent correspondence: *PFB* 3:232–247, 257–261, 276–298.

40. Neil Longley York, *Henry Hulton and the American Revolution: An Outsider's Inside View* (Boston: Colonial Society of Massachusetts, 2010), 44–49.

41. Henry Hulton, "Some Account of the Proceedings of the People in New England from the Establishment of a Board of Customs in America, to the

Breaking Out of the Rebellion in 1775," in York, *Henry Hulton,* 136; Tyler, *Smugglers and Patriots,* 135.

42. Francis Bernard to the Earl of Shelburne, 14 Nov. 1767, *PFB* 3:420–422.

{CHAPTER 3 · SMUGGLERS AND MOBS}

1. [Ann Hulton to Elizabeth Lightbody], 17 Dec. 1767, in H[arold] M[urdock] and C[harles] M[iner] T[hompson], eds., *Letters of a Loyalist Lady* (Cambridge, MA: Harvard University Press, 1927), 8; *HPMB* 3:181.

2. Otis: *BEP,* 23 Nov. 1767; *BG,* 9 Nov. 1767, 14 Mar. 1768. Dorr's annotated copies of the two issues of the *Gazette* are available online at http://www.masshist.org/dorr/browse-np/title/BGCJ. The *Gazette* item from 14 Mar. 1768 does not appear in Samuel Adams's collected writings, though another letter signed "Populus" does; see *WSA,* 1:xiv, 378–380.

3. John W. Tyler, *Smugglers and Patriots: Boston Merchants and the Advent of the American Revolution* (Boston: Northeastern University Press, 1986), 3–23, and appendix, pp. 253–277.

4. Tyler, *Smugglers and Patriots,* 65–107; see also Dirk Hoerder, *Crowd Action in Revolutionary Massachusetts, 1765–1780* (New York: Academic Press, 1977), 119–143, and Pauline Maier, *From Resistance to Revolution: Colonial Radicals and the Development of American Opposition to Britain, 1765–1776* (New York: Knopf, 1972), 77–112.

5. Tyler, *Smugglers and Patriots,* 60–63; *HPMB* 3:126. On McIntosh, see George P. Anderson, "Ebenezer Mackintosh: Stamp Act Rioter and Patriot," *Publications of the Colonial Society of Massachusetts* 26 (1927): 15–64, 348–361, and Hoerder, *Crowd Action,* 90–118, 138–143.

6. Hoerder, *Crowd Action,* 138.

7. For the text of the Townshend Revenue Act, see http://avalon.law.yale.edu /18th_century/townsend_act_1767.asp; Tyler, *Smugglers and Patriots,* 109–111 and following; Hancock to William Reeve, 3 Sept. 1767, quoted in Tyler, *Smugglers and Patriots,* 110. See also Bernard to Shelburne, 21 Mar. 1768, *PFB* 4:135–139.

8. John S. Farmer and W. E. Henley, *A Dictionary of Slang and Colloquial English* (London: George Routledge and Sons, 1905), 290.

9. Gustave Le Bon, *La psychologie des foules* (Paris: F. Alcan, 1895), translated as *The Crowd: A Study of the Popular Mind* (London: T. F. Unwin, 1896); Elias Canetti, *Masse und Macht* (Munich: Hanser, 1960), translated as *Crowds and Power* (New York: Viking, 1962).

10. George Rudé, *The Crowd in the French Revolution* (Oxford: Clarendon Press, 1959), and *The Crowd in History: A Study of Popular Disturbances*

in France and England, 1730–1848 (New York: Wiley, 1964); see also, e.g., E. P. Thompson, "The Moral Economy of the English Crowd in the Eighteenth Century," *Past and Present* 50 (1971): 76–136.

11. A similar point has been made by Jesse Lemisch: "Communications: The 'Mob' versus the 'Crowd'—the British Marxists and Early American History; and a Word about 'Empiricism' and 'Theory,'" *WMQ* 56 (1999): 231–237.

12. Bernard to the Earl of Shelburne, 14 Nov. 1767, *PFB* 3:420–422.

13. Bernard to Barrington, 4 Mar. 1768, and, for Malcom, Bernard to Shelburne, 21 Mar. 1768, *PFB* 4:108–110, 135–139.

14. Bernard to Shelburne, 5 Mar. 1768, *PFB* 4:112–118; Massachusetts Circular Letter to the Colonial Legislatures, February 11, 1768, http://avalon.law.yale.edu/18th_century/mass_circ_let_1768.asp; *BG,* 29 Feb. 1768; Bernard to Jackson, 6 Mar. 1768, *PFB* 4:119.

15. Tyler, *Smugglers and Patriots,* 25–63 and following.

16. W. T. Baxter, *The House of Hancock: Business in Boston, 1724–1775* (Cambridge, MA: Harvard University Press, 1945), 146–150, 223–226 and following.

17. Baxter, *House of Hancock,* 260–268; Hoerder, *Crowd Action,* 164–165 and following.

18. Among the many accounts of the *Liberty* affair, see Henry Hulton, "Some Account of the Proceedings of the People in New England from the Establishment of a Board of Customs in America, to the Breaking Out of the Rebellion in 1775," in Neil Longley York, *Henry Hulton and the American Revolution: An Outsider's Inside View* (Boston: Colonial Society of Massachusetts, 2010), 126–128, along with the account in York's volume introduction, 59–64. Quotes: American Board of Customs to Bernard, 11 June 1768, *PFB* 4:10–181.

19. [Ann Hulton to Elizabeth Lightbody], 30 June 1768, in M[urdock] and T[hompson], *Letters of a Loyalist Lady,* 11–14.

20. Gage to Bernard, 24 June 1768, GPAS, vol. 78.

21. Bernard to Gage, 2 July and 18 July 1768, GPAS, vol. 78.

22. Hillsborough to Gage, 8 June 1768, *CGTG* 2:68–69.

23. Gage to Bernard, 31 Aug. 1768, GPAS, vol. 78.

24. Hillsborough to Gage, 30 July 1768, *CGTG* 2:72–74.

25. Meeting of 13 Sept. 1768, in *BR* 16:261–264; quote: 264; Gage to Hillsborough, 26 Sept. 1768, *CGTG* 1:195–197.

26. Bernard to Gage, 24 Sept. 1768, GPAS, vol. 81.

27. Ibid.

28. Gage to Hillsborough, 7 Sept. 1768, *CGTG* 1:191; Gage to Bernard, 25 Sept. 1768, and Gage to Dalrymple, 25 Sept. 1768, GPAS, vol. 81.

29. Gage to Dalrymple, 25 Sept. 1768, GPAS, vol. 81.

{CHAPTER 4 · IMPERIAL SPACES}

1. See especially Eliga Gould, *Among the Powers of the Earth: The American Revolution and the Making of a New World Empire* (Cambridge, MA: Harvard University Press, 2012).

2. Lauren Benton, *A Search for Sovereignty: Law and Geography in European Empires, 1400–1900* (New York: Cambridge University Press, 2010), chap. 1, "Anomalies of Empire," 1–39; quotes: 10, 2.

3. For an especially provocative account of Boston as self-created and self-sustaining, see Mark A. Peterson, *The City-State of Boston* (New Haven, CT: Yale University Press, forthcoming).

4. See especially John Brewer, *The Sinews of Power: War, Money, and the English State, 1688–1783* (Cambridge, MA: Harvard University Press, 1990); Lawrence Stone, ed., *An Imperial State at War: Britain from 1689 to 1815* (New York: Routledge, 1993); and Stephen Conway, *War, State, and Society in Mid-Eighteenth-Century Britain and Ireland* (Oxford: Oxford University Press, 2006).

5. On the problem of European geographical ignorance in North America, see especially Paul W. Mapp, *The Elusive West and the Contest for Empire, 1713–1763* (Chapel Hill: University of North Carolina Press, 2011), and on post–Seven Years' War cartographic efforts, S. Max Edelson, "Mapping the New Empire: Britain's General Survey of North America, 1763–1782," Library of Congress Webcasts, http://loc.gov/today/cyberlc/feature_wdesc .php?rec=4304.

6. For an introduction to the Bourbon reforms in Latin America, see David A. Brading, "Bourbon Spain and Its American Empire," in *The Cambridge History of Latin America,* vol. 1, *Colonial Latin America,* ed. Leslie Bethell (Cambridge, UK: Cambridge University Press, 1984), 389–439; for Halifax and British reforms, see Andrew D. M. Beaumont, *Colonial America and the Earl of Halifax, 1748–1761* (Oxford: Oxford University Press, 2015).

7. John R. Alden, *General Gage in America: Being Principally a History of His Role in the American Revolution* (Baton Rouge: Louisiana State University Press, 1948), 11–14 and following.

8. On the transformation of Britain's empire that accompanied the Treaty of Paris, see especially Fred Anderson, *Crucible of War: The Seven Years' War and the Fate of Empire in British North America, 1754–1766* (New York: Knopf, 2000), 453–734.

9. Lois G. Schwoerer, *"No Standing Armies!": The Antiarmy Ideology in Seventeenth-Century England* (Baltimore: Johns Hopkins University Press, 1974); John Trenchard, *An Argument, shewing that a Standing Army is inconsistent with a Free Government, and absolutely destructive to the Constitution of the English Monarchy* (London, 1697), in *A Collection of Tracts.*

By the Late John Trenchard, Esq; and Thomas Gordon, Esq; the First Volume (London: F. Cogan, 1751), 29, online at http://oll.libertyfund.org/titles /2315#Gordon_1548-01_73.

10. John L. Bullion, "'The Ten Thousand in America': More Light on the Decision on the American Army, 1762–1763," *WMQ* 43 (1986): 646–657; J. A. Houlding, *Fit for Service: The Training of the British Army, 1715–1795* (Oxford: Clarendon Press, 1981), appendix B, p. 412. At the same time, more than seventeen thousand sailors continued to serve in the Royal Navy; see N. A. M. Rodger, *The Command of the Ocean: A Naval History of Britain, 1649–1815* (New York: W. W. Norton, 2004), appendix 6, p. 638.

11. The Petition of Right, 1628, online at http://www.legislation.gov.uk/aep /Cha1/3/1; the Bill of Rights, 1689, online at http://www.legislation.gov .uk/aep/WillandMarSess2/1/2/introduction.

12. Steve Pincus, *1688: The First Modern Revolution* (New Haven, CT: Yale University Press, 2009), 145, 147.

13. Charles Ivar McGrath, *Ireland and Empire, 1692–1770* (London: Pickering and Chatto, 2012), 69–106; see also Alan J. Guy, "The Irish Military Establishment, 1660–1776," and S. J. Connolly, "The Defence of Protestant Ireland, 1660–1760," in *A Military History of Ireland,* ed. Thomas Bartlett and Keith Jeffery (Cambridge, UK: Cambridge University Press, 1996), 211–230, 231–246. On the evolution of the barracks system, see James Douet, *British Barracks, 1600–1914: Their Architecture and Role in Society* (London: Stationery Office, 1998). On the growth of army contracting in Britain, see Gordon E. Bannerman, *Merchants and the Military in Eighteenth-Century Britain: British Army Contracts and Domestic Supply, 1739–1763* (London: Pickering and Chatto, 2008).

14. [Anon.], "Quarters of the Army in Ireland, 1769," *Irish Sword: The Journal of the Military History Society of Ireland* 2 (1955): 230–231; Guy, "Irish Military Establishment," 222–224 and following. See also the website entitled *Army Barracks of Eighteenth-Century Ireland,* maintained by a team headed by Ivar McGrath and Patrick Walsh, which aims to map all of Ireland's barracks sites active between 1690 and 1815. Currently over 270 sites are identified, including those for 1769: https://barracks18c.ucd.ie.

15. Wade quoted in H. C. B. Rogers, *The British Army in the Eighteenth Century* (London: George Allen and Unwin, 1977), 38, where Rogers also discusses billeting practices; for troop deployments, 1764–1767, see Houlding, *Fit for Service,* appendix A, tables A8 and A9, pp. 402–403, and more generally 1–98. For the challenges associated with provisioning encamped troops, see Bannerman, *Merchants and the Military,* 59–88.

16. On Scotland, see Victoria Henshaw, *Scotland and the British Army, 1700–1750: Defending the Union* (London: Bloomsbury Press, 2014), esp. 149–195, and McGrath, *Ireland and Empire,* 74–75; for Minorca, Desmond

Gregory, *Minorca, the Illusory Prize: A History of the British Occupation of Minorca between 1708 and 1802* (Cranbury, NJ: Associated University Presses, 1990), esp. 54–55, 78–81, 167, 179–183 and following; for Gibraltar, Ilya Berkovich, "Discipline and Control in Eighteenth-Century Gibraltar," in *Britain's Soldiers: Rethinking War and Society, 1715–1815,* ed. Kevin Linch and Matthew McCormack (Liverpool: Liverpool University Press, 2014), 114–130.

17. Bannerman, *Merchants and the Military,* 23; McGrath, *Ireland and Empire,* 73.

18. For the failed Canada expeditions and concerns about Boston's fortifications, see Samuel Drake, *The History and Antiquities of Boston* (Boston: L. Stevens, 1876), 491, 505–506, 511; for borderlands warfare more generally in this era, see especially Evan Haefeli and Kevin Sweeney, *Captors and Captives: The 1704 French and Indian Raid on Deerfield* (Amherst: University of Massachusetts Press, 2003). For Romer and the fort-building project, see "The memorial of Wolfgang William Romer, His Majesty's chief engineer in America, touching Castle Island in the bay of Boston," 20 June 1699, CO 5/860, NAUK, and *DNB* 49:184–185. A map depicting the island's defenses in 1699 and Romer's plan for their reconstruction accompanied his memorial, but no longer resides with it, and I have been unable to locate it. The fort was named for King William two years after its completion, in 1705: Drake, *History of Boston,* 531. My description of the fort is based in part on two later manuscript plans of the island's defenses, both of which include later improvements but depict Romer's fort and batteries. See Thomas Pownall, "A Plan of Castle William and the Island at Boston," 1758, MPG 1/123, NAUK; and John Montresor, "A General and Particular Plan of the Island of Castle William Near Boston," 1771, MR 1/19, NAUK, a digital copy of which is available at http://www.loc.gov/item/gm71000936/.

19. Anderson, *Crucible of War,* 136–141, 200–201, 317–320, 387–389, 288–289.

20. Pownall, "A Plan of Castle William and the Island at Boston," 1758.

21. Gary B. Nash, *The Urban Crucible: Social Change, Political Consciousness, and the Origins of the American Revolution* (Cambridge, MA: Harvard University Press, 1979), 169; Stanley M. Pargellis, *Lord Loudoun in North America* (New Haven, CT: Yale University Press, 1933), 132–166, 190–191.

22. John Shy, *Toward Lexington: The Role of the British Army in the Coming of the American Revolution* (Princeton, NJ: Princeton University Press, 1965), 238. For an analysis of the work routines and material conditions of the peacetime army in the western posts, see Michael N. McConnell, *Army and Empire: British Soldiers on the American Frontier, 1758–1775* (Lincoln: University of Nebraska Press, 2004).

23. For Gage's career, see John Richard Alden, *General Gage in America: Being Principally a History of His Role in the American Revolution* (Baton Rouge: Louisiana State University Press, 1948). The two-volume edition of Gage's correspondence with London — *CGTG* — offers only a small window into the rigors of his administrative duties. To gain a full appreciation for the scope of his work, it is necessary to survey the manuscript materials in the Gage Papers, housed in the William L. Clements Library at the University of Michigan, where they occupy seventy linear feet of space. The bulk of the material is organized into an English series, which has been bound into 30 volumes, and an American series, which has been bound into 139 volumes. The Warrants series (GPW) fills another forty boxes. For an overview of the collection, see http://quod.lib.umich.edu/c/clementsmss /umich-wcl-M-341gag?view=text.

24. Gage to Barrington, 11 Oct. 1766, *CGTG* 2:382–383.

25. The British army established a shipyard on Navy Island in the Niagara River for this purpose. Between 1761 and 1764 four schooners and two sloops were built there; in 1771 Detroit replaced Navy Island as the site of Britain's shipyard for the upper Great Lakes. See http://www.maritime historyofthegreatlakes.ca/Documents/shiplists/macpherson.htm.

26. Houlding, *Fit for Service,* 13–25.

27. Shy, *Toward Lexington,* 163–178; John G. McCurdy, " 'For the Better Payment of the Army and Their Quarters': Rethinking the Quartering Act of 1765," paper presented at the Eighteenth Annual Conference of the Omohundro Institute of Early American History and Culture, Huntington Library, San Marino, CA, June 2012. For the New York barracks, see *A Plan of the City of New York, Drawn by Major Holland, Surveyor General, 1776,* engraved for D. T. Valentine's Manual by G. Hayward, 1863, online at http://collections.mcny.org/Collection/A-Plan-of-the-City-of-New-York -drawn-by-Major-Holland,-Surveyor-General,-1776-2F3XC5ORP4Q.html.

28. Gage to the Earl of Halifax, 23 Jan. 1765, *CGTG* 1:47–49; quotes: 49.

29. Shy, *Toward Lexington,* 181–189; quote: 189. The text of the Quartering Act can be found at http://avalon.law.yale.edu/18th_century/quartering _act_165.asp. For the crown's intention to offload costs in North America, see Bullion, " 'The Ten Thousand in America.' "

30. For the New York episode, see Joseph S. Tiedemann, *Reluctant Revolutionaries: New York City and the Road to Independence, 1763–1776* (Ithaca, NY: Cornell University Press, 1997), 117–124.

31. This paragraph and the three that follow draw upon *Annual Report of the American Historical Association for the Year 1945,* vol. 2, *Spain in the Mississippi Valley, 1765–1794,* ed. Lawrence Kinnaird, *Part 1: The Revolutionary Period, 1765–1781* (Washington, DC: GPO, 1949), xv–xxxi; John Preston

Moore, *Revolt in Louisiana: The Spanish Occupation, 1766–1770* (Baton Rouge: Louisiana State University Press, 1976), 1–20, 42–59.

32. Ulloa to Señor Marqués Jerónimo Grimaldi [Spanish minister of state], 10 Oct. 1768, in *Spain in the Mississippi Valley, 1765–1794, Part 1: The Revolutionary Period, 1765–1781,* ed. Lawrence Kinnaird, 76–77.

33. Ibid.; Ulloa to Grimaldi, 6 Oct. 1768, in Kinnaird, *Spain in the Mississippi Valley, Part 1,* 76–77, 71–72.

34. Ulloa to Grimaldi, 23 Aug. 1768 and 6 Oct. 1768, in Kinnaird, *Spain in the Mississippi Valley, Part 1,* 69–70, 71–72.

35. Hillsborough to Gage, 15 Apr. 1768, *CGTG* 2:61–66; Gage to Lord William Campbell, 24 June 1768; Gage to Lord Charles Montague, 24 June 1768; Gage to James Wright, 24 June 1768; Gage to Governor James Grant, 25 June 1768; in GPAS, vol. 78.

36. Ulloa to Grimaldi, 6 Oct. 1768, in Kinnaird, *Spain in the Mississippi Valley, Part 1,* 71–72.

{CHAPTER 5 · SETTLING IN}

1. Martha J. McNamara, *From Tavern to Courthouse: Architecture and Ritual in American Law, 1658–1860* (Baltimore: Johns Hopkins University Press, 2004), 47–51; Hutchinson quote: 48.

2. Thomas Preston, "Case of Captain Thomas Preston," encl. Lieut.-Col. William Dalrymple to Earl of Hillsborough, 13 Mar. 1770, *DAR* 2:66.

3. Gage to Hillsborough, 7 Sept. 1768 and 10 Sept. 1768, in *CTG* 1:191, 195; Dalrymple to Gage, 9 Oct. 1768, GPAS, vol. 81. The terms "regiment" and "battalion" are distinct but closely related. Formally, regiments were administrative echelons, run by colonels commandant and their staffs. Battalions, generally commanded by lieutenant colonels, comprised the operational units of regiments. By the end of the Seven Years' War, most regiments (including all those posted to Boston) had a single battalion, making the two terms seem functionally interchangeable. In fact, however, because the administrative echelons of these regiments did not relocate to Boston during the occupation, it is more accurate to speak (for example) of the battalion of the 29th Regiment of Foot occupying the town. I am indebted to Fred Anderson for clarifying this distinction. For the sake of brevity and familiarity, however, I will generally refer to regiments in the colloquial understanding of the term.

4. Gage to Bernard, 2 Oct. 1768, and Gage to Montresor, 25 Sept. 1768, GPAS, vol. 81.

5. Bernard to Hillsborough, 1 Oct. 1768, and to Gage, 1 Oct. 1768, *PFB* 5:63–65, 68–70; Dalrymple to Gage, 2 Oct. 1768, GPAS, vol. 81.

6. Bernard to Gage, 1 Oct. 1768, *PFB* 5:68–70; Dalrymple to Gage, 2 Oct. 1768, and Montresor to Gage, 2 Oct. 1768, GPAS, vol. 81.

7. *A View of Part of the Town of Boston and Brittish Ships of War Landing Their Troops, 1768,* engraved and printed by Paul Revere, online at http://www.americanantiquarian.org/Inventories/Revere/b2.htm; Oliver Morton Dickerson, ed., *Boston under Military Rule, 1768–1769, as Revealed in a Journal of the Times* (New York: Da Capo Press, 1970 [orig. pub. 1936]), 1. For the use of springs on cables, see, e.g., Sam Willis, *Fighting at Sea in the Eighteenth Century: The Art of Sailing Warfare* (Woodbridge, Suffolk, UK: Boydell and Brewer, 2008), 160. The Revere print is based on a watercolor sketch executed by Christian Remick in the fall of 1769; Revere first made the print available for sale in April 1770, after the shootings in King Street. See Clarence S. Brigham, *Paul Revere's Engravings* (New York: Atheneum, 1969 [orig. pub. Worcester: American Antiquarian Society, 1954]), 79–80 and following.

8. *A View of Part of the Town of Boston . . . , 1768.* I am indebted to Justin Clement for originally alerting me to this feature of the print. For the use of an Indian as a symbol of American identity, see Lester C. Olson, *Emblems of American Community in the Revolutionary Era: A Study in Rhetorical Iconology* (Washington, DC: Smithsonian Institution Press, 1991), 75–123.

9. *A View of Part of the Town of Boston . . . , 1768;* Unknown to [John Robinson], 7 July 1768, *PFB* 4:390–391; Declaration of Richard Silvester, 23 Jan. 1769, *PFB* 5:167–171; Dalrymple to Gage, 2 Oct. 1768, GPAS, vol. 81. In the week before the troops arrived, Boston had called together a convention of representatives from neighboring towns to consider what to do about the troops' landing. Though Boston leaders hoped to whip up strong opposition, most delegates favored a more moderate approach, and the convention was dissolved after taking no action except to formulate a mildly worded petition to the king. See *HPMB* 3:205–212; Bernard to Hillsborough, 3 Oct. 1768, *PFB* 5:75–77.

10. Gage to Hillsborough, 31 Oct. 1768, *CGTG* 1:202–205; Bernard to Dalrymple, 2 Oct. 1768, *PFB* 5:70–71; *HPMB* 3:212–217; Dickerson, *Boston under Military Rule,* 2.

11. Dickerson, *Boston under Military Rule,* entries for 1, 18, 19, 20, 21, and 22 Oct., pp. 2, 7–9; *Pennsylvania Gazette,* 3 Nov. 1768; Gage to Bernard, 2 Oct. 1768, GPAS, vol. 81. Bernard claimed that the "faction" had moved residents from the workhouse to the Manufactory House in anticipation of the troops' arrival, coached Brown and his fellow occupants on the points of law to invoke, and threatened anyone who left the building with banishment or death; see Bernard to Hillsborough, 1 Nov. 1768, *PFB* 5:96–101.

The assembly had been prorogued at Hillsborough's direction after it refused to rescind its circular letter of February; see *PFB* 4:24–25 and following.

12. For the location of soldiers' lodgings, see Hiller B. Zobel, *The Boston Massacre* (New York: W. W. Norton, 1970), 104; Hugh Everard, *History of Thomas Farrington's Regiment: Subsequently Designated the 29th (Worcestershire) Foot, 1694–1891* (Worcester, UK: Littlebury and Co., 1891), online at http://www.worcestershireregiment.com/wr.php?main=inc/29hist _chapter4; John Rowe, *Letters and Diary of John Rowe,* ed. Anne Rowe Cunningham (New York: Arno Press, 1969 [orig. pub. Boston, 1903]), 177. Gage to Hillsborough, 31 Oct. 1768, *CGTG* 1:202–205.

13. Stephen Brumwell, *Redcoats: The British Soldier and the War in the Americas, 1755–1763* (Cambridge, UK: Cambridge University Press, 2002), 69–84 and appendix, tables 2, 5, and 8, pp. 316, 318, 320.

14. Brumwell, *Redcoats,* 84–98 and appendix, table 6, p. 319.

15. In her analysis of British soldiers who fought in the American Revolution, Sylvia R. Frey concludes, "The average soldier in the British army was a mature man of about thirty years of age who had joined the army when he was around twenty years old." Frey, *The British Soldier in America: A Social History of Military Life in the Revolutionary Period* (Austin: University of Texas Press, 1981), 23–27 and tables 2–9.

16. Richard Cannon, *Historical Record of the Fourteenth, or Buckinghamshire Regiment of Foot: Containing an Account of the Formation of the Regiment in 1685, and of Its Subsequent Services to 1845* (London: Parker, Furnivall, and Parker, 1845), 27–34, online at http://archive.org/stream/recordoffour teenoocanniala/recordoffourteenoocanniala_djvu.txt; Everard, *History of . . . the 29th Foot,* chap. 4; "59th (2nd Nottinghamshire) Regiment of Foot," on the National Army Museum website at http://www.nam.ac.uk /research/famous-units/59th-2nd-nottinghamshire-regiment-foot; "History of the 64th," on HM 64th Regiment of Foot website at http://64throf .com; "65th (2nd Yorkshire, North Riding) Regiment of Foot," on the National Army Museum website at http://www.nam.ac.uk/research /famous-units/65th-2nd-yorkshire-north-riding-regiment-foot.

17. Dalrymple to Gage, 28 Oct. 1769, GPAS, vol. 88.

18. Riot Act (1714), 1 Geo. 1 st. 2 c.5; Massachusetts passed its own version of the Riot Act in 1751, entitled An Act for Preventing and Suppressing of Riots, Routs and Unlawful Assemblies, in *The Acts and Resolves, Public and Private, of the Province of the Massachusetts Bay,* 21 vols. (Boston: Wright and Potter, 1869–1922), 3:544–546. Tony Hayter, *The Army and the Crowd in Mid-Georgian England* (London: Macmillan, 1978), 9–15; Nicholas Rogers, *Crowds, Culture and Politics in Georgian Britain* (Oxford: Clarendon Press, 1998), 35–37, 64–65; quote: Welbore Ellis to O. C. Guards at the Tower, 16 May 1765, in Hayter, *The Army and the Crowd,* 13.

19. Hayter, *The Army and the Crowd*, 31–32; Colonel Francis Leighton to General Wade, 24 Sept. 1740, and Lt.-Col. Fitzwilliam to Col. Fleming, 4 June 1743, quoted in ibid., 32.

20. J. H. Benton Jr., *Early Census Making in Massachusetts, 1643–1765* (Boston: Charles E. Goodspeed, 1905), 74–75.

21. Dickerson, *Boston under Military Rule*, 3, 17.

22. *HPMB* 3:224; Pomeroy to Gage, 12 Dec. 1768, and "Province of Massachusetts Bay in Council 7th December 1768" (enclosed); Pomeroy to Gage, 2 Feb. 1769, and enclosure, GPAS, vol. 83.

23. Gage to Pomeroy, 19 Dec. 1768, GPAS, vol. 83.

24. Pomeroy to Gage, 22 Dec. 1768, GPAS, vol. 83.

25. Rowe, *Diary*, entries for 16 Oct. 1768, 26 Mar. 1769, 5 Mar. 1769, pp. 177, 185, 184. For Rowe's interest in the supply contract, see John W. Tyler, *Smugglers and Patriots: Boston Merchants and the Advent of the American Revolution* (Boston: Northeastern University Press, 1986), 115.

26. Rowe, *Diary*, introduction and (for example) entries for 8 July 1769, Oct.–Dec. 1770, and Aug.–Sept. 1772, pp. 10–14, 189, 209–211, 233–234.

27. J. L. Bell, "Captain Ponsonby Molesworth: Officer, Freemason," *Boston 1775*, http://boston1775.blogspot.com/2009/11/capt-ponsonby-molesworth -officer.html; Bell, "Captain Molesworth Falls in Love," *Boston 1775*, http:// boston1775.blogspot.com/2009/11/capt-molesworth-falls-in-love.html; Bell, " 'Carried Miss Suky Sheaffe to Hampton,' " *Boston 1775*, http:// boston1775.blogspot.com/2009/11/carried-miss-suky-sheaffe-to-hampton .html; Zobel, *Boston Massacre*, 100.

28. For a much more sustained and thorough analysis of this topic, see Serena R. Zabin, *An Intimate History of the Boston Massacre* (New York: Houghton Mifflin Harcourt, forthcoming).

29. Depositions of Mary Thayer (no. 11), Mary Brailsford (no. 12), Asa Copeland (no. 13), John Wilme (no. 1), Sarah Wilme (no. 2), David Cockran (no. 3), John Brailsford (no. 14), and Richard Ward (no. 16), *SNHM*, appendix, pp. 37–45; *LPJA* 3:9n18; cf. Zobel, *Boston Massacre*, 107. For the widely misunderstood warning-out process, see Cornelia H. Dayton and Sharon V. Salinger, *Robert Love's Warnings: Searching for Strangers in Colonial Boston* (Philadelphia: University of Pennsylvania Press, 2014).

30. This and the following paragraph are based on *BR* 23:19–54; quote: 19.

31. Quote: *BR* 23:42. For the location of the Orange Tree, see Annie Haven Thwing, *Inhabitants and Estates of the Town of Boston, 1630–1800*, and *The Crooked and Narrow Streets of Boston, 1630–1822*, CD-ROM (Boston: NEHGS and Massachusetts Historical Society, 2001), refcode 59983.

32. Eighteenth-century currency values are incommensurate with modern ones, so there is no simple way to estimate the value of £314,000 in modern terms. A simple purchasing power calculator would suggest that this

amount is roughly equivalent to £33,950,000 in 2010 values. A labor value calculator produces an equivalent of £472,200,000, while an income value calculator produces an equivalent of £598,100,000. These calculations come from http://www.measuringworth.com/ppoweruk/. In 2010 a British pound was worth about $1.50; thus, a rough estimate of the modern value of Britain's annual expenditures in North America ranges from $50,925,000 (purchasing power value) to $897,150,000 (income value) per year.

33. John Shy, *Toward Lexington: The Role of the British Army in the Coming of the American Revolution* (Princeton, NJ: Princeton University Press, 1965), 338–340.

34. During wartime, a full regiment consisted of 1,000 men. Following the Seven Years' War, in order to reduce the size of the army without shrinking the number of regiments, the size of a regiment was halved, to 500. Fifteen regiments were posted to North America; thus, the theoretical size of this force was 7,500 men. In practice, most regiments fell short of their full complement of soldiers, though by what percentage it is impossible to say. In fall 1768 Gage ordered the battalions of four regiments to Boston, along with detachments from two others: the 14th and 29th Regiments of Foot, two companies of the 59th, and a detachment of the Royal Regiment of Artillery arrived in October, to be joined in November by the 64th and the 65th. At full strength, this force should have numbered about twenty-one hundred. Gage arranged for six months' provisions for two thousand men; see Delaney and Watts to Gage, 10 Oct. 1768, GPAS, vol. 81. After July 1769, only the 14th and the 29th were left. At full capacity they would have numbered about a thousand, but they were often shorthanded; see, e.g., Gage to Dalrymple, 29 Oct. 1769, GPAS, vol. 88.

35. The regimental records that once existed to document pay are no longer extant. My estimate for the year 1769 assumes that 25 percent of this expense was paid into Boston from January through July, and 12.5 percent was paid into Boston thereafter.

36. GPW 21:64; warrant dated 31 July 1769.

37. GPW 23:157; warrant dated 31 Jan. 1770. The seventeen posts were Halifax, Annapolis Royal, Fort Frederick, Fort Cumberland, Louisbourg, Fort Amherst, St. Johns, Placentia, Crown Point, Ticonderoga, Albany, Fort Ontario, Fort Stanwix, Detroit, Michilimackinac, Fort Pitt, and Fort Chartres.

38. GPW 18:41; warrant dated 20 Dec. 1768.

39. GPW 18:41, 21:63; Samuel Adams Drake, *Old Landmarks and Historic Personages of Boston* (Boston: James R. Osgood and Co., 1873), 358. Besides Molineux and Green, the following property owners made buildings available as barracks: James Smith, James Forrest, John Gooch, Francis Wright,

John Rowe, Jacob Thayer, Benjamin Davis, and Simeon Stoddard. Dr. Gardner rented a house to Montresor to serve as a hospital. Robertson's accounts also include rent payments, which suggests that Montresor made the initial arrangements, while Robertson kept up the agreements thereafter.

40. GPW 21:69.

{CHAPTER 6 · PROVOCATIONS}

1. Oliver Morton Dickerson, ed., *Boston under Military Rule, 1768–1769, as Revealed in a Journal of the Times* (New York: Da Capo Press, 1970 [orig. pub. 1936]), vii–xiii. Dickerson's collection brings together all the Journal pieces in a single publication; most are drawn from the *New-York Journal*, with comparisons to the versions that appeared in the *Boston Evening-Post.*

2. Quotes: Dickerson, *Boston under Military Rule,* entries for 29 Oct. and 15 Oct. 1768, pp. 15–16, 6; see also, e.g., entries for 29 Oct., 1 Nov., and 9 Nov. 1768, and 17 May 1769, pp. 15–16, 17, 20–21, 100. For an extended discussion of the practice of flogging soldiers, see the entry for 15 Dec. 1768, pp. 35–36.

3. Ibid., entries for 6 Nov. and 11 Nov. 1768, pp. 19, 21.

4. Bernard to Hillsborough, 25 Feb. 1769, *PFB* 5:216–218; Pomeroy to Gage, 23 Feb. 1769, GPAS, vol. 84.

5. Selectmen's Meeting minutes, 16 Feb. 1769, *BR* 23:6–7. For Adams's essays in the *Boston Gazette,* see *WSA* 1:249–278, 306–309.

6. *BR* 23:6–7.

7. Ibid., 7–9.

8. The best account of the effort to secure and publish Bernard's letters is in Colin Nicholson, "Introduction," *PFB* 5:14–31. Hillsborough to Bernard, 24 Mar. 1769, *PFB* 5:234–235.

9. In North America during the Seven Years' War, soldiers were recruited for life "if possible," and otherwise for a term of at least three years; see Stephen Brumwell, *Redcoats: The British Soldier and War in the Americas, 1755–1763* (New York: Cambridge University Press, 2002), 59. In practice, "for life" meant until they wore out; most would not have served more than twenty years or so. For the 60th Regiment, see John Shy, *Toward Lexington: The Role of the British Army in the Coming of the American Revolution* (Princeton, NJ: Princeton University Press, 1965), 172–175 and following; for desertion in the British army, see Arthur N. Gilbert, "Why Men Deserted from the Eighteenth-Century British Army," *Armed Forces and Society* 6 (1980): 553–567, especially 556–557; and William P. Tatum III, "'The Soldiers Murmured Much on Account of This Usage': Military

Justice and Negotiated Authority in the Eighteenth-Century British Army," in *Britain's Soldiers: Rethinking War and Society, 1715–1815,* ed. Kevin Linch and Matthew McCormack (Liverpool: Liverpool University Press, 2014), 95–113.

10. Samuel Cooper to Thomas Pownall, 18 Feb. 1769, in Frederick Tuckerman, "Letters of Samuel Cooper to Thomas Pownall, 1769–1777," *AHR* 8 (1903): 301–330; quote: 305.

11. Pomeroy to Gage, 12 Jan. 1769, GPAS, vol. 83 and enclosed testimony.

12. Gage to Pomeroy, 23 Jan. 1769; Pomeroy to Gage, 2 Feb. 1769; and Wentworth to Pomeroy, 20 Feb. 1769, GPAS, vol. 83.

13. Gage to Pomeroy, 23 Jan. 1769, GPAS, vol. 83; Gage to Pomeroy, 13 Feb. 1769, GPAS, vol. 84.

14. Gage to Pomeroy, 6 Mar. 1769, GPAS, vol. 84.

15. Maurice Carr to Gage, 6 Mar. 1769, and Gage to Carr, 13 Mar. 1769, GPAS, vol. 84.

16. Pomeroy to Gage, 27 Feb. 1769, and Gage to Pomeroy, 6 Mar. 1769, GPAS, vol. 84.

17. Pomeroy to Gage, 6 Mar. 1769, and Carr to Gage, 6 Mar. 1769, GPAS, vol. 84.

18. For correspondence about particular deserters, see, e.g., Alex[ande]r McMillan to Mackay, 4 May 1769, and Mackay to Gage, 8 May 1769; quote: Gage to Mackay, 15 May 1769; amnesty: Mackay to Gage, 25 May 1769; GPAS, vol. 85.

19. Gage to Dalrymple, 10 Sept. 1769; Dalrymple to Gage, 24 Sept. and 4 Sept. 1769, GPAS, vol. 87.

20. Dalrymple to Gage, 24 Sept. and 28 Oct. 1769; Gage to Dalrymple, 29 Oct. 1769; GPAS, vols. 87, 88.

21. Gage to Commodore Samuel Hood, 5 June 1769, GPAS, vol. 86; Bernard to Hillsborough, 25 June 1769, *PFB* 5:300–302.

22. Mackay to Gage, 12 June 1769 [#1], GPAS, vol. 86.

23. Gage to Pomeroy, 13 Feb. 1769, GPAS, vol. 84.

24. Pomeroy to Gage, 27 Feb. 1769, GPAS, vol. 84.

25. Mackay to Gage, 29 May 1769, GPAS, vol. 85.

26. See, e.g., Gage to Dalrymple, 25 Sept. 1769, vol. 87.

27. Dalrymple to Gage, 6 Sept. and 7 Sept. 1769; Gage to Dalrymple, 18 Sept. 1769; Dalrymple to Gage, 9 Oct. 1769; Dalrymple to Gage, 29 Oct. 1769; Dalrymple to Gage, 3 Nov. 1769; Dalrymple to Gage, 18 Jan. and 20 Jan. 1770; Dalrymple to Gage, 19 Feb. 1770; GPAS, vols. 87–90. For detailed accounts of these events, see Hiller B. Zobel, *The Boston Massacre* (New York: W. W. Norton, 1970), 145–179; John W. Tyler, *Smugglers and Patriots: Boston Merchants and the Advent of the American Revolution*

(Boston: Northeastern University Press, 1986), 118–152; and Richard Archer, *As If an Enemy's Country: The British Occupation of Boston and the Origins of Revolution* (New York: Oxford University Press, 2010), 144–178.

28. Dalrymple to Gage, 19 Feb. 1770, GPAS, vol. 90.

29. References to vexatious suits appear in Mackay to Gage, 12 June 1769, and Gage to Mackay, 2 July 1769, GPAS, vol. 86; Mackay to Gage, 18 Aug. 1769, GPAS, vol. 87. Gage's letter of 2 July asked Mackay to keep track of expenses associated with such suits; in his August accounts, Mackay included an expenditure of £3 6s. 1½d. "for a vexatious Law Suit against a Serjeant of the 29th Regiment." GPW 21:67. For the tension between local law and imperial law, see especially John Phillip Reid, *In Defiance of the Law: The Standing-Army Controversy, the Two Constitutions, and the Coming of the American Revolution* (Chapel Hill: University of North Carolina Press, 1981), esp. 177–188.

30. Mackay to Gage, 25 May 1769, GPAS, vol. 85.

31. Mackay to Gage, 19 June 1769, and enclosures: Suffolk County court proceedings and Dalrymple to Mackay; GPAS, vol. 86.

32. Mackay to Gage, 12 June 1769; Gage to Mackay, 18 June 1769; Dalrymple to Mackay, encl. in Mackay to Gage, 19 June 1769; Gage to Mackay, 28 June 1769; GPAS, vol. 86.

33. Mackay to Gage, 25 June 1769; Gage to Mackay, 2 July 1769; GPAS, vol. 86.

34. Mackay to Gage, 1 June 1769, GPAS, vol. 86; Massachusetts Bay Council to William Bollan, 27 Mar. 1770, encl. in Hutchinson to Gage, 1 Apr. 1770, GPAS, vol. 91; Dalrymple to Gage, 10 Dec. 1769, GPAS, vol. 88; Hutchinson to Gage, 29 Apr. 1770, GPAS, vol. 91. The General Court remained in Cambridge, against its collective will, for more than two years, where its members often refused to do business in protest. For a full account of the controversy, see Donald C. Lord and Robert M. Calhoon, "The Removal of the Massachusetts General Court from Boston, 1769–1772," *JAH* 55 (1969): 735–755.

35. Dalrymple to Gage, 27 Sept. 1769, GPAS, vol. 87. This paragraph and the three following rely on Hiller Zobel's masterful reconstruction of a tangled series of legal processes; see *Boston Massacre*, 139–143.

36. Dalrymple to Gage, 30 Nov. 1769, and deposition of Ensign John Ness, 3 Nov. 1769, encl. in Dalrymple to Gage, 12 Nov. 1769, GPAS, vol. 88.

37. Deposition of Ponsonby Molesworth, 3 Nov. 1769, encl. in Dalrymple to Gage, 12 Nov. 1769, GPAS, vol. 88.

38. Quotations: deposition of Lieut. Hugh Dickson and Lieut. Thomas Buckley, encl. in Dalrymple to Gage, 12 Nov. 1769, GPAS, vol. 88.

{CHAPTER 7 · UNCERTAIN OUTCOMES}

1. Among the deponents in the *SNHM*, Samuel Bostwick recalled that laborer William Green insulted a soldier as he approached the ropewalk: asked whether he was looking for work, the soldier said yes. Green replied, "Then go and clean my shithouse." According to Bostwick, the soldier swore at Green, returned to his barracks, and came back a short time later with thirty or forty soldiers. Thirteen or fourteen ropewalk workers "turn'd out and beat them off, considerably bruised." Nicholas Ferreter claimed that a single soldier came to the ropewalks spoiling for a fight; Ferreter "stept out of the window and speedily knock'd up his heels." The soldier went back to his barracks and returned with eight or nine more soldiers, armed with clubs; they, too, were beaten and went back to their barracks. Soon a still larger party of thirty or forty soldiers arrived, "*armed with clubs and cutlasses, and headed by a tall negro drummer.*" Without any weapons but their wouldring sticks (eighteen to twenty-four inches in length, these were used to braid hemp into rope), a group of ten or eleven ropemakers "beat them off." Three more deponents — Jeffrey Richardson, John Fisher, and John Hill — began their accounts of the incident with the approach of a small group of between six and ten soldiers, spoiling for a fight, who were beaten and then returned with a larger party of thirty or forty. The insult recounted by Bostwick did not appear in any other deposition in the *Short Narrative,* but once it was reported many people repeated it, including Ferreter when he testified in the soldiers' trial. It is the kind of detail that historians love as well, and nearly every account of the ropewalk melee begins with this colorful anecdote. But in Bostwick's account the insulted soldier left without picking a fight; thus, it does not align with Ferreter's deposition. See depositions no. 23 (Bostwick), no. 5 (Ferreter), no. 6 (Richardson), no. 7 (Fisher), and no. 8 (Hill), *SNHM*, pp. 13, 3–5. Warren and Kilroy present: testimony of Ferreter, *TWW,* 44–45; Gray targeted by Kilroy: testimony of Edward G. Langford, *TWW,* 16–19; description of Gray's wounds: *BG,* 12 Mar. 1770.

2. *BG,* 12 Mar. 1770; for Attucks's misidentification, see the inquest document, printed in *The Boston Massacre: A History with Documents,* ed. Neil L. York (New York: Routledge, 2010), 123–125. For attempts to reconstruct his biography, which necessarily require extensive speculation, see Bill Belton, "The Indian Heritage of Crispus Attucks," *Negro History Bulletin* 35 (1972): 149–152; and Harry M. Ward, "Attucks, Crispus," *ANB* 1:728.

3. *BG,* 12 Mar. 1770; J. L. Bell, "Who Was Caldwell's Captain Morton?," *Boston 1775,* http://boston1775.blogspot.com/2006/09/who-was-caldwells -capt-morton.html; Charles R. E. Koch, "A History of the Development of

Dentistry," in Koch, ed., *History of Dental Surgery,* 3 vols. (Chicago: National Art Publishing Co., 1909), 1:81–82.

4. *BG,* 12 Mar. 1770; J. L. Bell, "The Last Victim of the Boston Massacre?," *Boston 1775,* http://boston1775.blogspot.com/2008/05/last-victim-of -boston-massacre.html; J. L. Bell, "Patrick Carr: Breeches-Maker, Massacre Victim," *Boston 1775,* http://boston1775.blogspot.com/2007/03/patrick -carr-breeches-maker-massacre.html. For Carr's death, see *BG,* 19 Mar. 1770; for Monk, see also Chapter 9.

5. *BG,* 12 Mar. 1770.

6. For Land Pattern Muskets, see, e.g., Gunther E. Rothenberg, *The Art of Warfare in the Age of Napoleon* (Bloomington: Indiana University Press, 1978), 63–64. Two of the balls fired that night were recovered and now reside in the collections of the Massachusetts Historical Society, allowing us to see both their size and shape; see http://www.masshist.org/database /3056?ft=Boston%20Massacre&from=/features/massacre&noalt=1&pid =34. The Land Pattern Musket is popularly known today as the "Brown Bess," but that nickname is a modern coinage; see "Brown Bess"—Musket Misconception, The Lincoln Minute Men, http://www.lincolnminutemen .org/brown-bess-musket-misconception/.

7. The members of the town's committee were John Hancock, Samuel Adams, William Molineux, Joshua Henshaw, William Phillips, Joseph Warren, and Samuel Pemberton. The justices of the peace who collected affidavits were Richard Dana, John Hill, Belcher Noyes, Samuel Pemberton, Edmund Quincy, John Ruddock, and John Tudor. Of the ninety-six affidavits published with the *Short Narrative,* nine were given on March 19 and forty-four from March 20 to March 24; one was undated. *SNHM,* throughout.

8. *SNHM,* [4], 86–88. A manuscript version of the cover letter to the Duke of Richmond and the longer list of recipients is in the Winthrop Papers, reel 47, Bowdoin-Temple Papers, MHS.

9. Macaulay to the gentlemen of Boston, 9 May 1770, RWMC-BPL, https:// archive.org/details/lettertogentlemeoomaca; Bollan to James Bowdoin and others, 11 May 1770, RWMC-BPL, https://archive.org/details /lettertojamesbowooboll; Pownall to Bowdoin et al., 11 May 1770, RWMC-BPL, https://archive.org/details/lettertojamesbowoopown; and Trecothick to Boston selectmen, 10 May 1770, RWMC-BPL, https://archive.org /details/lettertobostonseootrec.

10. Pownall to Bowdoin et al., 11 May 1770; Trecothick to Boston selectmen, 10 May 1770.

11. Hutchinson to John Pownall (private), 21 Mar. 1770, MA 26:464, from the MHS typescript, 1007–1009 (John Pownall was secretary to the Board of Trade and the brother of Thomas, former governor of Massachusetts); Thomas Hutchinson Diary, British Library MS EG.2666, p. 55.

12. *The General Laws and Liberties of the Massachusetts Colony, Revised and Reprinted* (Boston, 1672), 90, printed in *The Colonial Laws of Massachusetts: Reprinted from the Edition of 1672* (Boston: Rockwell and Churchill, 1890); BR 18:1–19; quote: 2.

13. Hutchinson to Bernard, 25 Mar. 1770 (secret and confidential), MA 26:471–472, from the MHS typescript, 1023–1025; Hutchinson to Bernard, 30 Mar. 1770, MA 26:467, from the MHS typescript, 1015–1017; Hutchinson to Hillsborough, 27 Mar. 1770, MA 26:460–461, from the MHS typescript, 999–1001.

14. Hutchinson to Pownall, 21 Mar. 1770.

15. *SNHM*, 86. The town's grievances against the customs commissioners were further detailed in a supplemental pamphlet that appeared shortly after *SNHM*, entitled *Additional Observations to a Short Narrative of the Horrid Massacre in Boston, Perpetrated in the Evening of the 5th of March 1770* (Boston, 1770).

16. Hutchinson to Hillsborough, Mar. 1770, MA 26:452–455, from the MHS typescript, 985–990a. This is a draft of the letter Hutchinson sent on 12 Mar., which is printed in *DAR* 2:58–60, but it varies considerably from the final version. The quotation comes from the deleted passage on 990a. Minutes of the selectmen's meeting, 7 Mar. 1770, *BR* 23:57–58; *SNHM*, 37–38.

17. Dalrymple to Gage, 8 Mar. 1770, GPAS, vol. 90.

18. Ibid.; Dalrymple to Gage, 12 Mar. 1770, GPAS, vol. 90.

19. Gage to Hutchinson, 12 Mar. 1770, and to Dalrymple, 12 Mar. 1770, GPAS, vol. 90.

20. Gage to Dalrymple, 14 Mar. 1770, GPAS, vol. 90.

21. Hutchinson to Gage, 18 Mar. 1770, GPAS, vol. 90.

22. Dalrymple to Gage, 19 Mar. 1770, GPAS, vol. 90; *BR* 18:8–9, 10, 14–15, 16; Gage to Hutchinson, 28 Apr. 1770, Gage to Dalrymple, 28 Apr. 1770, and Dalrymple to Gage, 5 May 1770, GPAS, vol. 91; Dalrymple to Gage, 21 May 1770, GPAS, vol. 92.

23. For Quincy's recruitment, see *PJQJ* 1:22; for Adams, see John Adams autobiography, part 1, "John Adams," through 1776, sheet 12 of 53, 1769–1770, MHS, online at https://www.masshist.org/digitaladams/archive/doc?id =A1_12&bc=%2Fdigitaladams%2Farchive%2Fbrowse%2Fautobio1.php; Josiah Quincy Sr. to Josiah Quincy Jr., 22 Mar. 1770, and Josiah Quincy Jr. to Josiah Quincy Sr., 26 Mar. 1770, *PJQJ* 6:50–52.

24. William Molineux to Robert Treat Paine, Esq., 9 Mar. 1770, RTPP, Notes and Letters on the Boston Massacre Trial, 1770–1771, reel 14, MHS; *BR* 18:14; *LPJA* 3:7–8.

25. Molineux to Paine, 9 Mar. 1770.

26. *BR* 18:1–2.

27. Molineux to Paine, 9 Mar. 1770.
28. *BG,* 19 Mar. 1770; *BR* 18:8, 16; Hutchinson to Gage, 27 Mar. 1770 and 18 Mar. 1770, GPAS, vol. 90.
29. Dalrymple to Gage, 12 Mar. 1770, GPAS, vol. 90; *BG,* 12 and 19 Mar. 1770.
30. Preston's case was published first in London's *Public Advertiser,* 28 Apr. 1770; Albert Matthews, "Capt. Thomas Preston and the Boston Massacre," in *Publications of the Colonial Society of Massachusetts,* vol. 7 (Boston, 1905), 2–7; Gage to Dalrymple, 26 Mar. 1770, GPAS, vol. 90; Dalrymple to Gage, 5 May 1770, GPAS, vol. 91.
31. Hutchinson to Gage, 23 June 1770, GPAS, vol. 93.
32. *BR* 18:34; Thomas Cushing et al. to Preston, 11 July 1770, encl. in Preston to Gage, 6 Aug. 1770, GPAS, vol. 94.
33. For the tension between older notions of justice and the new practice of using soldiers as a police force, see John Phillip Reid, *In Defiance of the Law: The Standing-Army Controversy, the Two Constitutions, and the Coming of the American Revolution* (Chapel Hill: University of North Carolina Press, 1981), esp. 112–120.
34. The Duke of Richmond was one observer who "advise[d] the Town, in case Capt. Preston and the Soldiers should be convicted, to intercede for a respite that they might be recommended to the King for mercy": Hutchinson to Gage, 29 July 1770; [anonymous] to Preston, 20 July 1770, encl. in Preston to Gage, 6 Aug. 1770, GPAS, vol. 94.
35. Hutchinson to Gage, 22 June 1770, GPAS, vol. 93.
36. James Murray to Dalrymple, 27 July 1770, encl. in Dalrymple to Gage, 12 Aug. 1770, GPAS, vol. 94.
37. John W. Tyler, *Smugglers and Patriots: Boston Merchants and the Advent of the American Revolution* (Boston: Northeastern University Press, 1986), appendix, pp. 270–271.
38. Dalrymple to Gage, 12 Aug. 1770, and Gage to Dalrymple, 19 Aug. 1770, GPAS, vol. 94; Dalrymple to Gage, 27 Aug. 1770, GPAS, vol. 95.
39. Gage to Dalrymple, 19 Aug. 1770, GPAS, vol. 94. Hillsborough, too, compared events in Boston unfavorably to those in New York; see Hillsborough to Gage, 12 June 1770, *CGTG* 2:103–105.
40. Thomas Hutchinson to Francis Bernard, 2 July 1770, MA 26:515, from the MHS typescript.
41. Hillsborough to Gage, 12 June and 6 July 1770, *CGTG* 2:103–107.
42. Gage to Dalrymple, 2 Sept. 1770, GPAS, vol. 94; *BG,* 17 Sept. and 8 Oct. 1770.
43. *BG,* 17 and 24 Sept. 1770.
44. *BG,* 15 Oct. 1770.
45. The town meeting convened in August, September, and October, but attended only to routine business; see *BR* 18:35–38. For the proceedings

of the General Court, see *BG,* 22 and 29 Oct. 1770. Hutchinson to Hillsborough, 30 Oct. 1770, MA 27:46–47, from the MHS typescript, 70.

46. Dalrymple to Gage, 3 Sept. 1770, GPAS, vol. 94; *LPJA* 3:14–17.

47. Petition of Hugh White, James Hartigan, and Mat[t]hew Killroy [*sic*], 24 Oct. 1770, *LPJA* 3:17.

48. Ibid.

{CHAPTER 8 · FOUR TRIALS}

1. For Auchmuty and the *Liberty* case, see *LPJA* 2:173–193; Dalrymple to Gage, 12 Aug. 1770, GPAS, vol. 94; Hutchinson to Bernard, 30 Mar. 1770, MA 26:467, from the MHS typescript, 1015–1017; Preston to Gage, 31 Oct. 1770, GPAS, vol. 97.

2. John Adams Autobiography, part 1, "John Adams," through 1776, sheet 12 of 53 [electronic edition], *Adams Family Papers: An Electronic Archive,* MHS, http://www.masshist.org/digitaladams/. A guinea was a gold coin worth twenty-one shillings; Adams's eighteen guineas amounted to a little less than £19. For a penetrating sketch of Adams's character as a young man, see Bernard Bailyn, "Butterfield's Adams: Notes for a Sketch," *WMQ* 19 (1962): 238–256, reprinted without notes as "John Adams: 'It Is My Destiny to Dig Treasures with My Own Fingers,'" in *Faces of Revolution: Personalities and Themes in the Struggle for Independence* (New York: Knopf, 1990), 3–21.

3. *PJQJ* 1:16–21; Thomas Hutchinson, memoranda and diary for 1770, Egerton MS 2666, British Library.

4. *PJQJ* 1:18, 24–25.

5. Stephen Thomas Riley, "Robert Treat Paine and His Papers" (Ph.D. diss., Clark University, 1953), iii–xxviii; entry for Tues., Dec. 3 or 4, 1758, John Adams diary 2, 5 Oct. 1758–9 Apr. 1759 [electronic edition], *Adams Family Papers: An Electronic Archive,* MHS, http://www.masshist.org/digitaladams/.

6. Hiller B. Zobel, *The Boston Massacre* (New York: W. W. Norton, 1970), 241–266; quotes: 246, 248. Zobel's scholarship on these trials is unparalleled; anyone interested in them should begin by consulting the relevant chapters there, and also *LPJA,* vol. 3 in its entirety.

7. Hutchinson to Gage, 29 July 1770, Preston to Gage, 6 Aug. 1770, and Gage to Preston, 12 Aug. 1770, GPAS, vol. 94; Hutchinson, memoranda and diary for 1770, Egerton MS 2666, British Library; Hutchinson to Hillsborough, 30 Oct. 1770, MA 27:46–47, from the MHS typescript, 70. Neil Longley York has argued that town leaders had concluded that they did not have to provoke a confrontation at the trials, since the significance of the "massacre" had already been established in the minds of Bostonians and

the residents of other Massachusetts towns: see York, "Rival Truths, Political Accommodation, and the Boston 'Massacre,'" *MHR* 11 (2009): 57–95. He makes a persuasive case, but if he is correct it is puzzling why the prosecution efforts were so strenuous, and why Samuel Adams was offering advice to the prosecution team from the sidelines during the soldiers' trial (see Chapter 9, note 3).

8. According to Hutchinson, Preston's trial was the first in the Massachusetts courts to adjourn before the proceedings were completed. "The Jury," he wrote, "have never separated which is excessive hard upon them." Hutchinson to Gage, 28 Oct. 1770, GPAS, vol. 97.

9. Robert Treat Paine, notes for closing argument in the Preston trial, RTPP. There is no published account of the Preston trial. The official transcript, which includes only summaries of witness testimony, is in CO 5/759, NAUK; quotes: 713, 717, 718.

10. CO 5/759, NAUK; quotes: 714–715.

11. Ibid.; quote: Edward Hill, 721.

12. Ibid.; quotes: 727.

13. Ibid.; quotes: 727–728.

14. Ibid.; quotes: 729, 724.

15. Dalrymple to Gage, 1 Nov. 1770, Hutchinson to Gage, 5 Nov. 1770, and Preston to Gage, 31 Oct. 1770, GPAS, vol. 97.

16. The most thorough treatments of the soldiers' trial are in Zobel, *Boston Massacre,* 267–294, and *LPJA,* vol. 3.

17. There are two contemporary accounts of the soldiers' trial, one published and one in manuscript. The published version, which includes summaries of lawyers' arguments and judges' instructions as well as testimony, is *TWW,* based on a shorthand transcription by John Hodgson. The official transcript, like that of the Preston trial, is in CO 5/759, NAUK. *TWW* identifies thirty-two witnesses for the crown; two additional witnesses, Samuel Emmons and John Williams, appear only in the manuscript account of the trial. Quote: CO 5/759: 767. For background on Hodgson, see "John Hodgson, Court Transcriber and Book Binder," *Boston 1775,* http://boston1775.blogspot.com/2011/09/john-hodgson-court-transcriber-and.html.

18. See Appendix.

19. The eight new witnesses testifying to knowledge of the soldiers were Ebenezer Bridgham, James Dodge, Samuel Clarke, James Brewer, James Bailey, John Danbrook, Jedediah Bass, and Thomas Wilkinson. The five who had previously given accounts of March 5 were Jonathan Williams Austin, Edward Langsford, Francis Archbald Jr., Richard Palmes, and Josiah Simpson. CO 5/759, NAUK.

20. Ibid.; quote: 786.

21. Quincy argument: *TWW*, 68–80; quotes: 73, 75.

22. Thomas Hutchinson, memoranda and diary for 1770, Egerton MS 2666, British Library; Hiller B. Zobel, "Newer Light on the Boston Massacre," *Proceedings of the American Antiquarian Society* 78 (1968): 119–128.

23. Adams argument: *TWW*, 148–178; quote: 153–154.

24. Ibid., 153.

25. Ibid., 113–114. Andrew offered substantially the same testimony at both trials, and Hodgson's published account closely accords with the manuscript record; see the trial transcripts in CO 5/759, NAUK.

26. *TWW*, 12–13, 27–28, 101, 23, 31, 103; Paine, Notes and Letters, RTPP, reel 14. (These notes relate to Paine's closing argument in the Preston trial, where Andrew gave substantially the same testimony.)

27. *TWW*, 174.

28. Ibid., 176.

29. Ibid.

30. Hutchinson to Bernard, 25 Mar. 1770 (secret and confidential), MA 26:471–472, from the MHS typescript, 1023–1025; Hutchinson to John Pownall (private), 21 Mar. 1770, MA 26:464, from the MHS typescript, 1007–1009. This view of Boston's politics is also apparent in Peter Oliver's vitriolic account of Boston in the 1760s and 1770s: *Peter Oliver's Origin and Progress of the American Rebellion: A Tory View*, ed. Douglass Adair and John A. Schutz (Stanford: Stanford University Press, 1961).

31. *BR* 14:127. For the Knowles riot, see especially John Lax and William Pencak, "The Knowles Riot and the Crisis of the 1740's in Massachusetts," *Perspectives in American History* 10 (1976): 163–214.

32. *TWW*, 174.

33. Trowbridge instructions: *TWW*, 178–197; quote: 193; *BEP*, 10 Dec. and 17 Dec. 1770. Originally a privilege extended to clergymen, who could claim to be subject to canon law in ecclesiastical courts rather than criminal law in secular courts, by the eighteenth century the benefit of clergy had evolved into a provision allowing leniency to first-time offenders. They were branded on the thumb to prevent them from claiming the privilege a second time.

34. Deposition of Charlotte [Charles] Bourgate [*sic*] (no. 58), *SNHM*, 44–46.

35. Ibid.

36. Ibid.

37. Thomas Hutchinson, memoranda and diary for 1770, Egerton MS 2666, British Library; *BG*, 18 Mar. 1771; Hutchinson to Gage, 1 Apr. 1770, GPAS, vol. 91.

38. Samuel Quincy to Robert Treat Paine, 16 Dec. 1770, RTPP.

39. *TWW*, 215.

40. For the possibility of double loading, see *LPJA* 3:30. The coroner's inquest report for Crispus Attucks is reproduced in Neil L. York, ed., *The Boston*

Massacre: A History with Documents (New York: Routledge, 2010), 125. (The report originally identified Attucks as Michael Johnson, for reasons that are unclear.) For the mechanics of loading a musket and the use of buck and ball in the American Revolution, see Lawrence E. Babits, *A Devil of a Whipping: The Battle of Cowpens* (Chapel Hill: University of North Carolina Press, 1998), 11–13. For an X-ray image of a recently recovered eighteenth-century musket that clearly illustrates a musket loaded with buck and ball, see https://en.wikipedia.org/wiki/Buck_and_ball#/media /File:Buck%26Ball_musket_StormWreck.jpg. I am indebted to Neil York and Fred Anderson for illuminating conversations on this topic.

41. Depositions of Jeremiah Allen (no. 64), George Costar (no. 67), Gillam Bass (no. 59), Francis Read (no. 61), Benjamin Frizel (no. 63), Samuel Drowne (no. 68), and Cato (no. 70), *SNHM,* 46–56.

42. There is an extensive scientific literature on false memory. Much of it relates to falsely recovered memories of traumatic childhood experiences; because this involves false memories of supposedly long-past and repressed events, it bears little relation to the massacre depositions. But there is also a literature on "reality-monitoring errors," which could plausibly shed light on these depositions. See, e.g., Brian Gonsalves and Ken A. Paller, "Neural Events That Underlie Remembering Something That Never Happened," *Nature Neuroscience* 3 (2000): 1316–1321.

43. O. M. Dickerson, "The Commissioners of Customs and the 'Boston Massacre,'" *NEQ* 27 (1954): 307–325; affidavit of Thomas Greenwood (no. 96), *SNHM,* 75–77.

44. Edward Manwaring, petition to the Lords of the Treasury, 23 July 1771, T1/486, NAUK (this is the first of three Manwaring petitions in the file; it is undated, but the subsequent petition of 14 Aug. 1771 assigns it the date I have provided). For the port of Gaspé, see Mario Mimeault, *Gaspésie: A Brief History* (Quebec: L'Université Laval, 2005), 75–81.

45. Manwaring petition, 23 July 1771.

46. Testimony of Wyat and Goddard at Preston's trial, CO 5/759, NAUK; Bridgham, *TWW,* 14; "Case of Captain Preston," encl. in Preston to the Earl of Chatham, 17 Mar. 1770, 30/8/97 (Pt. 1), NAUK.

47. *TWW,* 51–52.

48. *Massachusetts Gazette: and the Boston Weekly News-Letter,* 21 Mar. 1771; *BG,* 1 April 1771; Edward Manwaring, memorial to the Lords of the Treasury, 14 Aug. 1771, T1/486, NAUK.

{CHAPTER 9 · CONTESTED MEANINGS}

1. *BEP,* 22 Oct. 1770; *BG,* 22 Oct. 1770; "Damages at Boston," encl. in Montresor to Gage, 22 Oct. 1770, GPAS, vol. 97.

2. Montresor to Gage, 22 Oct. 1770, GPAS, vol. 97.
3. Samuel Adams, Suggestions and remarks during the trial of the soldiers, 2 Dec. 1770 [?], reel 14, RTPP.
4. Samuel Quincy to Robert Treat Paine, 16 Dec. 1770, reel 14, RTPP; Proclamation, *BEP*, 17 Dec. 1770.
5. Vindex: *BG*, 10 Dec. 1770 and 28 Jan. 1771; Philanthrop: *BEP*, 17 Dec. 1770 and 18 Feb. 1771; Molineux: *BG*, 18 Mar. 1771; Palmes: *BG*, 25 Mar. 1771.
6. *BR* 18:49–50.
7. John Rowe, *Letters and Diary of John Rowe*, ed. Anne Rowe Cunningham (New York: Arno Press, 1969 [orig. pub. Boston, 1903]), entries for 8 and 17 Mar., 199; *BG*, 12 Mar. 1770. See also the accounts in *BEP*, 12 Mar. 1770; *Massachusetts Gazette, and Boston Post-Boy and Advertiser*, 12 Mar. 1770; [Salem] *Essex Gazette*, 13 Mar. 1770; and *Boston News-Letter*, 15 Mar. 1770.
8. Much has been written about these prints. Presently, the best account of them, and the one I have relied upon here, is Clarence S. Brigham, *Paul Revere's Engravings* (New York: Atheneum, 1969 [orig. pub. Worcester, MA: American Antiquarian Society, 1954]), 52–78; Pelham quoted at 52–53. Theresa Fairbanks-Harris, Senior Conservator of Works on Paper at the Yale University Art Gallery and the Yale Center for British Art, is part of a collaborative, interdisciplinary research project that is likely to update Brigham's findings, but for now Brigham's is the most reliable analysis of these images.
9. Brigham, *Revere's Engravings*, 64–71.
10. For the town meeting's effort to prevent the *SNHM* from circulating in Boston, see *BR* 18:20, and Samuel Cooper to Thomas Pownall, 2 July 1770, "Letters of Samuel Cooper to Thomas Pownall, 1769–1777," *AHR* 8 (1903): 318–320. For the availability of the *SNHM* beginning in the summer and its presence at the trials, see Hiller B. Zobel, *The Boston Massacre* (New York: W. W. Norton, 1970), 236, 246–247. Quote: Josiah Quincy Jr., opening statement, *TWW*, 77.
11. Brigham, *Revere's Engravings*, 58–61, 64.
12. I am indebted to Patrick Spero for sharing his research on almanacs from the period; for his larger work, see "The Revolution in Popular Publications: The Almanac and New England Primer, 1750–1800," *Early American Studies* 8 (2010): 41–74. This paragraph is based on a search of almanacs digitized in *Early American Imprints, Series I: Evans, 1639–1800*, part of the Archive of Americana database owned by Readex Corp., for the years 1771 to 1786.
13. *BG*, 11 Mar. 1771.
14. *BR* 18:47–52; for Hunt's and Lovell's employment, see *BR* 18:57–58.
15. *BR* 18:62–63, 108–110, 149–150.
16. James Lovell, A.M., *An Oration Delivered April 2d, 1771. At the Request of the Inhabitants of the Town of Boston; to Commemorate the Bloody Tragedy of the Fifth of March, 1770* (Boston: Edes and Gill, 1771), 6.

17. Dr. Joseph Warren, *An Oration Delivered March 5, 1772. At the Request of the Inhabitants of the Town of Boston; to Commemorate the Bloody Tragedy of the Fifth of March, 1770* (Boston: Edes and Gill, 1772), 12–13.
18. John Adams diary, 29 Dec. 1772 [electronic edition], *Adams Family Papers: An Electronic Archive,* MHS, http://www.masshist.org/digitaladams/.
19. Gage to Barrington, 29 June 1772, *CGTG* 2:607–608; Hillsborough to Gage, 2 and 22 Jan. 1771, *CGTG* 2:122–124, 125–126; Gage to Dalrymple, 24 Mar. 1771, and to Lt. Col. Bruce, Gambier, and Hutchinson, 25 Mar. 1771, GPAS, vol. 101; Gage to Dalrymple, 15 and 21 Apr. 1771, GPAS, vol. 102; Dalrymple to Gage, 13 May 1771, GPAS, vol. 103. Robertson's expenses can be estimated from the following warrants: June 1769–30 Dec. 1770, £3601 14s. 1d., GPW 27:43; [?]–5 Oct. 1771, £647 19s., GPW 29:39; 1 July–31 Dec. 1772, £472 6s., GPW 30:28; 1 Jan.–30 June 1772, £824 3s., GPW 31:71; 1 July–31 Dec. 1772, £719 8s. 5d. Montresor's expenses: 8 Mar.–8 Dec. 1770, £2,965 14s. 1½d., GPW 27:41; [1771], £380 3s., GPW 30:3; 25 June–25 Dec. 1771, £3,000, GPW 30:99; 19 Oct. 1771–8 Aug. 1772, £7,287 5s. 5¼d., GPW 33:46; Dec. 1770–June 1771, Aug.–Oct. 1772, £326 19s., GPW 33:53.
20. John Shy, *Toward Lexington: The Role of the British Army in the Coming of the American Revolution* (Princeton, NJ: Princeton University Press, 1965), 412–413; Montresor's expenses: GPW 36:35, 36:68; Spry's expenses: GPW 36:34.
21. John Barker, *The British in Boston: The Diary of Lt. John Barker,* ed. Elizabeth Ellery Dana (New York: Arno Press, 1969 [orig. pub. Cambridge, MA: Harvard University Press, 1924]), 20–21; Edward Griffin Porter, "Remarks Describing a Visit to New England in 1897 of Lieutenant-General George Digny Barker, C.B., and the Diary of His Grandfather, Lieutenant John Barker, 1774–1776," *Publications of the Colonial Society of Massachusetts,* vol. 5, *Transactions, 1897 and 1898* (Boston: Colonial Society of Massachusetts, 1902), 49–55.
22. Barker, *Diary,* 21; John Andrews, *The Letters of John Andrews, Esq., of Boston, 1772–1776,* comp. and ed. Winthrop Sargent (Cambridge, MA: Press of John Wilson and Sons, 1866), entry for 19 Jan. 1775, 80.
23. The best modern biography of Warren is still John Cary, *Joseph Warren: Physician, Politician, Patriot* (Urbana: University of Illinois Press, 1961).
24. Frederick Mackenzie, diary entry for 6 Mar. 1775, in *A British Fusilier in Revolutionary Boston: Being the Diary of Lieutenant Frederick Mackenzie, Adjutant of the Royal Welch Fusiliers, January 5–April 30, 1775, with a Letter Describing His Voyage to America,* ed. Allen French (Cambridge, MA: Harvard University Press, 1926), 36–39; quotes: 37.
25. Because March 5 fell on a Sunday, Warren's oration was delivered on Monday, March 6. Joseph Warren, *An Oration; delivered March Sixth,*

1775, At the Request of the Inhabitants of the town of Boston, to commemorate the Bloody Tragedy of the Fifth of March, 1770 (Boston: Edes and Gill and Joseph Greenleaf, 1775), 5, 7.

26. Ibid., 14.

27. Ibid., 15.

28. Ibid., 15–17.

29. Ibid., 17, 23.

30. *BG*, 13 Mar. 1775; *BR* 18:215–216; Mackenzie, *British Fusilier*, 37; "Old Bostonian," *Columbian Centinel*, 12 Sept. 1821. Six months afterward, a British officer named Colonel James told Thomas Hutchinson that there were three hundred officers present; Mackenzie and Barker both used the phrase "a great number." *DLTH* 1:528; Mackenzie, *British Fusilier*, 37; Barker, *Diary*, 25. Writing half a century after the fact, the "Old Bostonian" remembered that "more than a hundred" officers had been present.

31. The four eyewitness descriptions are Mackenzie, *British Fusilier*, 36–39; Barker, *Diary*, 25–26; "Extract of a Letter from Boston, March 9," *Rivington's New-York Gazeteer*, 16 Mar. 1775; "Extract of a Letter, dated Boston, March 9, 1775," *Rivington's New-York Gazeteer*, 23 Mar. 1775 (quoted). For derogatory references to Rivington's paper, see, e.g., *BEP*, 13 Mar. 1775; *Massachusetts Spy*, 9 and 17 Mar. 1775. The event was described briefly, in passing, in a letter from Samuel Adams to [?], 12 Mar. 1775, *WSA* 3:198–200, and in John Andrews to William Barrell, 18 Mar. 1775, *Letters of John Andrews, Esq., of Boston, 1772–1776*, comp. and ed. Winthrop Sargent (Cambridge, MA: John Wilson and Sons, 1866), 113. The local papers made only passing references to the event; see, e.g., the *Massachusetts Spy*, 9 Mar. 1775, and *BG*, 13 Mar. 1775. Thomas Hutchinson's diary contains a secondhand account based on his conversation with Colonel James in September 1775; see *DLTH* 1:528–529.

32. *DLTH* 1:528–529; Mackenzie, *A British Fusilier*, 37; "Extract of a Letter," *Rivington's New-York Gazeteer*, 23 Mar. 1775; Adams to [?], 12 Mar. 1775, *WSA* 3:199.

33. "Extract of a Letter," *Rivington's New-York Gazeteer*, 23 Mar. 1775.

34. Barker, *Diary*, 26; "Extract of a Letter," *Rivington's New-York Gazeteer*, 16 Mar. 1775; Mackenzie, *A British Fusilier*, 38.

35. Mackenzie, *A British Fusilier*, 38; Andrews to Barrell, 18 Mar. 1775, in *Letters of John Andrews*, 113.

36. Mackenzie, *A British Fusilier*, 38; Adams to [?], 12 Mar. 1775, *WSA* 3:199.

37. "Extract of a Letter," *Rivington's New-York Gazeteer*, 16 Mar. 1775.

38. The toga was not widely reported as fact until the twentieth century. See, e.g., Ellen Chase, *The Beginnings of the American Revolution, Based on Contemporary Letters, Diaries, and Other Documents*, 2 vols. (New York: Kennikat Press, 1970 [orig. pub. New York: Baker and Taylor, 1910]),

2:268; Esther Forbes, *Paul Revere and the World He Lived In* (Cambridge, MA: Harvard University Press, 1942), 230; Eran Shalev, "Dr. Warren's Ciceronian Toga," *Common-Place* 7 (2007), http://www.common-place -archives.org/vol-07/no-02/shalev/. Warren's entry by means of a ladder appeared first in Samuel L. Knapp, *Biographical Sketches of Eminent Lawyers, Statesmen, and Men of Letters* (Boston: Richardson and Lord, 1821), 113, and was repeated in Rebecca Warren Brown, *Stories about General Warren, in Relation to the Fifth of March Massacre, and the Battle of Bunker Hill, by a Lady of Boston* (Boston: James Loring, 1835), 39–40. Neither of these accounts describes a disturbance at the end of the oration. John Cary resists both the toga and the ladder, but adopts the handkerchief; see Cary, *Joseph Warren*, 174–177.

39. In response to the publication of Knapp's *Biographical Sketches*, "Old Bostonian" wrote to the *Columbian Centinel* to add details to the oration scene. He recalled that the officers were "secretly armed." He attributed the disturbance to Captain Chapman of the Welch Fusiliers, noted that he held three bullets in his hand, and credited Cooper with the "fire of envy" remark. *Columbian Centinel*, 12 Sept. 1821. The earliest account I have found of Warren dropping his handkerchief on an officer's hand is Chase, *Beginnings of the American Revolution*, 2:270; the anecdote is repeated in Forbes, *Paul Revere*, 230.

40. BR 18:225–226, 267–269. For the fate of the Old South, see the church's website: http://www.oldsouthmeetinghouse.org/history/protest-and -revolution.

41. BR 18:149; 26:170–172, 47–49; 18:267–269; 26:1–2, 106–108, 170–172, 224–226, 289–291.

42. *BR* 26:291; *BR* 26:305; *Orations Delivered at the Request of the Inhabitants of the Town of Boston, to Commemorate the Evening of the Fifth of March, 1770; When a number of Citizens were killed by a party of British troops, quartered among them, in a time of Peace* (Boston: Peter Edes, 1785).

{CHAPTER 10 · A USABLE PAST}

1. David Ramsay, *The History of the American Revolution*, 2 vols. (Philadelphia: R. Aitken and Son, 1789). For Ramsay's life, see Arthur H. Shaffer, *To Be an American: David Ramsay and the Making of the American Consciousness* (Columbia: University of South Carolina Press, 1991).

2. Mercy Otis Warren, *History of the Rise, Progress and Termination of the American Revolution: Interspersed with Biographical, Political and Moral Observations*, 3 vols. (Boston: E. Larkin, 1805). For Warren's life, see especially Rosemarie Zagarri, *A Woman's Dilemma: Mercy Otis Warren and the American Revolution*, 2nd ed. (Malden, MA: John Wiley and Sons, 2015).

3. Ramsay, *History of the American Revolution,* 1:90–91.
4. Ibid., 91.
5. Warren, *History of the . . . American Revolution,* 1:89–93.
6. Ibid., 93–94.
7. Alfred F. Young, *The Shoemaker and the Tea Party: Memory and the American Revolution* (Boston: Beacon Press, 1999), esp. 155–165.
8. Mitch Kachun, "From Forgotten Founder to Indispensable Icon: Crispus Attucks, Black Citizenship, and Collective Memory, 1770–1865," *Journal of the Early Republic* 29 (2009): 269–271; Stephen Kantrowitz, "A Place for 'Colored Patriots': Crispus Attucks among the Abolitionists, 1842–1863," *Massachusetts Historical Review* 11 (2009): 96–117; Tavia Nyong'o, "'The Black First': Crispus Attucks and William Cooper Nell," *Dublin Center for New England Folklife Annual Proceedings* 28 (2003): 141–152.
9. Charles Botta, *History of the War of the Independence of the United States of America,* 2 vols., trans. George Alexander Otis (Philadelphia, 1820); quotes from the third edition (New Haven, CT, 1834), book 3, p. 113. The seventh edition was published in New Haven in 1837.
10. William C. Nell, *The Colored Patriots of the American Revolution* (Boston: Robert F. Wallcut, 1855), 13–14.
11. Harriet Beecher Stowe, *Uncle Tom's Cabin; or, Life among the Lowly,* 2 vols. (Boston: John P. Jewett and Co., 1852); Albert J. von Frank, *The Trials of Anthony Burns: Freedom and Slavery in Emerson's Boston* (Cambridge, MA: Harvard University Press, 1998).
12. James Oliver Horton and Lois E. Horton, *Black Bostonians: Family Life and Community Struggle in the Antebellum North* (New York: Holmes and Meier, 1979); To the editor, *Boston Evening Transcript,* 7 Mar. 1851, 2.
13. Nell, *Colored Patriots,* 16–18.
14. Kachun, "Forgotten Founder to Indispensable Icon," 273–278; Kantrowitz, "A Place for 'Colored Patriots,'" 97; Nyong'o, "'The Black First,'" 146–148.
15. On Hayden, see Dale H. Freeman, "The Crispus Attucks Monument Dedication," *Historical Journal of Massachusetts* 25 (1997): 128; Horton and Horton, *Black Bostonians,* 54–56 and following. The petition appears in *A Memorial of Crispus Attucks, Samuel Maverick, James Caldwell, Samuel Gray, and Patrick Carr from the City of Boston* (Boston, 1889), 11–12. A list of Massachusetts governors can be found at http://www.netstate.com/states /government/ma_formergov.htm. The seven governors who signed the petition were Henry Joseph Gardner ("Know-Nothing," 1855–1858), Nathaniel Prentice Banks (R, 1858–1861), William Claflin (R, 1869–1872), William Barrett Washburn (R, 1872–1874), William Gaston (D, 1875–1876), Alexander Hamilton Rice (R, 1876–1879), John Davis Long (R, 1880–1883),

NOTES TO PAGES 268–277

Benjamin Franklin Butler (D, 1883–1884), and George Dexter Robinson (R, 1884–1887).

16. *Proceedings of the Massachusetts Historical Society,* vol. 23, *1886–1887* (Boston: MHS, 1888), 313–318; quotes: 314.

17. Ibid., 314, 317.

18. Ibid., 315–316.

19. Ibid., 315, 317–318. It should be noted that numerous members of the MHS publicly supported the monument. Henry Cabot Lodge, Phillips Brooks, Abner C. Goodell Jr., Martin Brimmer, and Francis Amasa Walker, all MHS members, signed the petition but presumably did not attend the May meeting. John Fiske, who delivered the address at the monument dedication, was elected to membership four years later, in 1892. *List of Officers and Members of the Massachusetts Historical Society, January, 1791–September, 1897* (Boston, 1897).

20. *Memorial of Crispus Attucks,* 31–39, quotes: 31, 39.

21. Ibid., 19, 46–47, 51–56.

22. Ibid., 94, 59–89; quotes: 75, 78, 81.

23. Ibid., 61, 84–85.

24. Ibid., 26–28. For the popular reception of the monument, see Freeman, "Crispus Attucks Monument Dedication," 134–136.

25. John H. Fenton, "Negro Clergymen Press Fund Drive: At Attucks Statue in Boston, National Campaign Urged," *NYT,* 1 June 1967, 23; "Newark Will Honor Negro Killed in 1770," *NYT,* 5 Mar. 1968, 31; "25,000 March in Newark in Honor of Crispus Attucks," *NYT,* 25 Mar. 1968, 47. For additional Attucks-related occurrences, see Robert J. Allison, *The Boston Massacre* (Beverly, MA: Commonwealth Editions, 2006), xi–xii, 66.

26. Among the many versions of these events that are available, I have relied here on the day-by-day reconstruction at http://www.kentstate1970.org/.

27. The comparison is developed in Ronald L. Hatzenbuehler, "Assessing the Meaning of Massacre: Boston (1770) and Kent State (1970)," *Peace and Change* 21 (1996): 208–220. The SBS Creative Designs poster is exhibited on the website of the Oakland Museum of California: http://collections.museumca.org/?q=collection-item/2010541241.

28. "Anti-war Protests Go On; Nixon Backers March Here," *NYT,* 14 May 1970, 20; "The View from Kent State: 11 Speak Out," *NYT,* 11 May 1970, 1, 23; John J. Guiniven, MIT '71, to the editor, *Time,* 1 June 1970, E2. The Guiniven letter supplied the text for a poster that is exhibited on the website of the Oakland Museum of California: http://collections.museumca.org/?q=collection-item/2010542057.

29. Peter Stone, "Afraid of Revolution?," *NYT,* 3 Oct. 1970, 31. For Stone's career, see especially his obituary in *Playbill:* http://www.playbill.com

/news/article/peter-stone-tony-award-winning-librettist-of-titanic-1776
-dead-at-73-112867.

30. The literature on Kent State is enormous, nearly all of it strongly sympathetic to the victims. The novelist James A. Michener and the investigative journalist I. F. Stone both wrote accounts of the shootings that were published in the following year: Michener, *Kent State: What Happened and Why* (New York: Random House, 1971), and Stone, *The Killings at Kent State: How Murder Went Unpunished* (New York: New York Review, 1971). Other especially useful accounts include Peter Davies, *The Truth about Kent State: A Challenge to the American Conscience* (New York: Farrar, Straus, Giroux, 1973); Scott L. Bills, ed., *Kent State/May 4: Echoes through a Decade* (Kent, OH: Kent State University Press, 1982); and William A. Gordon, *The Fourth of May: Killings and Coverups at Kent State* (Buffalo, NY: Prometheus Books, 1990). A new wave of books has appeared more recently, including Thomas R. Hensley and Jerry M. Lewis, eds., *Kent State and May 4th: A Social Science Perspective,* 3rd ed., rev. and expanded (Kent, OH: Kent State University Press, 2010); Carole A. Barbato, Laura L. Davis, and Mark F. Seeman, *This We Know* (Kent, OH: Kent State University Press, 2012); Carole A. Barbato and Laura L. Davis, eds., *Democratic Narrative, History, and Memory* (Kent, OH: Kent State University Press, 2012). Two websites offer extensive resources related to the shootings: http://www.kentstate1970.org/ and http://www.may4.org/, both accessed 20 Jan. 2016.

31. Publications that appeared in the aftermath of the shootings include Bill Warren, ed., *The Middle of the Country: The Events of May 4th as Seen by Students and Faculty at Kent State University* (New York: Avon, 1970). At the University of Utah, students in the English Department quickly assembled a series of impressionistic responses: [Anon., ed.,] *A Spectrum of Student Reactions to the Tragic Incident Last Week at Kent State University* (Salt Lake City, 1970). For the legal resolution of the Kent State shootings, see Joseph Kelner and James Munves, *The Kent State Coverup* (New York: Harper and Row, 1980).

32. See especially John Fitzgerald O'Hara, "Kent State/May 4 and Postwar Memory," *American Quarterly* 58 (2006): 301–328.

33. Rev. William S. Reisman, letter to the editor, *NYT,* 13 Oct. 1970, 44.

34. Diane Foster, letter to the editor, *Record Courier,* p. 2, quoted in Erica Eckert, "Learning from the Tragedy at Kent State: Forty Years after May 4," *About Campus,* March–April 2010, 7; Gordon, *The Fourth of May,* 18.

35. Tim Spofford, *Lynch Street: The May 1970 Slayings at Jackson State College* (Kent, OH: Kent State University Press, 1988), esp. 53–79; *The Report of the President's Commission on Campus Unrest, Including Special Reports:*

The Killings at Jackson State and the Kent State Tragedy (New York: Arno Press, 1970), 421–436.

36. Gene Cornelius Young, "May 15, 1970: The Miracle at Jackson State College," and Susie Erenrich, "Introduction to the Second Edition," in *Kent and Jackson State, 1970–1990,* ed. Susie Erenrich, 2nd ed. (Woodbridge, CT: Viet Nam Generation Inc. and Burning Cities Press, 1995), 87, 10. For the "Orangeburg Massacre," see Jack Shuler, *Blood and Bone: Truth and Reconciliation in a Southern Town* (Columbia: University of South Carolina Press, 2012).

37. Jesse Jackson, "The Rev. Jesse Jackson Tells What Blacks of Chicago Want," *Chicago Tribune,* 19 July 1970, 1-1, 1A1–2.

38. For concerns over militarized policing, see, e.g., Kurt Andrew Schlichter, "Locked and Loaded: Taking Aim at the Growing Use of the American Military in Civilian Law Enforcement Operations," 26 *Loyola of Los Angeles Law Review* 1291 (1993), and *War Comes Home: The Excessive Militarization of American Policing,* June 2014, American Civil Liberties Union, https://www.aclu.org/feature/war-comes-home?redirect=war-comes-home -excessive-militarization-american-policing. For Black Lives Matter, see http://blacklivesmatter.com/. For links between Crispus Attucks and Michael Brown, see, e.g., "Killing of an African-American and Racial Profiling in USA," *Financial Express* (Bangladesh), 18 Aug. 2014; "Ferguson Jury Echoes 18th C Boston Court," *Timaru Herald* (New Zealand), 2 Dec. 2014; Amy Goodman with Denis Moynihan, "From Crispus Attucks to Michael Brown: Race and Revolution," *Democracy Now!,* 5 Mar. 2015, http://www.democracynow.org/2015/3/5/from_crispus_attucks_to _michael_brown; and Dayo Olopade, "Race Aside, There's a Constitutional Reason the Ferguson Grand Jury Was Wrong," *Quartz,* 26 Nov. 2014, http://qz.com/302980/race-aside-theres-a-constitutional-reason-the -ferguson-grand-jury-was-wrong/.

Acknowledgments

IT IS WITH GREAT PLEASURE that I reflect on the many forms of assistance, kindness, and friendship that have made this book possible. I am fortunate to work at the University of Utah, where I have received abundant aid for this project. Two department chairs, Jim Lehning and Isabel Moreira, and two deans, Robert Newman and Dianne Harris, have generously supported me in my research and writing. I am grateful for a Faculty Fellow Award granted by the University Research Committee. I am especially appreciative of the Obert C. and Grace A. Tanner Humanities Center, which gave me a collegial home in my final year of writing. Under the leadership of my colleague Bob Goldberg, with the able support of Beth Tracy, John Boyack, and Susan Anderson, and with the stimulating company of Hugh Cagle, Kate Coles, Maeera Schreiber, David Kieran, Martin Padget, Jessica Alexander, Daniel Auerbach, Stanley Thayne, and Joshua Lipman, the Tanner Humanities Center was a valuable spur to the writing process.

I am indebted to many institutions and individuals who helped me along the way. The book delivery service and interlibrary loans at Marriott Library at the University of Utah were indispensable to this project. The staffs of the National Archives of the United Kingdom, the Massachusetts Historical Society (whose research programs are ably led by Conrad Wright), the Massachusetts Archives, Houghton

Library at Harvard University, and the William L. Clements Library at the University of Michigan (where I especially benefited from the help of Brian Dunnigan and Cheney Schopieray) were unfailingly generous. I am also grateful for the rich resources available online from the Library of Congress, the American Antiquarian Society, and the Boston Public Library (the latter housed at archive.org), without which the research for this book would have been much more laborious. Thanks, too, to institutions that made images available for publication in the book: in addition to those named above, the Frick Art Reference Library and the Metropolitan Museum of Art, both in New York, and the Museum of Fine Arts in Boston.

I learned a great deal from the opportunity to present earlier formulations of the arguments in this book and receive feedback from numerous audiences. Attendees at the Omohundro Institute's annual conference in New Paltz, a meeting of the Bay Area Seminar hosted by Alan Taylor, and the Circum-Atlantic Studies Seminar at Vanderbilt University heard early versions of my attempt to make sense of the topic. I shared preliminary drafts of Chapter 4 at meetings of the British Studies Reading Group at the University of Utah and the British Historical Studies Colloquium at Yale and at a conference at the Massachusetts Historical Society, and versions of Chapter 10 at the Tanner Humanities Center at the University of Utah and at Utah Valley University. A symposium sponsored by the Early Modern Studies Institute at USC and the *William and Mary Quarterly,* and splendidly hosted by Peter Mancall and the Institute's excellent staff, afforded me an opportunity to think about the subject of the book in a broader comparative frame. Many people offered helpful comments in these settings and in personal interactions. At the risk of forgetting more names than I recall, I want to thank Fred Anderson, Juliana Barr, Matt Basso, Hugh Cagle, Ben Carp, Celso Castilho, Vince Cheng, Justin Clement, Ben Cohen, Ed Davies, Nina Dayton, Nadja Durbach, Michael Goode, Eliga Gould, Chris Grasso, Karen Haltunnen, Chris Hodson, Woody Holton, Rebecca Horn, Howard Horwitz, David Kieran, Jane Landers, Peter Mancall, Matt Mason, Dave Mickelsen, Catherine Molineux, Jenna Nigro, Peter Paret, Mark Peterson, Josh Piker, Steve Pincus, Richard Preiss, Alyssa Reichardt, Dan Richter, Brett Rushforth, Patrick Spero, Tom Stillinger, Alan Taylor, Dan Usner, Sophie White, Michelle Wolfe, and Serena Zabin for their questions, suggestions, and support.

I must single out Neil York for thanks. A scholar of the Boston Massacre in his own right who has published both an excellent journal article and an extensive document collection on the subject, he expressed interest and enthusiasm from the start and offered many forms of assistance. Most materially, he deposited a very large box of research materials in my lap, thereby saving me countless hours of archival and library work. Just as important, he heard me out as I puzzled through the research and writing problems associated with the project, offering good advice and a sympathetic ear. When I finished the first draft of the manuscript, he read it with great care and corrected a variety of errors. Neil knows as much about Boston in the 1760s and 1770s as anyone I know, and I am grateful to him for sharing so much with me.

Others offered many forms of assistance. John Tyler, Editor of Publications at the Colonial Society of Massachusetts, generously provided two volumes of the Bernard Papers in PDF page proofs before they appeared in print. Patrick Spero shared the portion of his research on almanacs that related to the Boston Massacre and responded to my queries about his database. Hunter Harris offered crucial assistance in my research in the Gage Papers. Ron Hatzenbuehler sent me a copy of his essay comparing the Boston Massacre and Kent State. Late in the project, Nadja Durbach generously took time out of her own research to photograph a document in the United Kingdom's National Archives. J. L. Bell, author of the incomparable *Boston 1775* website, replied to several queries about the geography of Boston. My former student Jared R. Larson has generously supported a research fund that helped with travel to archives. Woody Holton and Mark Peterson served as readers for the Press and offered both penetrating critiques and helpful suggestions. Fred Anderson read the manuscript in its entirety with his characteristic thoroughness, precision, and insight. Serena Zabin and I have been working in parallel on Boston Massacre book projects for more than five years, and she has been unfailingly open, supportive, and collegial in all our interactions.

I was fortunate to spend a month at the Huntington Library as I was finishing the final draft of the manuscript. Thanks to Steve Hindle, the Director of Research, and the marvelous staff of the Huntington, for helping to make it such a productive stay. Thanks are also due to Daniela Bleichmar and Andy Lakoff for their hospitality and the chance to stay in their beautiful casita, and to the circle of friends who made my time there especially enjoyable: Peter Mancall, Lisa Bitel, David Igler, Cindy Willard, Juliana Barr, Roy Ritchie, François Furstenberg, Bill Deverell, Carla Pestana, Tawny Paul, Alex Dubé, Brett Rushforth, and Josh Piker.

At Harvard University Press, Kathleen McDermott has championed this project from the beginning; I am especially grateful for her confidence and support. Everyone at the Press has been a pleasure to work with, including Editor-in-Chief Susan Wallace Boehmer, Anne Zarrella, Michael Higgins, and Katrina Vassallo. Kim Giambattisto and Barb Goodhouse at Westchester Publishing Services offered superb editorial support. I benefited immensely from the efforts of my agent, Lisa Adams at Garamond Agency. Isabelle Lewis worked with great care and precision on the beautiful maps.

My family has been with me through it all. Michael and Samuel, now young adults, have sometimes listened patiently to the book's stories and ideas and, more often, diverted me from them. Carrie, my touchstone in all things, has listened to my many concerns about the

ACKNOWLEDGMENTS

project since its inception and read the manuscript with care. She has always offered sound and sage advice, about writing and everything else. My mother, Eula Mae Jertson Hinderaker, who died while I was working on this book, and my father, Irving Alden Hinderaker, instilled in me a love of language and a deep sense of freedom, my two most precious inheritances. This book is dedicated to them with love and gratitude.

Illustration Credits

ILLUSTRATION CREDITS

Index

Adams, Abigail Smith, 3, 191
Adams, John, 3, 45, 173, 186,
189, 191–192; argument in the
soldiers' trial, 201–210; declines
to deliver massacre oration, 238;
legacy of, in later accounts of the
massacre, 259, 261–262, 264,
273, 279, 283–284
Adams, Samuel, Jr., 3, 30, 40,
60, 62, 66, 68, 122, 208, 226,
242; emergence and character
of, 44–46; writing as "Populus," 58; urges resistance to
the occupation of Boston, 112;
identified as author of Journal of the Times, 136; and
relationship between civil and
military authority, 137–138;
and committee to pressure the
Superior Court, 166; consults
with Josiah Quincy Jr., about
defending Preston, 173; visits
Preston in his cell, 178; advice
to Robert Treat Paine at soldiers' trial, 223–224; writing as
"Vindex," 224, 236; and Joseph
Warren's 1774 massacre oration,
248–250

Adams, Samuel, Sr., 36, 40, 42, 45
Addonizio, Hugh J., 275
Allen, James, 36, 39–40, 42, 44
Allen, Jeremiah, 214–215
Allen, Mary Adams, 40
American Revolution, meanings of,
283–284
Ames, Governor Oliver, 267,
269–270
Ames, Richard, 120
Amherst, Jeffrey, 80
Andrew (slave owned by Oliver
Wendell), 195–197, 202,
204–205, 264, 271
Andrews, John, 250
Apthorp, Charles, 42, 89, 130, 191
Archbald, Edward, 11
Ast, Bruno, 279
Attucks, Crispus, 7–8, 160, 162,
205–207, 209–210, 213–214,
263–275, 282–284
Attucks Guards, 267
Atwood, Samuel, 11–12
Auchmuty, Robert Jr., 173,
188–189, 198, 201
Augustus, Prince William.
See Cumberland, Duke of
Austin, Jonathan William, 253